A Demonstration of Patriotism as Expressed Throughout the
United States

At Independence Hall, on the ground where, 141 years ago, the fathers of our
republic declared belief in the inalienable right of man to life, liberty and the pursuit
of happiness, 100,000 citizens of Philadelphia renewed their oath of allegiance to
the Constitution and pledged loyal support in any action necessary to the protection
of American rights upon land and sea.

AMERICA AND THE GREAT WAR FOR HUMANITY AND FREEDOM

——BY——

WILLIS FLETCHER JOHNSON, A.M., L.H.D.

Honorary Professor of the History of American Foreign Relations in
New York University;

AUTHOR OF

"America's Foreign Relations," "A Century of Expansion," Etc., Etc.

ILLUSTRATED

WITH MORE THAN 100 PLANS, MAPS,
DIAGRAMS, DRAWINGS AND REPRO-
DUCTIONS OF PHOTOGRAPHS

Copyright, 1917, by
L. T. MYERS

To
Our Allies

AUTHOR'S NOTE

Portions of some chapters of this work have hitherto been printed in signed articles by the author
in *The New York Tribune, The Boston Evening
Transcript,* and *The Newark News,* to which jour-
nals grateful acknowledgments are made.

PREFACE

IT IS MY PURPOSE in this volume to give an account of the entry of America into the War of the Nations. I shall relate the histories of some of the chief belligerents sufficiently to indicate the trend of their policies toward those conditions and complications which afforded pretexts for the war; and the history of the war itself sufficiently to make clear the manner in which it was begun and the manner in which it has been waged. In this we shall see not only the abundant justification but also the imperative necessity of our participation in the conflict.

I shall endeavor to give some account of the military and other potency of the various belligerent nations, and of the resources upon which they rely for support in the struggle; of the disregard of law and humanity which has characterized the conduct of the war; of its unparalleled and almost incredible destructiveness, much of it wanton and malicious; and of the transcendent world-wide issues which are at stake.

I shall give much attention to the army and navy establishments of the United States and the details of their organization and operation; to the gross lack of adequate preparedness from which we suffered at the time of our entry into the war, and in the early stages of our participation therein, due to our fatuous disregard of the admonitions of the founders of the Republic and our abandonment of the wise and prudent policy which they enunciated; and to the vital need of our promptly awakening to a realization of what it means to be engaged in a world-wide war in which the integrity and the very lives of nations, including our own, are at stake.

PREFACE

I shall also attempt to show how crucial was the situation in Europe at the "psychological moment" of our declaration of war, and how truly at that time the fate of humanity seemed to be hanging upon our decision and our action; and how momentous for ourselves and for others was the action of our government in accepting the hostile challenge of the German Empire.

Concerning the magnitude of the theme there can be no question. The war which was begun by the Teutonic powers in the summer of 1914 brought the world face to face with what is probably the greatest crisis in its whole history. We might compare it with the Punic wars, which decided whether Rome or Carthage should rule the Mediterranean and its shores; with the Greek and Persian wars, which determined whether European or Asiatic civilization should be dominant; with the Fall of Rome; with the Mohammedan conquests and the Crusades; with the Napoleonic wars. But not one of these approximated the physical magnitude of this War of the Nations, or its moral and spiritual importance to the future of the whole human race.

For the first time in our history, all the highest material and intellectual resources of civilization are arrayed in an effort to subvert and to destroy the moral and spiritual fruits of human progress. The drunken helot of Sparta is invested with all the arts of Athens. To such a conflict are we called, to declare, as truly as in 1776, that states and peoples have a right to independent government of their own choice; and to see to it, as truly as in 1863, that "government of the people, by the people, for the people, shall not perish from the earth."

W. F. J.

CONTENTS

CONTENTS

6

CONTENTS

CONTENTS

INTRODUCTION

Argumentum ad Humanitatem

AMERICAN intervention in the War of the Nations was most timely, and most untimely. That is a paradox that is in both its statements entirely true and pertinent.

It was timely and something more, so far as the needs of the Allies were concerned, for they were approaching perilously near to the limit of their strength and their endurance. The greatness of their need and the imminence of their peril were not generally understood, or known. It was not the policy of governments to publish all the facts of their extremities and distresses to the world. But though unpublished, the grim facts were there. For the third time a psychological moment had come, and the cry "Help, or we perish!" was heard.

The first such occasion was at the very beginning, when Belgium with almost godlike heroism and sacrifice withstood for a little space the German onset, holding out in sheer desperation for a few days until France could mobilize her forces. Then Belgium broke, and the burden of the day fell upon France.

The second was when, after the immortal Marne, the rallied armies of France "against great odds bare up the war" until England could be aroused from her non-militarist lethargy and could be brought to the aid of France. Not Leonidas at Thermopylae was more resolute than France when she said of the Hunnish hordes, "They shall not pass."

The third came when the allied hosts of France and Eng-

9

land were threatened with exhaustion, not of valor but of supplies; and all they could do was to hold on grimly until we could come to their relief. They could fight. But they could not continue fighting without supplies, and those supplies must largely come from America, and with such coming the submarine pirates of Germany were ominously interfering.

In spite of all that the Allies could do, the submarines were destroying their commerce far faster than they could replace it by building or by purchase. The losses amounted to hundreds of thousands of tons in a single week. At that rate even the gigantic mercantile marine of England would in a not long time be so depleted as to be quite insufficient for the carrying trade; and when thus supplies failed, the Allies would have to succumb. That was the condition with which the Allies were confronted at the beginning of April, 1917.

The question has been asked, why the Allies did not use submarines, too, to counteract the German use of them. The answer is simple. There was nothing for them to be used against. Germany had no commercial marine at sea, and her fighting navy was fenced and screened in inland waters. She had no vessels at sea except the submarines, and they were practically immune against the attacks of others of the same kind. Submarines could not efficiently fight other submarines. There was thus nothing to do but to endure their losses as best they could, in earnest hope that America would come to their relief and rescue before those losses became so great as to be fatal.

France had been performing miracles of heroism for two years and a half. But she could not keep on forever. Her population was little more than half that of her chief adversary, and her store of manhood on which she could draw was correspondingly less. By the spring of 1917 she was feeling the strain and the drain almost to desperation. She was in need of our help, even more than we had been in need of hers in the dark days of the Revolution.

Italy was practically at a standstill. For months her armies had made no advance, so that it was possible to withdraw many Teutonic troops from that front for service in Northern France.

Russia, after a long period of inactivity, had plunged into an anti-dynastic revolution. From one point of view, that was a great gain for the Allies, for it checked the German propaganda and meddling which had during much of the war thus far been costly and at times disastrous to the Russian arms. Also, the example of the Russian democracy expelling the imperial dynasty and establishing a popular government had some effect upon the German proletariat and incited talk and agitation for radical reforms and even of a revolution in that country. On the other hand, it for the time greatly weakened the Russian military aggressive, and left the Russian armies for a time so nearly a negligible a quantity that the Germans felt safe in transferring hundreds of thousands of troops from the eastern to the western frontier.

Great Britain was at the height of her power on land, and was maintaining her power at sea in all respects excepting against the elusive submarines. But she was of all the belligerents most dependent upon lands across the sea for the supplies which were essential not only to efficiency in the field but also to life itself. Already the pinch of restricted food supplies was felt, reserves were much depleted, and the nation felt that it was living practically from hand to mouth. The stoppage of supplies, or even the considerable reduction of them, would be disastrous.

Indeed, not since the German drive at Paris was checked at the Marne had there been so ominous an outlook for the allied powers, or had the possibility of German victory been so great. It was in such a time of trial and almost of desperation that America projected herself into the war, with the immediate contribution of vast sums of money, with the promise of ships and troops a little later—at the middle of May American destroyers were cooperating with the British navy in the North Sea and American soldiers were on their way to France—and with the incalculable moral encouragement that such adherence afforded. It was timely, indeed, from the European point of view, and was thus recognized and gratefully acclaimed by the Allies. As for Germany, she was obviously much perturbed; she realized how heavy a weight had been thrown into the scale against her. But she assumed to regard it lightly, and even refused to recognize the United States as a belligerent against her.

The declaration of war was, on the other hand, most untimely for the United States itself. That was because of our condition of gross unreadiness. For years, and especially ever since the outbreak of the war, thoughtful and far-seeing men had been preaching the gospel of preparedness, but to little avail. The government itself set its face like a flint against it. "We have not been unmindful of our defenses," it said. "We are not unready. If the President called for a million men at daybreak, they would all be in the ranks by sunset."

With such siren songs America had lulled herself to sleep while all the world around her was in flames. The government made no preparations for war, nor even any plans for preparation. The result was that after the declaration of war there was deplorable and costly delay in preparing our military establishment. It was not until after the middle of May, nearly six weeks after the declaration, that Congress agreed upon a law for the increase of the army by conscription. But even then the Secretary of War announced that while the conscription would be held on June 5, there would be no summoning of the men to the colors before about the first of September, because of lack of supplies for their equipment. That is to say, after nearly three years' warning we were so unready for war that nearly five months must elapse after our declaration of war before we could so much as send recruits to training camps to begin their preparation for service on the battle front; and even then, as we shall see, camps were still unfinished, while there was a woeful lack of the most essential supplies of arms and clothing. The event was as untimely for us as it was timely for our allies.

Nevertheless, it was inevitable; and it was well that it was precipitated upon us even in all our unreadiness. That is because without it we should never have taken a single effective step toward getting ready. It needed the rude shock of war to rouse the government and the people to a realization of their necessities, to a realization of the fact that "It's war we're in, not politics." In fact, even the declaration of war was scarcely sufficient to bring that realization home to all. It was said, and truly, that England did not fully realize that she was at war with Germany so long as the fighting was confined to France and Flanders. It was not until German cruisers bombarded unfortified residence villages along the coast, and German Zeppelins dropped incendiary and murderous bombs upon defenseless towns and cities, that the nation was fully roused. No such shock as that was given to America, and the popular recognition of the state of war was consequently less prompt and less keen.

But the realization grew, and became sufficiently clear to the majority of the people, and then preparation for the strife was pressed with inexorable resolution. Even in the latter part of 1917, months after our nominal entry into the war, the danger was not wholly past. The most judicious and informed men perceived that there was still a possibility that Germany might win the war with her piratical submarines before America would be able to make her power felt. A year before Mr. Lloyd George was lamenting that in so many things England had been "Too late; always too late!" The balance quivered on the turning of a hair to decide whether our entry into the war was too late or was just in time.

It was evident that to make it just in time and not too late, the American nation must send men and ships to Europe as quickly as possible; that it must organize and operate a gigantic system of ocean transportation of supplies; and that it must so conserve its food supplies as to be able to feed its allies as well as itself for a year or two years to come. These were the conditions on which haply we could hope to avoid having the war transferred from Flanders and Picardy to our own Atlantic littoral.

It was the psychological moment for America to intervene in the war. It was the psychological moment for every American to intervene with all his individual, personal might, to help the nation and its allies to win a victory commensurate in magnitude with the magnitude of the war itself; a victory for humanity as great as is the menace to humanity in the arrogant challenge of the Huns.

PROLOGUE

THE BATTLE HYMN OF THE REPUBLIC

Mine eyes have seen the glory of the coming of the Lord;
He is trampling out the vintage where the grapes of wrath are
stored;
He hath loosed the fateful lightning of His terrible swift sword;
His truth is marching on.

I have seen Him in the watch-fires of a hundred circling
camps;
They have builded Him an altar in the evening dews and
damps;
I can read His righteous sentence by the dim and flaring
lamps.
His day is marching on.

I have read a fiery gospel, writ in burnished rows of steel;
"As ye deal with my contemners, so with you my grace shall
deal;
Let the hero, born of woman, crush the serpent with his heel,
Since God is marching on."

He has sounded forth the trumpet that shall never call retreat;
He is sifting out the hearts of men before His judgment-seat;
Oh, be swift, my soul, to answer Him! be jubilant, my feet!
Our God is marching on.

In the beauty of the lilies Christ was born across the sea,
With a glory in His bosom that transfigures you and me;
As He died to make men holy, let us die to make men free,
While God is marching on.

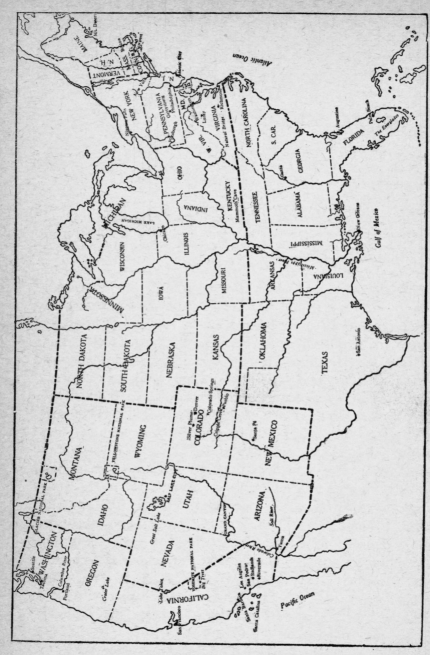

MAP OF THE UNITED STATES SHOWING THE IMMENSE LENGTH OF COAST-LINE TO BE DEFENDED

CHAPTER I

THE CALL TO RIGHTEOUS BATTLE

Another Great Event in April, the Month of Great Events — A Memorable Session of Congress — The President's Address Calling for a Declaration of War with Germany — His Review of the Train of Events and Grievances which had Led to that Necessity — A War to be Waged for no Selfish Purpose, but for Humanity and for the Freedom of the World — Full Text of a Memorable Message — Its Favorable Reception by Congress and the Nation — How It was Regarded in Foreign Lands — Prompt Action by Congress in Adopting a Resolution Declaring that Germany had Begun War Against Us — The President's Proclamation of Our Entry into the World War.

IT WAS April, the most famous month in American History. It was in April, 1135, that the Norsemen discovered Greenland on their way to the pre-Columbian discovery of America, and it was in April, 1492, that Columbus was recalled to the Spanish Court and was commissioned to sail upon his epoch-making voyage. It was in that same month, the "Month of Openings," that Ponce de Leon landed in Florida; that Cortez began the conquest of Mexico; that the Virginia colony was chartered; that Henry Hudson began the voyage in which he discovered the river which bears his name; that the Plymouth Pilgrims received their patent; that La Salle took possession of the Mississippi Valley for France; that the French and Indian War was begun; that taxation of the Colonies by Parliament without their representation was first proposed. It was in April that our Revolution began at Lexington, Concord and Boston; that the American navy took its first prize in war; that Lafayette landed on our shores; that Arnold began his treason;

that the first American man-of-war was built; that the British Government sent peace commissioners to meet our own; that George III ratified the treaty of peace with America, and that the ending of the War for Independence was proclaimed. It was in April that Washington designed the Stars and Stripes, and that the flag in its present form was first displayed. It was in April that Washington was elected and inaugurated President; that Louisiana was purchased; that the United States Mint was established; that the Mexican War was begun; that the Civil War was begun, and ended; that the Spanish War was begun and that the treaty of peace at its end was proclaimed. It was in April that Putnam, Jefferson, Monroe, Clay and Grant were born, and that Lincoln suffered martyrdom.

It was the latest April in our history, in the year of our era 1917, and the second day of the month. Woodrow Wilson had less than a month before been installed as President of the United States for a second term. He had severed diplomatic relations with the German Empire, because of its atrocious and intolerable disregard of our rights and of the rights of humanity in the war which for two and a half years had been convulsing the continent of Europe; and he had called the newly elected Congress together in special session to consider what further steps were necessary for the safeguarding of American citizens and the vindication of the honor of the nation.

Washington was thronged with interested citizens of eminence and influence from all parts of the country. The streets were crowded with spectators as the President, accompanied by a glittering cavalcade of guards, passed from the White House to the Capitol on one of the most momentous errands ever undertaken by an American

18

WOODROW WILSON
Commander-in-Chief of the Army and Navy of the United States

THEODORE ROOSEVELT

Chief of State. The great hall of the House of Representatives was thronged with a brilliant company—the two Houses of Congress on the floor and diplomats, officials of civil and military service, and citizens, in the galleries—as at half-past eight the President stepped upon the Speaker's platform, and voiced the demand of the American nation for a war for the freedom of the world. This is what he said:

THE PRESIDENT'S WAR MESSAGE

I have called the Congress into extraordinary session because there are serious, very serious, choices of policy to be made, and made immediately, which it was neither right nor constitutionally permissible that I should assume the responsibility of making.

On the 3d of February last I officially laid before you the extraordinary announcement of the Imperial German Government, that on and after the 1st day of February it was its purpose to put aside all restraints of law or of humanity and use its submarines to sink every vessel that sought to approach either the ports of Great Britain and Ireland or the western coasts of Europe, or any of the ports controlled by the enemies of Germany within the Mediterranean.

That had seemed to be the object of the German submarine warfare earlier in the war, but since April of last year the imperial government had somewhat restrained the commanders of its under-sea craft, in conformity with its promise then given to us that passenger boats should not be sunk, and that due warning would be given to all other vessels which its submarines might seek to destroy, when no resistance was offered or escape attempted, and care taken that their crews were given at least a fair chance to save their lives in their open boats. The precautions taken were meagre and haphazard enough, as was proved in distressing instance after instance in the progress of the cruel and unmanly business, but a certain degree of restraint was observed.

FINAL INDICTMENT OF GERMAN FRIGHTFULNESS

The new policy has swept every restriction aside. Vessels of every kind, whatever their flag, their character, their cargo, their destination, their errand, have been ruthlessly sent to the bottom without warning and without thought of help or mercy for those on board, the vessels of friendly neutrals along with those of belligerents. Even hospital ships and ships carrying relief to the sorely bereaved and stricken people of Belgium, though the latter were provided with safe conduct through the prescribed areas by the German Government itself, and were distinguished by unmistakable marks of identity, have been sunk with the same reckless lack of compassion or of principle.

I was for a little while unable to believe that such things would in fact be done by any government that had hitherto subscribed to the humane practices of civilized nations. International law had its origin in the attempt to set up some law, which would be respected and observed upon the seas, where no nation had right of dominion and where lay the free highways of the world. By painful stage after stage has that law been built up, with meagre enough results, indeed, after all was accomplished that could be accomplished, but always with a clear view at least of what the heart and conscience of mankind demanded.

BECAUSE IT HAD NO WEAPONS BUT THESE

This minimum of right the German Government has swept aside under the plea of retaliation and necessity, and because it had no weapons which it could use at sea except these, which it is impossible to employ as it is employing them without throwing to the winds all scruples of humanity or of respect for the understandings that were supposed to underlie the intercourse of the world.

I am not now thinking of the loss of property involved, immense and serious as that is, but only of the wanton and wholesale destruction of the lives of non-combatants, men, women and children, engaged in pursuits which have always, even in the darkest periods of modern history, been deemed innocent and legitimate. Property can be paid for; the lives of peaceful and innocent people cannot be.

GERMAN WARFARE IS AGAINST MANKIND

The present German warfare against commerce is a warfare against mankind. It is a war against all nations. American ships have been sunk, American lives taken, in ways which it has stirred us very deeply to learn of, but the ships and people of other neutral and friendly

20

nations have been sunk and overwhelmed in the waters in the same way. There has been no discrimination. The challenge is to all mankind. Each nation must decide for itself how it will meet it. The choice we make for ourselves must be made with a moderation of counsel and a temperateness of judgment befitting our character and our motives as a nation. We must put excited feeling away. Our motive will not be revenge or the victorious assertion of the physical might of the nation, but only the vindication of right, of human right, of which we are only a single champion.

IT NOW APPEARS ARMED NEUTRALITY IS IMPRACTICABLE

When I addressed the Congress on the 26th of February last I thought that it would suffice to assert our neutral rights with arms, our right to use the seas against unlawful interference, our right to keep our people safe against unlawful violence. But armed neutrality, it now appears, is impracticable.

Because submarines are in effect outlaws when used as the German submarines have been used, against merchant shipping, it is impossible to defend ships against their attacks, as the law of nations has assumed that merchantmen would defend themselves against privateers or cruisers, visible craft giving chase upon the open sea. It is common prudence in such circumstances—grim necessity, indeed— to endeavor to destroy them before they have shown their own intention. They must be dealt with upon sight, if dealt with at all.

The German Government denies the right of neutrals to use arms at all within the areas of the sea which it has proscribed, even in the defense of rights which no modern publicist has ever before questioned their right to defend. The intimation is conveyed that the armed guards which we have placed on our merchant ships will be treated as beyond the pale of law and subject to be dealt with as pirates would be.

Armed neutrality is ineffectual enough at best; in such circumstances and in the face of such pretensions it is worse than ineffectual; it is likely to produce what it was meant to prevent; it is practically certain to draw us into the war without either the rights or the effectiveness of belligerents.

THERE IS ONE CHOICE WE CANNOT MAKE

There is one choice we cannot make, we are incapable of making: We will not choose the path of submission and suffer the most sacred

21

rights of our nation and our people to be ignored or violated. The wrongs against which we now array ourselves are not common wrongs; they cut to the very roots of human life.

IN FACT NOTHING LESS THAN WAR

With a profound sense of the solemn and even tragical character of the step I am taking and of the grave responsibilities which it involves, but in unhesitating obedience to what I deem my constitutional duty, I advise that the Congress declare the recent course of the Imperial German Government to be in fact nothing less than war against the government and people of the United States; that it formally accept the status of belligerent which has thus been thrust upon it, and that it take immediate steps not only to put the country in a more thorough state of defense, but also to exert all its power and employ all its resources to bring the government of the German Empire to terms and end the war.

WHAT THIS WILL INVOLVE IS CLEAR

What this will involve is clear. It will involve the utmost practicable cooperation in counsel and action with the governments now at war with Germany, and, as incident to that, the extension to those governments of the most liberal financial credits in order that our resources may, so far as possible, be added to theirs.

It will involve the organization and mobilization of all the material resources of the country to supply the materials of war and serve the incidental needs of the nation in the most abundant and yet the most economical and efficient way possible.

It will involve the immediate full equipment of the navy in all respects, but particularly in supplying it with the best means of dealing with the enemy's submarines. It will involve the immediate addition to the armed forces of the United States, already provided for by law in case of war, at least 500,000 men, who should, in my opinion, be chosen upon the principle of universal liability to service; and also the authorization of subsequent additional increments of equal force so soon as they may be needed and can be handled in training.

It will involve also, of course, the granting of adequate credits to the government, sustained, I hope, so far as they can equitably be sustained by the present generation, by well-conceived taxation. I say sustained so far as may be by equitable taxation because it seems to me that it would be most unwise to base the credits which will now be necessary entirely on money borrowed. It is our duty, I most respectfully urge, to protect our people so far as we may against the very serious hardships and evils which would be likely to arise out of the inflation which would be produced by vast loans.

MUST NOT INTERFERE WITH ALLIED MUNITIONS

In carrying out the measures by which these things are to be accomplished we should keep constantly in mind the wisdom of interfering as little as possible in our own preparation and in the equipment of our own military forces with the duty—for it will be a very practical duty—of supplying the nations already at war with Germany with the materials which they can obtain only from us or by our assistance. They are in the field, and we should help them in every way to be effective there.

I shall take the liberty of suggesting, through the several executive departments of the government, for the consideration of your committees measures for the accomplishment of the several objects I have mentioned. I hope that it will be your pleasure to deal with them as having been framed after very careful thought by the branch of the government upon which the responsibility of conducting the war and safeguarding the nation will most directly fall.

WHILE WE DO THESE THINGS

While we do these things, these deeply momentous things, let us be very clear, and make very clear to all the world what our motives and our objects are. My own thought has not been driven from its habitual and normal course by the unhappy events of the last two months, and I do not believe that the thought of the nation has been altered or clouded by them.

I have exactly the same thing in mind now that I had in mind when I addressed the Senate on the 22d of January last; the same that I had in mind when I addressed the Congress on the 3d of February and on the 26th of February. Our object now, as then, is to vindicate the principles of peace and the justice in the life of the world as against selfish and autocratic power and to set up among the really free and self-governed peoples of the world such a concert of purpose and of action as will henceforth insure the observance of those principles.

ONE MORALITY FOR NATIONS AND PERSONS

Neutrality is no longer feasible or desirable where the peace of the world is involved and the freedom of its peoples, and the menace to that peace and freedom lies in the existence of autocratic governments backed by organized force which is controlled wholly by their will, not by the will of their people. We have seen the last of neutrality in such circumstances.

We are at the beginning of an age in which it will be insisted that the same standards of conduct and of responsibility for wrong done shall be observed among nations and their governments that are observed among the individual citizens of civilized states.

WE HAVE NO QUARREL WITH THE GERMAN PEOPLE

We have no quarrel with the German people. We have no feeling toward them but one of sympathy and friendship. It was not upon their impulse that their government acted in entering this war. It was not with their previous knowledge or approval.

It was a war determined upon as wars used to be determined upon in the old unhappy days when peoples were nowhere consulted by their rulers and wars were provoked and waged in the interest of dynasties or of little groups of ambitious men who were accustomed to use their fellowmen as pawns and tools.

Self-governed nations do not fill their neighbor states with spies or set the course of intrigue to bring about some critical posture of affairs which will give them an opportunity to strike and make conquest. Such designs can be successfully worked only under cover and where no one has the right to ask questions.

Cunningly contrived plans of deception or aggression, carried, it may be, from generation to generation, can be worked out and kept from the light only within the privacy of courts or behind the carefully guarded confidences of a narrow and privileged class. They are happily impossible where public opinion commands and insists upon full information concerning all the nation's affairs.

24

IT MUST BE A LEAGUE OF HONOR

A steadfast concert for peace can never be maintained except by a partnership of democratic nations. No autocratic government could be trusted to keep faith within it or observe its covenants.

It must be a league of honor, a partnership of opinion. Intrigue would eat its vitals away; the plottings of inner circles who could plan what they would and render account to no one would be a corruption seated at its very heart.

Only free peoples can hold their purpose and their honor steady to a common end and prefer the interests of mankind to any narrow interest of their own.

HERE IS A FIT PARTNER

Does not every American feel that assurance has been added to our hope for the future peace of the world by the wonderful and heartening things that have been happening within the last few weeks in Russia?

Russia was known by those who knew it best to have been always in fact democratic at heart, in all the vital habits of her thought, in all the intimate relationships of her people that spoke for their natural instinct, their habitual attitude toward life.

Autocracy that crowned the summit of her political structure, long as it had stood and terrible as was the reality of its power, was not in fact Russian in origin, in character or purpose, and now it has been shaken, and the great, generous Russian people have been added in all their native majesty and might to the forces that are fighting for freedom in the world, for justice and for peace. Here is a fit partner for a league of honor.

SPIES WERE HERE BEFORE THE WAR BEGAN

One of the things that have served to convince us that the Prussian autocracy was not and could never be our friend is that from the very outset of the present war it has filled our unsuspecting communities and even our offices of government with spies and set criminal intrigues everywhere afoot against our national unity of council, our peace within and without, our industries and our commerce.

Indeed, it is now evident that its spies were here even before the war began; and it is unhappily not a matter of conjecture, but a fact proved in our courts of justice, that the intrigues, which have more than once come perilously near to disturbing the peace and dislocating the industries of the country, have been carried on at the instigation, with the support, and even under the personal direction, of official agents of the imperial government accredited to the government of the United States.

Even in checking these things and trying to extirpate them we have sought to put the most generous interpretation possible upon them, because we knew that their source lay, not in any hostile feeling or purpose of the German people toward us (who were, no doubt, as ignorant of them as we ourselves were), but only in the selfish designs of a government that did what it pleased and told its people nothing. But they have played their part in serving to convince us at last that that government entertains no real friendship for us, and means to act against our peace and security at its convenience.

FOR THE ULTIMATE PEACE OF THE WORLD

That it means to stir up enemies against us at our very doors the intercepted note to the German Minister at Mexico City is eloquent evidence.

We are accepting this challenge of hostile purpose because we know that in such a government, following such methods, we can never have a friend, and that in the presence of its organized power, always lying in wait to accomplish we know not what purpose, there can be no assured security for the democratic governments of the world.

We are now about to accept gage of battle with this natural foe to liberty and shall, if necessary, spend the whole force of the nation to check and nullify its pretensions and its power. We are glad, now that we see the facts with no veil of false pretence about them, to fight thus for the ultimate peace of the world and for the liberation of its peoples, the German peoples included, for the rights of nations great and small, and the privilege of men everywhere to choose their way of life and of obedience.

The world must be made safe for democracy. Its peace must be planted upon the trusted foundations of political liberty.

We have no selfish ends to serve. We desire no conquest, no dominion. We seek no indemnities for ourselves, no material compensation for the sacrifices we shall freely make. We are but one of the champions of the rights of mankind. We shall be satisfied when those rights have been as secure as the faith and the freedom of the nation can make them.

Just because we fight without rancor and without selfish objects, seeking nothing for ourselves but what we shall wish to share with all free peoples, we shall, I feel confident, conduct our operations as belligerents without passion and ourselves observe with proud punctilio the principles of right and of fair play we profess to be fighting for.

WILL DEAL WITH AUSTRIA LATER

I have said nothing of the governments allied with the imperial government of Germany, because they have not made war upon us or challenged us to defend our right and our honor. The Austro-Hungarian Government has, indeed, avowed its unqualified endorsement and acceptance of the reckless and lawless submarine warfare adopted now without disguise by the imperial government, and it has therefore not been possible for this government to receive Count Tarnowski, the ambassador recently accredited to this government by the imperial and royal government of Austria-Hungary, but that government has not actually engaged in warfare against citizens of the United States on the seas, and I take the liberty, for the present at least, of postponing a discussion of our relations with the authorities at Vienna. We enter this war only where we are clearly forced into it because there are no other means of defending our rights.

BECAUSE WE ACT WITHOUT ANIMUS

It will be all the easier for us to conduct ourselves as belligerents in a high spirit of right and fairness because we act without animus, not in enmity toward a people or with the desire to bring any injury or disadvantage upon them, but only in armed opposition to an irresponsible government which has thrown aside all considerations of humanity and of right and is running amuck.

We are, let me say again, the sincere friends of the German people, and shall desire nothing so much as the early re-establishment of intimate relations of mutual advantage between us—however hard it may be for them, for the time being, to believe that this is spoken from our hearts. We have borne with their present government through all these bitter months because of that friendship—exercising a patience and forbearance which would otherwise have been impossible.

THE MILLIONS OF GERMAN BIRTH WHO LIVE AMONG US

We shall, happily, still have an opportunity to prove that friendship in our daily attitude and actions toward the millions of men and women of German birth and native sympathy who live amongst us and share our life, and we shall be proud to prove it toward all who are in fact loyal to their neighbors and to the government in the hour of test. They are, most of them, as true and loyal Americans as if they had never known any other fealty or allegiance. They will be prompt to stand with us in rebuking and restraining the few who may be of a different mind and purpose.

IF THERE SHOULD BE DISLOYALTY

If there should be disloyalty it will be dealt with with a firm hand of stern repression; but if it lifts its head at all, it will lift it only here and there, and without countenance, except from a lawless and malignant few.

It is a distressing and oppressive duty, gentlemen of the Congress, which I have performed in thus addressing you. There are, it may be, many months of fiery trial and sacrifice ahead of us. It is a fearful thing to lead this great peaceful people into war, into the most terrible and disastrous of all wars, civilization itself seeming to be in the balance.

But the right is more precious than peace, and we shall fight for the things which we have always carried nearest our hearts—for democracy, for the right of those who submit to authority to have a voice in their own governments, for the rights and liberties of small nations, for a universal dominion of right by such a concert of free peoples as shall bring peace and safety to all nations and make the world itself at last free.

PRIVILEGED TO SPEND HER BLOOD

To such a task we can dedicate our lives and our fortunes, everything that we are and everything that we have, with the pride of those who know that the day has come when America is privileged to spend her blood and her might for the principles that gave her birth and happiness and the peace which she has treasured. God helping her, she can do no other.

28

This address was received with extraordinary expressions of approval by the members of Congress present and by the occupants of the galleries. The press and public of America, with almost unprecedented unanimity hailed it with grateful satisfaction. It was similarly received in Great Britain, France, and the other allied nations of Europe, and also in South America, where Brazil and other powers immediately began considering the question of following the example of the United States in declaring war against the arch-foe of democracy and of humanity.

In Germany the full text of the address was withheld by the censorship from general circulation. Among the government officials it caused a mingling of rage and fear, the latter passion being but ill-concealed. There was at first an attempt made to pretend that it did not matter, that the United States would be a negligible quantity in the war; but such words rang hollow, and the real thought of official Germany was that fearful odds were being cast against the Central Powers by the entrance of America into the fray.

PROMPT ACTION OF CONGRESS

Immediately upon the conclusion of the President's address a resolution declaring war against Germany, or rather accepting the war which Germany had already begun against the United States, was introduced into both Houses of Congress. Brief debates followed, in which very few members ventured to oppose what was known to be the overwhelming will of the people. In the Senate one day's delay was caused by the opposition of Senator La Follette, of Wisconsin, but late on the evening of April 4th the resolution was adopted by a vote of 82 to 6.

29

The next day the House took it up, and before morning of April 6th adopted it by a vote of 373 to 50.

At eleven minutes after one o'clock on the afternoon of April 6th—Good Friday—the President affixed his signature to the resolution, and that moment marked the official entrance of the United States into the World War.

TEXT OF THE WAR ACT

The resolution declaring the war which Germany had forced upon us was as follows:

WHEREAS, *The Imperial German Government has committed repeated acts of war against the government and the people of the United States of America; therefore, be it*

RESOLVED, *By the Senate and House of Representatives of the United States of America, in Congress assembled, that the state of war between the United States and the Imperial German Government, which has thus been thrust upon the United States is hereby formally declared; and that the President be, and he is hereby authorized and directed to employ the entire naval and military forces of the United States and the resources of the government to carry on war against the Imperial German Government; and to bring the conflict to a successful termination all of the resources of the country are hereby pledged by the Congress of the United States.*

Immediately after affixing his signature to the war resolution, the President issued a proclamation announcing the same, calling upon all American citizens to give their loyal support to the government and the laws, and prescribing and establishing various rules and regulations concerning the conduct and disposition of alien enemies found within the jurisdiction of the United States.

CHAPTER II

ANTECEDENTS OF THE WORLD WAR

Pretexts and Causes — Ancient Inter-Racial Rivalries and Conflicts — Nations Seeking Places "In the Sun" — The Quest of Free Outlet to the High Seas — Russia's Age-Long Struggles Toward Open Water — Our Own Fight for the Sea — Austria and the Adriatic — Looking Toward Salonica — Serbia's Need of a Sea Coast — The Annexation of Novi Bazar — Austrian Designs Against Serbia — Germany the Master Hand — Imperial Schemes in Mesopotamia and the Far East — Planning for World-Wide Empire — The German North Sea Frontage — The War Begun on the World's Most Famous Battlefield.

BOTH THE pretexts and the causes of the World War— and pretexts and causes are often very different things— were varied and complex. The former were in some measure contradictory. First of all, there was Austria-Hungary's wrath over the assassination of the heir to the thrones, and her demands upon Serbia for such amends as could be made. Next there was Russia's preparation to protect Serbia against oppression and spoliation. Then there was Germany's intervention to protect her ally from Russian attack. There was Germany's complaint, afterward admitted to have been quite false, that French aviators had committed hostile invasion of the empire, on which account war was declared against France. Later there was the pretence that Germany had discovered a plot of the other powers to attack and oppress her and to deprive her of her rightful "place in the sun." But, as a matter of fact, there were involved certain racial rivalries and national ambitions dating much further back than any of these things; some of the principles being almost as old as human history.

31

From the earliest times nations have generally been divided into two rival camps, antagonistic if not openly belligerent; and at intervals during and since the classic age some nation sought and has been seeking a larger "place in the sun," or more free access to the high seas. The strife of Iran against Turan was the burden of the Epic of Kings. The strife of classic Greece, from Miltiades to Alexander of Macedon, was a war of continents and civilizations, the soul of Europe against the mass of Asia. Rome in turn long stood on the one side and the rest of the world on the other. Later the Western Empire was arrayed against the Gauls and Goths, and the Eastern Empire against the Slavs and the Turks. In the days of the Crusades Europe was again arrayed against Asia. After that it was the Latin against the Teutonic race, a strife which was maintained down to within our own recollection, in the "Terrible Year" between France and Germany.

The present war at first assumed the aspect of a new alignment, that of Teuton against Slav. That appeared in Austria's attack upon Serbia, Russia's championship of Serbia, and Germany's defiance to Russia. Later, however, such lines were largely swept aside in a mad welter of all races and nations. Teuton and Slav, Latin and Anglo-Saxon, Tartar and Turk, Hindoo and Mongolian, were all inextricably mingled.

THE QUEST OF THE SEA

As often of old, too, it was a fight for access to the sea. The cry of Xenophon's Ten Thousand, "Thalatta! Thalatta!" has been repeated, in desire or in realization, by many a nation in many a campaign. It was the sea that the Phœnicians sought in their colonizations, thirty-one centuries ago; and that the Dorians sought thirty centuries back, when they supplanted the Pelasgi in the Peloponnesus. It was the sea that the Assyrians sought when they overran Syria, and that the Babylonians sought when they conquered Judea and Egypt. It was the sea that Darius and his Persians sought when they invaded Thrace and oppressed the Greek colonies of Asia Minor.

When at last the powers fronting on the Great Sea were supreme over all others, the strife to reach the sea was ended for a time, and was transformed into a struggle for the sea's control. But later, when again great inland powers arose, the old quest was renewed. The so-called "Will of Peter the Great" is notoriously a sheer invention, sprung upon the world by Napoleon Bonaparte for the furtherance of his own purposes. But it is quite true in its expression of the unresting efforts of the great Slav power to gain an outlet upon an unfrozen sea.

"A WINDOW LOOKING UPON EUROPE"

Peter secured at the capital to which he gave his name what he described as "a window looking upon Europe"; but it was a window too much barred with frost, and the same is to be said of all the Russian conquests along the Baltic. The great Catherine gained a frontage on the Euxine, but the "narrowing Symplegades" were still between her and the high seas of the world. A march was made across Siberia to the Pacific, to get only an ice-locked harbor and to find Japan blocking the way to warmer waters. Longing eyes have been cast toward the North Atlantic, but miles of Sweden and Norway intervene. An essay has been made toward the Persian Gulf, but there Great Britain is in the way. Russian history for two hundred years has been a story of efforts to reach the open sea.

OUR OWN SEA-SEEKING

Nor has Russia been singular in that quest. Four times has our own country been party to it. Once was when we were ready to fight France and the world for an outlet down the Mississippi, and a second essay was at the same time, when pioneers were sent over the mountains to win a title to the Pacific Coast. The third time was in the days of "Fifty-four Forty or Fight!" with two nations contending for Oregon and its ocean frontage; and the fourth was when Canada vainly sought to break through our Alaskan Panhandle for a short cut from the Klondike to the sea.

AUSTRIA AND THE ADRIATIC

Still more to the present purpose, Austria-Hungary has long been seeking the sea, or more of the sea. There have been many ill-advised jests directed at Shakespeare for speaking of the sea-coast of Bohemia, showing chiefly the ignorance of those who make them; for the fact is, of course, that prior to Shakespeare's time, as that poet doubtless knew, Bohemia was a maritime power, with an extensive and important frontage upon the sea—much of the very same coast which Austria possessed after she had acquired Bohemia, and some of which she still possesses. It was largely for the frontage on the sea that Austria so prized and clung to Venetia, and it is for the same cause that she now chiefly values Kustenland.

But that Istrian frontage is insufficient and unsatisfactory. It contains only the one port of Trieste and the one watering place of Abbazia, while Croatia, adjoin-

34

ing, gives to Hungary only the one port of Fiume. No wonder that it was determined, at all hazards and at the sacrifice of plighted faith, to seize the Serb provinces of Bosnia and Herzegovina in order to secure an ample hinterland for the tenuous Dalmatian littoral, and thus to give the Dual Realm an effective sea-coast of more than three hundred miles. No wonder, either, that it was similarly determined to set up the puppet state of Albania, to be a practical appanage of Austria and to give that power some hundreds of miles more of coast, almost continuous from Dalmatia southward, to and beyond the Strait of Otranto, with a frontage not merely on the Adriatic, but also on the open Ionian Sea.

LOOKING TOWARD SALONICA

There was another and perhaps a still stronger purpose in the rape of the Serb provinces. That was to push toward another sea, the Ægean, by way of Novi Bazar, the Vardar Valley and Salonica. That had been Austria's ambition for many years. More than once she had practically offered to support Russia in seizing Constantinople if Russia would support her in seizing Salonica. She had sought to secure sanction for such expansion at the Berlin Congress of 1878, and though she then failed her whole Eastern policy thereafter had been directed to that end. To that end she had alternately cajoled and bullied Serbia, striving to make and keep that country dependent upon her. And the most maddening blow that Austria had received since the loss of Venetia was that inflicted by Serbia in the Balkan War of 1912, in annexing Novi Bazar and Kossovo and forming a political union with Montenegro, thus throwing a complete barrier across Austria's path to the Ægean. That barrier could not

35

be turned, and there is reason to believe that Austria in desperation resolved to break it down through the device of picking a quarrel with Serbia and waging a war of conquest.

SERBIA AND THE SEA

Serbia, too, had a desire for the sea. For centuries she had been shut up inland. Even when her independence was restored she remained occluded from the sea, and dependent upon Austria-Hungary for a route of communication with the rest of Europe. Naturally she desired her old sea frontage, of Dalmatia and Albania. The Austrian seizure of Bosnia and Herzegovina destroyed for a time her hope of an outlet in that direction. But she did expect as the fruit of her heroism in the war with Turkey to be permitted to take Scutari. When that was denied her, through Austrian opposition, her resentment against that power was greatly increased and confirmed.

More than that. She had at any rate taken Novi Bazar and thus made herself directly contiguous with Montenegro, a state as purely Serb as Serbia herself. The next step was logical and formidable. It was to make a compact with Montenegro for the organic union of the two nations. That was done just before the beginning of the World War. It was agreed that so long as Nicholas of Montenegro lived, he should remain an independent sovereign. But upon his death, his son should not succeed him but should abdicate in favor of the King of Serbia. Then the two kingdoms would become one.

AUSTRIAN DESPERATION

Now this Serbo-Montenegrin compact, which was for a time kept secret, became known at Vienna only a little

FRENCH SOLDIERS MARCHING TO THE MOBILIZATION POINT

France flamed with excitement when the news of the German invasion came. The troops, ready and anxious for war, proceeded smoothly and swiftly to their concentration points, blazing with zeal to repel the invaders and recover the territory lost to France in

GENERAL PERSHING AND MARSHAL JOFFRE

The Commander-in-Chief of the American Expeditionary Forces chatting with the veteran Marshal of
France, the hero of the first battle of the Marne.

while before the fatal visit of the Austrian heir-presumptive to Sarajevo. As might be supposed, it created a profound sensation and aroused both consternation and wrath. It was recognized as placing, if it were permitted to stand, the final seal of doom upon Austria's ambitions in that direction. Then it was determined, by hook or by crook, to have that compact broken. There seemed to be only one way in which to do this. That was to pick on some pretext a quarrel with Serbia, to wage war against that country, and to compel it to recede from the ground which it had thus taken. The pretext which was thus created proved to be much more tragic than had been intended, but, of course, it was not for that reason abandoned. So it came to pass that Austria practically demanded as an alternative to war that Serbia should abdicate her independent sovereignty and make herself an administrative appanage to Austria. All other demands than that Serbia was willing to grant, for the sake of peace. Her knowledge of her own government's integrity and blamelessness for the Sarajevo crime emboldened her to court all possible inquiry. But she could not and would not assent to having Austrian inquisitors usurp the places of Serbian judges and manufacture at Belgrade the spurious evidence which had been trumped up the year before at Agram. So she refused that one demand, and at that Austria, having anticipated such refusal, declared war.

DESIGNS AGAINST SERBIA

The purposes of Austria were threefold. One was to cripple Serbia, to humiliate her, to impose upon her a huge debt for war indemnity, and to exact from her in the peace treaty a practical acknowledgment of Austrian suzerainty.

The second was to compel Serbia to withdraw from Novi Bazar in favor of Austria, and thus let herself be separated from Montenegro by an Austrian wedge, and at the same time to compel her to renounce the projected union with Montenegro.

The third was to oppress Montenegro, as a penalty for her aid to Serbia, by taking from her the little sea-coast which she possessed, so as to make the Austrian littoral of Dalmatia extend unbroken down to the quasi-Austrian puppet state of Albania, which was to be ruled by the German Prince of Wied. Thus the whole eastern coast of the Adriatic would have become Austrian.

THE HAND OF GERMANY

In all these designs Austria was backed by Germany. Indeed, it was Germany that imperatively insisted that Austria should inexorably pursue them, particularly the second which we have mentioned, the seizure of the sanjak of Novi Bazar. There was a terrible scene at Vienna when it became known that Count Aerenthal, at the same time that he seized Bosnia and Herzegovina, committed his government to the relinquishment to Turkey of that limited occupation of Novi Bazar which it had exercised since 1878. His idea was, of course, thus to mollify the Turkish Government and minimize its objections and resentment over the theft of the Serb provinces. But the "forward" party at Vienna, and even the venerable Emperor himself, regarded it as a great mistake, which must at some time be rectified. "You should have seized the Serb provinces," Aerenthal was told, "but at the same time you should have held fast to the sanjak. Remember, it is to him that hath that more shall be given!"

This wrath was largely inspired from Berlin. For just

as Austria wanted to get down to Salonica, so did Germany
desire a highway to Constantinople and the East. The
German Emperor had visited Constantinople and Palestine.
He had secured concessions from the Sultan for railroads
in Asia Minor and Mesopotamia. He planned a great
German trade route, over German railroads, through
Serbia and Thrace to Constantinople, through Asia Minor
to Bagdad, and thence down Mesopotamia to the Persian
Gulf. Thus Germany would have direct outlets to the
Ægean and Mediterranean Seas, and to the Indian Ocean.
Germany would thus get into closer touch with her exten-
sive East Indian colonies, and with the province which
she had practically wrested from China, and would be in
a position to attack the British Empire in India.

THE NORTH SEA FRONTAGE

There was a lust for sea frontage in still another direction. Germany wanted to have a more commanding outlook upon that North Sea which she preferred to call the
German Ocean. It was to increase her frontage upon it
that Prussia seized Schleswig Holstein, and afterward
similarly acquired Hanover. But that was not sufficient.
The two Low Countries were in the way. Holland had
for years been the object of ardent German wooing, with
the hope of inducing her to become a member of the Empire;
and that hope was never abandoned down to the outbreak
of the war.

But Belgium was still more coveted. That was partly
because of that country's greater industrial and commercial importance, her port of Antwerp being the second
or third largest in the world, and partly because of her
geographical position, commanding the upper approaches
to the British Channel and affording a vantage point from

which the English coast itself might be attacked. It was therefore with an eye cast in each direction, toward the East and toward the West, that Germany thrust her ally forward into a position which gave pretext and provocation for war; a war which technically began in that southeastern corner of Europe which had more than once or twice before been the battlefield of the world.

THE FIRST GERMAN ARMY WHICH INVADED FRANCE (1,200,000) WOULD HAVE STRETCHED FROM PARIS INTO RUSSIA (1200 MILES) IF MARCHING IN SINGLE FILE

CHAPTER III

THE BALKAN BATTLEFIELD OF THE WORLD

"The Lumber Room of Europe" — A Land of Many Different Peoples — Its Early Importance as the Battleground between Europe and Asia — Byzantium, or Constantinople — Effects of Its Capture by the Turks — The Ancient Albanians — The Coming of the Bulgars — History of the Serbs and their Empire — The Black Mountain — Greece — Roumania — The Ottoman Turks — American Influences in the Balkans — The War of 1877 — The Congress of Berlin — Contempt of the Great Powers for the Rights of the Balkan States — The Turkish Revolution — Austria-Hungary's Seizure of the Serb Provinces — The Balkan League — The Amazing War of the United Balkans Against Turkey — More Meddling by the Great Powers for Selfish Ends — Resentment in Serbia — A Step Toward the World War.

THE AVERAGE person probably thinks of the Balkan peninsula in something like the words of Tennyson, as a land "where fragments of forgotten peoples dwelt." Macedonia in particular, which is that part of the region over which the recent Balkan war most directly rose, has long been described by diplomatists and journalists as "the lumber room of Europe." To change the figure, you may sometimes see at the bend of a swiftly flowing stream a little cove or bay, in which the water is almost motionless, or in which it simply eddies round and round, and into which has been whirled by the passing current all manner of flotsam and jetsam, good and bad, the living and the, dead. So it has been with this region of the southern Balkans. Into it have drifted men of every tribe and nation, inextricably mingled together in a slackwater, while the great stream of the world's progress has rushed by almost unheeded and unheeding. And yet that region

41

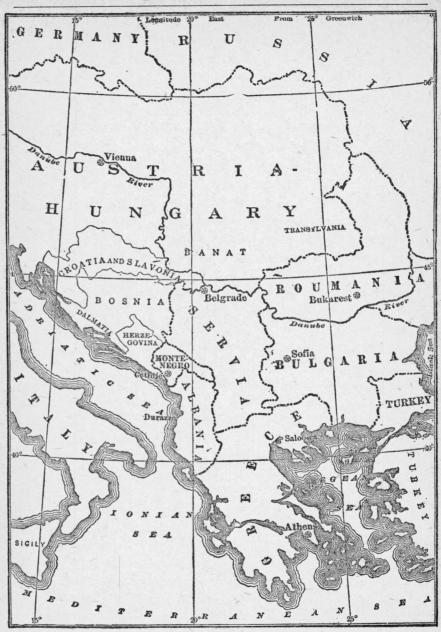

ATTLEGROUND OF SOUTHEASTERN EUROPE

is peopled with representatives of some of the greatest races that the world has ever known. There are the Arnauts of Albania, strange remnants of a prehistoric race of whose ancestry or origin the world knows nothing, save that before Greece and Rome were founded they were there, and now centuries after Greece and Rome have fallen they are still there—remote, unique, unconquerable. There are Greeks, who once made the plains of Thrace and the narrow seas the battlegrounds on which to protect the dawning soul of Europe from the decadent body of Asia. There are the Bulgars, who came down from the dreary plains between the Volga and the Urals to plant the rose garden of Europe. There are the Serbs, who wandered south from Poland to found a great though short-lived empire. There are the Ottoman Turks, who followed in the track of Darius and Xerxes and conquered where the Persians had failed, and who by their conquests changed all the subsequent history of the world. There are the Jews, most marvelous of peoples, who after more thousands of years than most nations know hundreds, are still distinct, immutable, with scarcely a change of character since the days of Solomon. There are Roumanians, who still proudly call themselves Romans; Russians, Germans, Italians, and a contingent of almost every nation under the sun.

THE CENTER OF THE OLD WORLD

And these are gathered together in that land which of all is perhaps most entitled to be known as the center of the world. There is no other country round which the history of the human race has so much revolved and upon which human interest has so much centered. Look at a map of the world as it was known by the ancients, or was imagined by them, and observe its place. It occupies the center of the stage, in full blazing spotlight of the world's attention. On the one hand, Europe; on the other, Asia. At the North, the vast regions of the Slavs, the Bulgars, the Tartars; at the South, the immemorial civilization of Egypt and Ethiopia. And this region, the point at which they all meet; the veritable Four Corners of the world. There is no more certain law of physics than that forces move along lines of least resistance. Forces moving North and South or East and West found the lines of least resistance leading them directly to the Bosporus and Dardanelles. Thousands of years ago it was recognized that the power which held those Straits controlled the destinies of the world. Later discoveries in geography, the opening of new routes of travel, and the invention of new methods and systems of transportation have greatly modified these conditions; yet even to this day those lands and waters retain a large degree of their old-time importance.

ON THE BOSPORUS

We speak familiarly of Constantinople with less of reverence or of awe than of Babylon, Rome, Athens, or Jerusalem, yet it easily ranks with them as one of the five or six greatest cities of the ancient world. More than six centuries before the Christian era it was founded by the Megarians and Argives, under the lead of Byzas, from whom it took its ancient name, Byzantium. Tradition has it that the site was divinely selected and directed by the Delphic Oracle. In the Greco-Persian Wars it was destroyed by the armies of Darius, but after the immortal battle of Platea the Spartan hero Pausanias regained it and rebuilt it. Alcibiades, Lysander, Xenophon and Epaminondas and many other great names in Grecian history are inseparably associated with the city upon the Bosporus; and after them the names of Roman emperors and conquerors. The place was attacked and largely destroyed by Alexander Severus, who thus unwittingly struck a deadly blow at his own Roman Empire. For with the fortifications of Byzantium destroyed, the fleets of the Goths were enabled to come down the Danube and other rivers into the Black Sea and thence through the Straits into the Mediterranean. It was not until the fourth century of our era that the city was rebuilt by Constantine the Great, endowed with his name and made the Eastern Capital of the Roman Empire, soon to become the capital of the Eastern Roman or Byzantine Empire. As such it played a great part in history for many centuries. You may still see there the stately ruins of the castle of Belisarius, the last of the great Roman conquerors. The tides of Turkish and Tartar invasion swept past the city into Europe, but could not overwhelm it. Even after the Ottoman Turks had conquered Bulgaria, Serbia, Macedonia and most of Thrace, and had established their capital at Adrianople, the city of Constantine still seemed impregnable. When at last, after one of the most famous and heroic defenses in history, deserted and betrayed by those who should have been its friends and defenders, it finally fell in 1453, a new epoch came upon the world. For the fall of Constantinople threw into Turkish hands that one great gateway between Europe and the East, and that was what set the Portuguese and other navigators, explorers and adventurers to seeking new routes to the Indies, and finally sent Columbus across the Atlantic to seek the back door of Asia but instead to find the front door of America. The rise of the new world dates from the triumph of the Crescent over the Cross on the banks of the Bosporus.

THE ALBANIANS

Now let us glance for a moment at some of the present dwellers in this historic land. In the extreme west, in the mountainous region along the Adriatic Coast, are the Albanians, or Arnauts, who have the distinction of being one of the only two or three peoples in Europe who so far as we know have never migrated but have been settled where they are today ever since the dawn of history. More than one thousand years before our era there occurred the Dorian invasion, and it was several centuries later before Greece attained the glory which made her unique among the nations of antiquity and still leaves her in memory the unrivaled wonder of the world. But long before the Dorian invasion this whole region was occupied by what the Greeks called the Pelasgian race. The origin or the meaning of that word Pelasgian is unknown. But that was what Homer and other ancient Greeks called the people who were there before them. They have all vanished save the Albanians, who today remain the unchanging representatives of the prehistoric Pelasgians. Centuries ago, when the Turks were striving for the conquest of all Europe, the Albanians produced in John Castriot, Prince of Croia, best known as Scanderbeg, one of the supreme, immortal heroes of the world; the man who held his rock citadel for a lifetime against all the might of Othman, and who with a handful of mountaineers rolled back in disaster and dismay the Turkish armies which were threatening all Europe, and sent the proudest and mightiest of the Ottoman Sultans back to Adrianople to die of chagrin and despair and a broken heart.   To this day the Albanians are still the same wild, daring, hospitable, indomitable mountaineers that they were of old, and though for centuries they have been nominally under Turkish rule, they have never fully acknowledged any other authority than their own.

THE BULGARS

The Bulgars are a Turanian people, kin to the Tartars, Huns and Finns, who had their former home at the earliest date of which we know of them on the vast plains and mountain slopes of Eastern Russia, between the Volga River and the Ural Mountains, where their kingdom was known as Great Bolgary for several centuries.   In the seventh century of our era they began their migration, by way of Astrakhan, the Crimea and the northern and western shores of the Black Sea, around to the Balkan region; a horde of wild and savage horsemen, practicing polygamy, and ruled despotically in patriarchal fashion by tribal chiefs.   Their invasion was a forerunner of the later Tartar invasions of Genghis-Khan and Timur Leng, but while not marked with so extensive conquests or so great savagery as theirs, it was more successful in being more permanent.   They marched to the very gates of Constantinople and compelled the Byzantine Emperor to pay them rich tribute and to grant them the extensive provinces which form the Bulgaria of today.   These savage invaders absorbed the civilization of the lands which they conquered and became a part of the Serbian empire which in the tenth and thirteenth centuries ranked among the great civilized powers of the world.   It extended from the Black Sea to the Adriatic and from Thessaly to the Carpathians, and its ruler bore the proud title of Emperor and Autocrat of All the Serbs.   In 1389 the fatal battle of Kossovo made the Turks masters of the Balkan peninsula, in 1393 Tirnovo was captured and destroyed by the Turks, and thereafter until our own time the Bulgars were crushed beneath the Ottoman heel. By the beginning of the nineteenth century their existence and their name were almost forgotten by the world.

THE SERBS

The Serbs are a Slavonic people, kin to the Croats, and first appear in history in the writings of Pliny, who described them as an agricultural people settled in Poland and especially in what is now known as Galicia. In the sixth century of our era they moved down the Danube and settled in what is now the kingdom of Serbia and the adjoining provinces, including Bosnia and Herzegovina, now claimed by Austria-Hungary, and the northern part of Macedonia and Albania. It was not until the twelfth century that their first ruler, Stephen Nemanya, organized them into an independent kingdom. Education, literature and the arts were greatly promoted, and Serbia became one of the most enlightened lands of Eastern Europe. Under Stephen Dushan, in the fourteenth century, the Serbian Empire attained the zenith of its greatness and glory. It comprised the whole Balkan peninsula, from Greece northward to Poland, and from the Black Sea to the Adriatic, excepting Constantinople itself and a small territory adjacent. In laws and civilization it was scarcely inferior to the most advanced nations of Western Europe. Near the end of that century the last great Serbian ruler, the Tsar Lazarus Hrebelianovich, sought to unite Greece and Constantinople itself with his empire to form an irresistible barrier against the advance of the Turks into Europe. But through the indifference of some and the

48

treason of others his plans failed and he was defeated in the great battle of Kossovo. On that fatal field both the Serbian Tsar Lazarus and the Turkish Sultan Amurath I were slain, and the Ottoman power became supreme. While, however, Bulgaria and other parts of the Serbian Empire fell under complete Turkish control, Serbia proper long maintained a semi-independent status. In the latter part of the fifteenth century, Serbia had become weakened by repeated Turkish assaults, no other nation in Europe would or could raise a hand to help her, and so at last she fell beneath the Ottoman yoke. But as she was the last of all the Christian states to be vanquished, she was in course of time also the first to strike a successful blow for the restoration of her freedom.

MONTENEGRO

After the fatal battle of Kossovo a number of the most valiant and resolute of the Serbian nobles and their retainers fled to the mountain fastnesses at the north of Albania and established themselves as an independent state. There they held their ground with unrivaled heroism against all the power of the Ottoman Empire, unconquerable as the rocky peaks amid which they made their home. In all the time during which the Turks were masters over the rest of the Balkan region, Montenegro alone retained its independence, and never until the present, in all the more than five centuries since, was the brave little mountain state subdued. It held its own through being a nation of warriors. Here we have a law forbidding men to carry deadly weapons. But in Montenegro they had a law which required every man to carry at least one loaded pistol in his belt at all times; at work and at play, in the family circle and in worship at church; and woe to the luckless man who was found without such equipment. The greatest of the early Montenegrin rulers was Ivan the Black, and there is to this day a legend among the people that he is not dead but merely sleeping in a mountain cavern, awaiting the call for the final expulsion of the Turks from Europe, when he will awaken again to lead his people.

GREECE

Of Greece it should scarcely be necessary to speak, so familiar is its history to the world. Twenty-four centuries ago it was the bulwark of Europe against Asiatic invasion. It rose to a height of intellectual and artistic splendor which the world for more than twenty centuries since has despaired of rivaling. It fell under alien subjection through its own intestine feuds. Seven years after the fall of Constantinople it was conquered by the Turks, and though Venice two centuries later wrested half of it from the Asiatic conquerors, in 1715 the whole of it fell back under the Ottoman yoke and there remained until, more than a century later, occurred the revolution adorned by the chivalric heroism of Byron, which in 1829 was finally successful. Since that time Greece has been an independent kingdom among the nations of the world.

ROUMANIA

One other kingdom demands at least passing notice. This is Roumania, the largest of them all, lying between Russia on the north, Bulgaria on the south, the Black Sea on the east and Hungary on the west. We first hear of that region as occupied by the Dacians, a brave and warlike tribe who for many years held their own against first the Greeks and then the Romans. The Emperor

Trajan at last subdued them and the region was then largely colonized by Romans. After the fall of Rome the province became a thoroughfare through which passed many hordes of invaders, coming from Russia and Asia into Southern Europe. The Goths, the Huns under Attila, the Lombards under Alboin, the Bulgars, the Magyars and the Wallachs successively traversed that region, leaving their imprint upon it, and the Wallachs particularly leaving many permanent settlers. In time the region became divided into the two provinces of Moldavia and Wallachia, long known as the Danubian provinces and ruled by independent chiefs. In the fifteenth and sixteenth centuries they were both so far conquered by the Turks as to be compelled to pay tribute to the Sultan, though they always retained a considerable measure of self-government. Under Peter the Great the Russians attempted the conquest of them, and for many years practically controlled the provinces. But in 1859 the two were united under a single prince whose independence of both Turkey and Russia was presently recognized, and in 1881 Roumania was erected into a kingdom, ranking in importance next to the great powers of Europe.

THE OTTOMAN TURKS

But we must not play Hamlet with the part of Hamlet left out; nor review the history of the Balkans without recalling that of the Ottoman Turks. This formidable tribe was first heard of at Khorassan, on the Afghan border of Persia. Driven westward by the Mongols it, early in the thirteenth century, entered Armenia and Asia Minor and gave much military assistance in a time of need to the Seljuk of Iconium, helping him to win the great battle of Angora against the Mongols. For this service the

Sultan gave to the tribe extensive lands at Sugut, in the ancient province of Phrygia, in Asia Minor. At that place was born the great leader, Osman, or Othman, from whom the tribe thereafter took its name of Osmanli or Ottoman Turks. He and his son conquered all that part of Asia Minor to the shores of the Dardanelles and Bosporus. There for years the tribe rested, developing one of the most marvelous and masterful civil and military systems in the world, and then, in the middle of the fourteenth century, they resumed their westward movement. Amurath I crossed the Dardanelles and soon conquered Adrianople, Philippopolis, most of Thrace, Bulgaria and Serbia and practically the whole Balkan country save Constantinople itself and the territory immediately adjacent. Constantinople itself would probably have been taken had not the Mongols under Timur Leng swept into Asia Minor and crushed the Ottoman army at Angora, on the very field where the Mongols had been defeated many years before. For a time the Ottoman Empire seemed destroyed, but its tremendous vitality survived and in a few years it had regained all that it had lost. Under Mohammed I the capital was transferred from Broussa, in Asia Minor, to Adrianople, in Thrace, and that is the reason why the Turks today regard Adrianople with peculiar veneration and were so reluctant to surrender it to the victorious allies of the Balkans. In time the Ottoman Empire extended from Persia at the east to Italy at the west, and from Poland at the north to Ethiopia at the south. Hungary for a century and a half was an Ottoman province, and the Austrian capital, Vienna, was twice attacked by Turkish besiegers and was saved from capture only by payment of a ransom.

THE DAWN OF BALKAN FREEDOM

At the middle of the sixteenth century the Turkish power reached its zenith, and thereafter it waned. In

THE BALKAN STATES, 1815–1885

the eighteenth century it was repeatedly attacked and despoiled by the rising power of Russia, at times aided by Austria, and in the nineteenth century its downward course was swift and sure. Greece won her independence. Serbia led the way in the Balkans toward the same end, and in 1866 expelled the last Turkish garrison. In that same year Roumania became independent, and then in 1874 came the beginning of the end. The disordered condition of Turkish finances led to fiscal intervention by the powers. An insurrection in the provinces of Bosnia and Herzegovina was suppressed with difficulty, and in 1875 a rebellion in Bulgaria was crushed with such savagery that when two Americans, J. A. MacGahan and Eugene Schuyler, exposed the atrocities, the civilized world stood appalled. Nor was the work of these two devoted men the only service America rendered to the Balkan peoples. Years before there had been founded at Constantinople by a New York philanthropist the great institution known by the name of its creator as Robert College. There many young men of Bulgaria were educated not only in the arts and sciences but also in the principles of free government and the rights of men. Many Bulgarians, too, came to America and were educated in our own schools and colleges. And thus from our own land the light of liberty and the spirit of independence were reflected into the dark places of the oppressed Balkan States. It was because of that American impulse that Bulgaria rebelled, and it was by the word of American witnesses that the unexampled horrors of Turkish repression were made known to the world. Following those appalling tragedies Serbia and Montenegro declared war against Turkey, but were quickly defeated. Then in the spring of 1877 Russia and Roumania declared war, ostensibly for the redemption of the Bulgarians and other Christian peoples from Turkish tyranny. The Roumanian Prince was made commander-in-chief of the allied forces, and though Russia contributed the major part of the army the most critical engagement in the war was won by the valor of the Roumanian troops. Adrianople was captured in January, 1878, and soon afterward Russia attempted to dictate terms to Turkey under which she would have taken for herself as spoils of war the larger part of the Ottoman Empire. Against this other great powers protested, and a European congress was held at Berlin in 1878 to arrange the final terms of peace and the readjustment of the political map of Europe.

BLUNDERS OF THE POWERS

Two stupendous errors were committed by the powers at that time. One was, that they largely ignored the natural rights of the Balkan peoples and looked chiefly to their own selfish aggrandizement. Serbia and Montenegro did receive slight advantages, but the two important provinces of Bosnia and Herzegovina which were almost purely Serbian, and which on every principle of right and justice belonged to that country, were placed under Austrian protection and thus the way was opened for Austria-Hungary years later to seize them and arbitrarily annex them to her own domain. Roumania, which had really won the war against Turkey, instead of being rewarded was actually despoiled by having the rich province of Bessarabia taken from her and given to Russia, her only compensation being a gift of the comparatively worthless region known as the Dobrudscha. Bulgaria was, it is true, erected into an autonomous state, under Turkish suzerainty, but with no thought of its ever becoming or long remaining really independent. Its crown was offered to a gallant German prince, Alexander of Battenberg, and when he asked the advice of Bismarck as to whether he should accept it or not, the Iron Chancellor, anticipating the speedy collapse of the new state, cynically replied,

"Oh, yes, take it; it will be a pleasant souvenir!" The fact was, Russia had waged the war against Turkey not so much for the liberation of the Balkan peoples as for her own aggrandizement, and she now intended presently to absorb Bulgaria and so to push on to her long coveted goal at Constantinople, upon which her eye had been fixed for a thousand years. On the other hand, Austria-Hungary was similarly intent upon absorbing Serbia and much of Macedonia, and so pushing down to Salonica, her goal on the Ægean Sea. Serbia and Bulgaria, with their former history of greatness, were ignored, or were used only as pawns in the game. And for many years thereafter, indeed down to half a dozen years ago, Russian and Austro-Hungarian diplomacy, intrigues, commercial influence and military threats were exercised to those same ends, to disturb the governments of Bulgaria and Serbia, to make their success as independent states impossible, and to compel them to fall into the hands of the two great powers.

MACEDONIA

The other capital error, which grew out of this first one, was in making no provision or in taking no steps for the enforcement of the European prescriptions of better government for Macedonia. The powers at the congress of Berlin demanded great reforms in that government and Turkey promised to grant them. But as a matter of fact immediately after the adjournment of the congress Turkish government in Macedonia and Albania became every whit as bad as it had been before, and atrocities similar to those which in Bulgaria had staggered humanity were of frequent occurrence. This disastrous policy had various results. It maintained and intensified the age-long hostility of the Serbs, Bulgars and Greeks against Turkey. It kept Albania in a state of chronic disaffection and revolt. It made of Macedonia a land of benighted lawlessness. It provoked occasional remonstrances from the powers and some acts of intervention, which were futile and ineffectual. It also for many years gave rise to bitter jealousies and animosities among the three states of Serbia, Bulgaria and Greece, each of them seeking to advance its own interests in Macedonia and each claiming to be the rightful owner of that region.

DEMORALIZED STATES

Both these causes, moreover, had a demoralizing effect upon the Balkan States themselves. In Serbia the intrigues of Austria corrupted the court and filled its career with repeated scandals, until at last the people could endure that state of affairs no longer. A military conspiracy was formed, which resulted in one of the most shocking tragedies in modern history, when the palace was forcibly entered and the king and queen were butchered in cold blood and the dynasty exterminated. Then a prince of a former dynasty was called to the throne, and is now the king of Serbia. In Bulgaria there was a succession of outrages and tragedies similarly brought about by the malevolent intrigues of Russia. Prince Alexander was one night seized in his palace by Russian kidnappers and forcibly carried out of the country and compelled under threats of death to abdicate his throne. On regaining his liberty he returned and for a time resumed his wise and patriotic rule, but again was compelled to abdicate as an alternative to having his country crushed by the overwhelming force of Russia. In his place Ferdinand of Saxe-Coburg-Gotha was elected prince. He was a grandson of Louis Philippe of France and related to four or five royal families, but at the time of his election he was a half-pay lieutenant in the Austrian army. A master of intrigue, of boundless ambition, and of more than ordinary ability in statecraft, he set himself to the task of restoring the ancient greatness of Bulgaria and at the same time of exalting himself among the great rulers of Europe. Stephen Stambuloff, the greatest statesman of modern Bulgaria and the real creator of that country's independence, was known not unfittingly as the Bismarck of the Balkans and for a time as Prime Minister of Bulgaria he overshadowed the young prince. In Germany, the young Emperor William II got rid of Bismarck by forcing his resignation from the chancellorship. In Bulgaria, Stambuloff was disposed of through brutal assassination, and thereafter Prince Ferdinand was the unchallenged head of the state.

TURKISH REVOLUTION

At last the evils of Turkish misgovernment, not merely in Macedonia and Albania but in Thrace and Constantinople itself, accumulated until they could no longer be endured, and a formidable organization known as the Young Turks arose whose aim was revolution. For a time the Sultan, Abdul Hamid II, strove to suppress it and its members worked chiefly in exile in other lands; but at last finding it too strong, he affected to yield to its demands. In 1908 the world was astonished and gratified by the announcement that a constitution had been proclaimed in Turkey and that under it a popular liberal government was being organized. It seemed for a time as though the tyrant who for a generation had been one of the worst criminals that ever defiled even the Turkish throne had transformed himself into a benevolent servant of the people. Religious freedom and equality were proclaimed, the people were no longer subjects but citizens, freedom of speech and of the press were guaranteed, universal suffrage and a representative legislature were established, and Turkey took its place for the first time among the free and enlightened nations of the earth. It was fondly thought that we should see the inspiring spectacle of a supposedly dying nation rising into newness of life. But the promise was not to be so easily fulfilled. The Sultan soon showed his lack of sympathy with the new era which he himself had inaugurated, and he was forcibly deposed and imprisoned and his kinsman, Mohammed V, who had spent many years in imprisonment, was placed upon the throne. After this, factional strife distracted the empire, old animosities between Moslem and Christian arose, old abuses were continued, and the experiment of popular government seemed to be in danger of failing.

THE RAPE OF THE PROVINCES

Meantime the great powers, or some of them, instead of encouraging the regeneration of Turkey, looked on with little sympathy and in some cases with actual hostility. One of them, Austria-Hungary, assumed an attitude of aggressive antagonism. It was evidently feared at Vienna and Budapest that Turkey might fully rehabilitate herself and become a great and enlightened power, and so might be entitled to reclaim the valuable provinces of Bosnia and Herzegovina which Austria-Hungary had been holding and governing in trust for her, and might so reform the government of Macedonia as to give no pretext for alien seizure of those provinces. Accordingly, with a sordid determination to make sure of those provinces which she had in charge, and with a malevolent determination to discourage and discredit the new order of things in Turkey as much as possible and to cause the experiment of liberal government to fail, Austria-Hungary arbitrarily seized Bosnia and Herzegovina and annexed them to her own conglomerate domain. It was a flagrant violation of the Berlin Treaty of 1878 and a cynical application of the piratical old rule of the age of force, "that they shall take who have the power, and they shall keep who can." Turkey protested vigorously against the outrage, and so did Serbia, to which the reversion of the provinces logically belonged, but all in vain. The other powers passively assented to or condoned the wholesale theft, and Turkey and Serbia were powerless before the huge army with which Austria-Hungary backed up her morally indefensible act. There was then every prospect that Austria-Hungary would presently continue her career of aggression and spoliation, by pushing down the Vardar Valley through Macedonia and seizing the city and port of Salonica, which she had long coveted, and which indeed all Europe had regarded as destined to fall into her hands.

THE BALKAN LEAGUE

But the rape of the two provinces had another result, quite unexpected and undesired by the perpetrator of that crime. It caused Serbia and her neighbors to open their eyes to the manner in which they were being used as pawns and playthings, and to realize the actual designs of the great powers toward them. They took to themselves the warning of Byron to the Greeks, "Trust not for freedom to the Franks," and became persuaded that "who would be free, themselves must strike the blow."

The Congress of Berlin, June 13, 1878, at the Close of the Russo-Turkish War

At this Congress was sown the seed of future troubles in the Balkan Peninsula, which culminated in the Great War.

American Troops Marching to their Camp in France.

A long column of "Sammees" just off the transport marching through a historic town "Somewhere in France" on their way to a training camp preparatory to taking their places in the front line trenches.

The Prince of Bulgaria took the initiative. Throwing off the last shadowy trace of Turkish suzerainty and of the tutelage of the great powers, he proclaimed himself no longer Prince, but King, Emperor and Tsar. In this assumption of dignity the powers acquiesced, partly because they could not easily prevent it and partly because they fondly imagined that it would amount to nothing more than a change of name. But it did amount to a great deal more. The government of Bulgaria and Serbia, which because of the rival intrigues and influences of Russia and Austria had long been unfriendly and at one time had been openly at war, realized that the interests of both would be promoted by the establishment of a friendly understanding. So negotiations to that end were quietly begun, and soon were extended to include also Montenegro and Greece. Meanwhile all these four powers began, in profound secrecy but with unmatched energy and devotion, to stock their arsenals, to recruit, and discipline their armies, and to prepare for a war which would be a war to the knife and the knife to the hilt.

Never, probably, in the history of the world was so important and extensive a movement conducted with so profound a degree of secrecy and so complete a measure of success. Turkey and all the powers of Europe knew, nothing and suspected nothing of what was going on, either in diplomacy or in the armies of the Balkan States. If any symptoms of the campaign were observed they were contemptuously disregarded because of the habit which all Europe had formed of refusing to take seriously anything which the Balkan States might do. But the rulers and the peoples of the Balkan States were tremendously in earnest. In the early fall of 1911 the Prime Ministers of Serbia and Bulgaria met in a railroad car on the frontier between the two countries. There the outline of a treaty of alliance, offensive and defensive, was formed and adopted. It was agreed that as Bulgaria was the largest of the four states, the headquarters of the alliance should be at her capital, Sophia, and in that city on the last day of February, 1912, a formal treaty between the two powers was signed. At the middle of May following a similar treaty was made with Greece and with Montenegro, so that by the beginning of summer all four states were firmly united in a Balkan League, which was to last for twenty-five years and the object of which was the waging of war upon Turkey and the partitioning among the allies of a large part of the Turkish domains. It was on August 13, 1912, that King Ferdinand of Bulgaria presided over a council of the four allies, at which it was formally resolved that if Turkey did not promptly grant and put into effective execution the reforms in Macedonia and elsewhere to which she was bound by the Berlin Treaty of 1878, then the four Balkan States should unitedly wage war upon her.

PLANS OF CONQUEST

That resolution was formed on August 13, 1912, and it was agreed that, in order to interfere as little as possible with the occupations of the people, the war should be started as soon as the farmers had gathered in their autumn harvests, which at that time were already beginning to ripen in the fields. And down to this time not another government in Europe outside of these four had the slightest inkling of what was going on and of what was about to occur. A few weeks later Bulgaria made peremptory demands upon Turkey for the granting of reforms in Macedonia, which were as usual, and as was expected, ignored. Then the military preparations and purposes of the allied states began to be hinted at. The great powers regarded them with mingled amusement, impatience and contempt. The armies and governments of the Balkan States had lately been travestied upon the stage as "chocolate soldiers" and "puppet kingdoms" and it was universally assumed that if they were so foolhardy and presumptuous as to begin war they would be speedily overwhelmed by the vast and invincible legions of the Turks. The Turks were a warrior race, who had no superiors in the world as first-class fighting men, and for the petty Balkan States to attack them would be much like committing suicide; of which fact the allies were solemnly warned by the powers.

But little the powers knew or dreamed of what had been going on behind the veil of secrecy which the four allies had so well maintained. In October came the declaration of war, and then there was seen the spectacle of four nations simultaneously springing forth in the panoply of war, like the fabled Minerva from the brow of Jove. In a twinkling, the streets of Athens, as of Belgrade and Sophia, were thronged with a populace frenzied with zeal to join the colors and to march to the conquest of the hated Turkish Empire. The cattle pastures of Serbia, the flower gardens of Bulgaria from which the world gets its supplies of attar of roses, the rocky heights of Montenegro, and the hills and valleys and fertile plains of classic Greece, were deserted by every able-bodied man, and even by many women who put on male attire and marched in the ranks. The ruined temples of Greece, which in their prime had seen the triumphs of Platea and Salamis and Marathon commemorated, and had echoed to the footsteps of Pericles and Xenophon and

Epaminondas, now saw stern musterings of men who had inherited the traditions of Thermopylae. And so while the great powers of Europe awaked from their slumber and gaped and gazed and wondered, there burst through the encircling mountain from four sides at once the storm of pent-up wrath of centuries upon the hated Turk.

A SHORT, SWIFT WAR

It was on October 8th that Montenegro declared war on Turkey, but her early operations were not important. It was not until October 17th that war began between Bulgaria and Serbia on the one hand and Turkey on the other, and the next day Greece also began to fight. Date the beginning of the war, then, at October 17th. In just eight days, on October 25th, the Bulgarians had swept half way across Thrace and had captured the important city of Kirk Kilisse, between Adrianople and Constantinople; capturing it after a battle and storm which made its streets a shambles and a wilderness of ruin. The next day a Serbian army, pressing far into the heart of Macedonia, captured the city of Uskub. By October 30th, scarcely a fortnight after the declaration of war, the Bulgarians had fought at Lule Burgas a four days' battle, extending over a line of more than thirty miles, had crumpled up and put to rout the main Turkish army of 150,000 men, had cut Adrianople off from Constantinople, and were closely besieging the ancient capital of the Sultans. On November 3d, only seventeen days after the declaration of war, the Turkish Government in its despair begged the great powers to intervene to save it from the victorious allies. But the powers, which a few weeks before had scorned those allies and had patronizingly warned them not to get into trouble by attacking the superior might

64

of Turkey, now stood in open-mouthed amazement and stupefaction, and ventured not to raise a hand or speak a word to stay the triumphant tide of war. Five days later the Greeks captured the great Macedonian city and seaport of Salonica, anciently known as Thessalonica to the church in which Paul's Epistle to the Thessalonians was addressed. On November 13th, less than a month from the beginning of the war, Turkey asked the allies for a cessation of hostilities to discuss terms of peace, but the conditions which she suggested were not acceptable and the campaign went on. On November 18th the completion of a month of war was celebrated by the Serbians in the capture of Monastir, the most important inland city of Macedonia, while the Bulgarian army drove the Turks within the lines of Tchataldja, in the very suburbs of Constantinople itself. Ten days later, when the Serbians triumphantly marched to the shore of the Adriatic at Durazzo, gaining the outlet to the sea which their country had long desired and needed, the Albanians raised a flag of their own, proclaimed their national independence, and called upon Austria-Hungary and Italy to recognize and protect them. Finally, on December 3d, an armistice was signed between Turkey and the allies at the village of Kadin Keni, and on December 16th, a day less than two months after the beginning of the war, the envoys of the five powers met in London to negotiate a treaty of peace. In two months' time those "puppet states," as they were contemptuously called, those "chocolate soldiers" who had been the favorite butts of ridicule and travesty in works of fiction and on the stage, had achieved a consummation which no great power would have undertaken. They had overthrown and practically annihilated the Turkish Empire in Europe, leaving it nothing of all its great domain but three or four cities and their environs, and these closely besieged. They had waged war in a singularly up-to-date method. Ferdinand, King or Tsar of Bulgaria, was the first sovereign who ever accompanied his armies to war in an automobile, but in such a vehicle he did accompany his army throughout its campaign. A fleet of aeroplanes was also employed by the allies. Lessons in sanitation were learned from the Japanese in their marvelous war with Russia. And in brief, the supposedly rude and uncouth farmers and mountaineers exhibited a degree of efficiency in civilized warfare such as had not been surpassed by any European nation.

MORE MEDDLING

Now, at the close of the war, the great powers played an ignoble part; as they had also done at its beginning. Let us consider their moral responsibilities and duties. It was because of their gross and incorrigible neglect to enforce their own decrees and to fulfill their own plain duty, that the war was provoked. That is the first indictment against them. The war was their fault. The second indictment is that when the war became imminent they made no serious efforts to avert it. They were morally bound by the treaty of The Hague to use all practicable efforts to preserve the peace, but they wholly neglected to do so and let the war come on without a single indictment against them. Then, when the war was ended, they repeated one of the capital blunders which they had made in 1878, by seeking to seize for themselves the prizes of others' victories. They objected especially to letting Serbia reap the rewards of her own labors and insisted that much of the territory which that gallant little power had won by conquest should be taken from her and put under Austrian protection. It was the same old policy of using the Balkan States as tools to serve the selfish ends of the great powers. Of course Serbia and her allies could scarcely hope to maintain their rights against Austria-Hungary and Germany and Italy united, and so they were forced reluctantly to yield and to be despoiled of much of the just fruits of their campaign. It was the old story of seeking to reap where other men had sown; and of ordering the affairs of the Balkans not in the interest of the Balkan peoples but for the sordid gain of outside powers.

Nevertheless, the great powers in self-interest could scarcely avoid doing some good work. When Turkey demurred to the proposals of the allies and threatened to break off negotiations and resume the war, the powers, fearful lest the conflict might extend to their own circle, exerted moral pressure upon the Porte with the result that at last, but most reluctantly, on January 22d, it yielded to the allies and consented even to the surrender of Adrianople and of the remaining islands of the Ægean Sea. That date may be regarded, therefore, as marking the assurance of peace, though it meant disaster to the Turkish Government, which the very next day was driven from office by an infuriated mob organized and led by the Young Turk Party. From the beginning of the war to the establishment of an armistice was only forty-seven days. From the signing of the armistice to the practical agreement on peace was just fifty days. In these ninety-seven days was undone the work of centuries. Four hundred and sixty years before the Turks had won all the Balkan peninsula save only Constantinople and its immediate suburbs. Now the conditions were exactly reversed, and Constantinople and its suburbs were all that was left to the once mighty and conquering tribe of Othman.

The evil meddling of the great powers, however, led to a breaking up of the Balkan League and to war among its members who had lately been loyal allies; particularly between Bulgaria and Serbia; while Austria's interference with Serbia, as already related, provided provocation to the still greater war which speedily followed.

PROVISIONS OF THE TREATY OF BUCHAREST, 1913

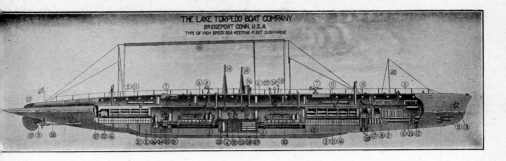

MODERN SUBMARINES

Top, type of high speed ocean-going submarine; center, a submarine about to submerge; below, a mine-planting submarine.

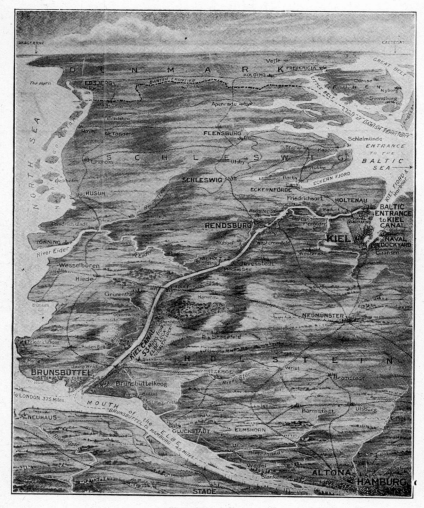

The Kiel Canal

The keystone of Germany's naval defence, the canal joining the Baltic and the North Sea, was deepened just in time for the beginning of the war.

CHAPTER IV

STORY OF THE CENTRAL POWERS

Twenty Centuries of German Ambition — Wars with Rome — The Germanic Invasion of Gaul — Charlemagne's Conquest and Empire — The First German Emperor Nearly a Thousand Years Ago — The Teutonic Order — The Rise of Prussia — The Napoleonic Wars — Prussian Militarism — The Creation of the Present German Empire — The Hohenzollern Dynasty — A Fortunate Marriage — The Electors — Frederick the Great — William I and William II — Twenty Sovereigns — The Polyglot Realm of Austria-Hungary — The German Hapsburgs and Their Slavic Subjects — Fortunes and Misfortunes of the House of Austria.

THE STORY of the Central Powers, the two Teutonic empires, dates back two thousand years and more. It was in the year 113 B. C. that Teutonic tribes first clashed with imperial Rome. They met in battle at Noreia, in Illyria, now the southern part of the Austrian Empire, and the Teutons and their Cymric allies were victorious over the Roman legions. It is interesting to recall the alliance of the Teutons and Cymri, because the latter were of the same stock as the ancient Britons. Eleven years later Marius avenged this defeat of the Roman arms by vanquishing the Teutons, after which there was peace for many years. Julius Caesar came into comparatively slight contact with the Teutonic or German tribes, with whom, however, he reported that the Belgians, who were the bravest of all the Gauls, were in almost incessant conflict.

Drusus Germanicus, in 12 B. C., was the first to engage in a general war between the Latin and Teutonic worlds. He invaded Germany in force and conquered the tribes between the Elbe and the Rhine, built a fort near the

69

present site of Liege, and was the first Roman to reach the shore of the North Sea, or German Ocean. His brilliant conquests, however, were not lasting, and they were followed a few years later by a campaign of disaster.

THE LOST LEGIONS OF VARUS

It was in 9 A. D. that the next great Roman expedition invaded Germany, under the lead of Varus. It penetrated as far as the Teutoberger Wald, the German Mountain Forest, near Osnabrueck, where it was met by a German army under Hermann, whom the Romans called Arminius. The result was that the three legions of Varus, the very flower of the Roman army, were annihilated; and Caesar Augustus groveled in pain upon the floor of his Roman palace, crying in anguish, "Varus! Give me back my legions!"

It was too late. The legions were gone, and what was still more ominous, the German fighting spirit was aroused. A little more than two centuries later, in 238, various Frankish tribes invaded Gaul, scorning the waning power of the empire whose borders the Goths and Vandals were ravaging, and in 450 the Germanic tribes began their wholesale irruption into Gaul. More than three centuries later Charlemagne subdued the Saxons and other German peoples, and on Christmas day in the year 800 was crowned by the Pope as Emperor of the West, that is, of Germany and Gaul. That potent monarch then, in 802, designed the two-headed eagle as his emblem, in token of his sovereignty over the dual empire of Rome and of Germany. That was the origin of the two-headed eagle which is now displayed in the imperial escutcheon of Austria, whose sovereigns were the last titular successors of Charlemagne; while the German coat-of-arms bears the single-headed black eagle of Prussia.

THE FRANCO-GERMAN FEUD

We may date the feud between Germany and France away back to the year 840. At that time Louis I, surnamed the Debonnair, separated those two countries and made them antagonistic to each other. France became independent, while for some years Germany remained subject to Rome. But in 896 the Germans under Arnulph marched upon Rome and captured that city, and then, on November 8, 911, declared their independence, with Conrad I of Franconia as their king A few days later the dukes and counts of the various states declared their local sovereignty, and their right to choose their own national sovereign, and thus constituted themselves Electors. So at the death of Conrad they selected Henry the Fowler as his successor, and thereafter for many centuries the kingly or imperial dignity remained elective.

OTTO THE FIRST EMPEROR

Otto I, in 962, was the first such Emperor to be formally recognized and crowned by the Pope at Rome. After him came a series of conquering emperors, who added Bohemia, Lorraine and other lands to the empire. Under Henry IV, surnamed Hildebrand, there came in 1075 a memorable conflict with Pope Gregory VII. This first led to the crushing defeat of Henry, who, in 1077, went to Canossa and did penance by standing in the snow, bareheaded, under the Pope's window, until that prelate was willing to receive him as a suppliant for mercy. But in 1084 Henry avenged himself by capturing the papal city and sending Gregory to die in exile the next year at Salerno. Then came on the Guelph and Ghibelline feuds, the wars which ravaged Italy, the establishment of the famous Teutonic Order of Knighthood in 1190, and the election of Rudolph, the first Hapsburg Emperor, in 1273. Finally, in 1439, the Pragmatic Sanction settled the imperial dignity in perpetuity upon the Hapsburgs, who held it until August 11, 1804, when Francis II formally resigned it, and the Holy Roman Empire—which, as Lord Bryce once wrote, was neither holy nor Roman, nor yet an empire—came to an end.

THE BEGINNING OF PRUSSIA

Meanwhile, Prussia arose, her rising in a subtle but potent manner stimulated by the Hapsburg monopoly of the imperial crown. It was in 1415 that Prussia had its origin. At that time a petty nobleman, Frederick IV of Nuremberg, founder of the Hohenzollern family, became Margrave of Brandenburg. He obtained that dignity by purchase, for so much cash, from the then Emperor, Sigismund of Bohemia, and that Mark of Brandenburg became the nucleus of what was to become the kingdom of Prussia. Presently the conquest of Porussia, as East Prussia was known, because of its proximity to Russia, was undertaken by the Teutonic Knights, while Casimir of Poland assisted the Porussians in their resistance. Albert of Brandenburg, the grand master of the Teutonic Knights, in 1575 so far succeeded in the conquest as to get himself recognized as Duke of Porussia, or East Prussia, though he was compelled to acknowledge the suzerainty of Poland. That was another striking incident, the beginning of Prussia as a fief of Poland! So it remained for more than a century and a quarter, until in 1657 Poland recognized the complete independence of Prussia, the latter state then being under the able reign of Frederick William, the Great Elector.

PRUSSIA A KINGDOM

After that events proceeded more swiftly. On January 18, 1701, Frederick III, Elector of Brandenburg and Duke of Prussia, crowned and proclaimed himself King of Prussia, and instituted the now famous Order of the Black Eagle. He was Frederick I of Prussia, and he considerably added to the extent of his domain by purchase and by seizure. Then came Frederick II the Great, whose reign marked an epoch in European history, and who at his death in 1786 left Prussia securely established among the great powers of the continent. It was Frederick the Great who not only threw off the last traces of Polish suzerainty over Prussia but also conceived and incited the first Partition of Poland. This he did in order to increase the area of his kingdom, in order to connect and consolidate East Prussia with Brandenburg instead of having them separated by Polish provinces, and in order to secure for himself the important Baltic seaport of Dantzig and the adjacent littoral. Twenty years after his death the kingdom was almost extinguished by Napoleon, in and after the battles of Jena and Auerstadt. But it was there that Von Stein's Tugendbund was organized, and that Scharnhorst secretly transformed the people into a nation of soldiers. On March 17, 1813, the Prussian nation rose, to lead all Germany in a war of liberation, which culminated at Waterloo.

PRUSSIAN RIVALRY WITH AUSTRIA

From Waterloo down to the revolutionary era of 1848 Prussia pursued a quiet and uneventful career. In 1848, however, a new Constitution was promulgated, and the next year a National Assembly of the German States elected the King of Prussia "hereditary Emperor of the

Germans." He declined the honor, but six months later it was again proposed for him by Bavaria; in the face of vigorous protests from Austria, not only against the imperial scheme, but even against any alliance between

EUROPE AFTER THE CONGRESS OF VIENNA

Prussia and any other German state. The result was that in the course of a few years most of the German states were allied with Austria, and Prussia was left almost alone.

SEEKING CONTINENTAL DOMINATION

With the accession of William I, in 1861, the Bismarckian era began. Autocratic absolutism suspended the Constitution in order to force the nation into extreme militarism. At that early date plans were made for the domination of the continent. First, in 1864, Denmark was despoiled of two provinces, and Austria was discredited. In 1866 the German states were peremptorily bidden to choose between Prussia and Austria; a federal Diet was held at Frankfort, which, under Austrian influence, voted for the demobilization of the Prussian army. Prussia replied by declaring the Germanic Confederation to be dissolved, and then came the war. Austria was crushed, a Diet at Augsburg recognized the dissolution of the Germanic Confederation, Prussia annexed Hanover, Electoral Hesse, Nassau and Frankfort and fully incorporated the Danish provinces, and a North German confederation was formed under Prussian hegemony, with Austria left out in the cold as Prussia had been before. The sequel—foreseen and planned for at the beginning—was the war of 1870, by which France was supposed to be forever crushed to the rank of a third-class power, and the new German Empire was formed, with Prussia at the head, including all of Germany but Austria. Since then, the Triple Alliance, the secret treaty with Russia, German colonial expansion, and now a war with nearly all the rest of Europe, which was meant to make the remainder of the European continent a mere appanage to the German Empire, but which may result in the ending of that empire.

THE STORY OF THE HOHENZOLLERNS

For "Germany" now read "Prussia," and for "Prussia" read "The Hohenzollerns." It will be fitting to review the career of that extraordinary family.

Albert Achilles stoutly maintained that he could trace the descent of the Hohenzollerns directly from one of the companions of the Pious Æneas in his flight from burning Troy, his episode with Queen Dido at Carthage, and his founding of the Latin State from which sprang Rome.

It does not appear, however, that he proved his claim to such ancestry; though neither did any one ever disprove it. The learned Herr Doctor Cernutius, the loyal historian of the house of Hohenzollern, was content with tracing the line back to the Italian family of Colonna; perhaps with more plausibility than marked the ambitious genealogy of Albert Achilles, and perhaps with no less distinction, since the ancestral pretensions of the Colonnas are among the most ancient and renowned in all the world.

FIRST APPEARANCE IN HISTORY

What is certain is that the Hohenzollern family first authentically appears in history at about the time when, in 1077, the Emperor Henry IV was humiliating himself before Pope Hildebrand at Canossa, and that it took its name from Hohen Zollern, or Upper Zollern, its ancestral seat among the Suabian Alps. In those days Suabia, under the Hohenstaufen dukes and emperors, was one of the chief feudatory states of the empire. But after the extinction of that dynasty, in 1268, Suabia became a "geographical expression," being broken up into a number of petty principalities.

Among these latter were Hohenzollern Sigmaringen and Hohenzollern Hechingen, which are now united into that single province of Hohenzollern which forms a detached and isolated part of Prussia, enclosed by southern Württemberg and Baden. Near the town of Hechingen there stands today a magnificent modern castle, erected by William II on the site of the ancient home of his ancestors.

MARRIAGE STARTS RISE

Like the rival house of Hapsburg, the Hohenzollern line owed its first great rise in life to a fortunate marriage.

It was at the middle of the twelfth century that Frederick, Count of Zollern, became by virtue of marriage Burgrave of Nuremberg. That gave him extensive and valuable possessions in various parts of Germany, and placed him among the most important princes—though not yet an Elector—of the empire. So great, indeed, were his possessions that his two sons divided them between themselves, one taking Nuremberg and the Burgraviate and the other taking Zollern and some other territories. It is with the former that we have now chiefly to do, as it was from that Franconian branch of the family that the Prussian line proceeded. From the other, the Suabian branch, came that Prince Leopold whose candidacy for the crown of Spain was a pretext for the Franco-German War of 1870, and that Prince Charles who is now King of Roumania.

THE ACQUISITION OF BRANDENBURG

The next great event in Hohenzollern history occurred in the early part of the fifteenth century. At that time the once important principality of Brandenburg had fallen into seemingly hopeless decay. The great Ascanian dynasty of Anhalt had become extinct, and under feudal law the territory had reverted to the Emperor. That monarch, Louis of Bavaria, gave it to his two sons, who still further ruined it by running it into bankruptcy and alienating a part of its area. Then Louis was deposed from the imperial throne and was succeeded by Charles of Moravia, who thus became proprietor of Brandenburg, and who also gave it to his two sons, Wencelaus and Sigismund. They, in turn, mortgaged it to their cousin, Justus, and the result was that when Sigismund became Emperor he found Brandenburg a heavy fiscal burden upon him.

For relief he turned to Frederick VI of Hohenzollern, Burgrave of Nuremberg. Finally, Frederick later was permitted to take possession of it. He became Frederick I, Margrave of Brandenburg and an elector of the empire. At his death in 1440 he ordered his possessions to be divided among his four sons. Two of them, however, waived their claims, and so the domain was temporarily divided into only two parts, Frederick II taking Brandenburg and Albert taking Nuremberg. Frederick was surnamed "The Iron" because of his firmness in subduing towns to his will, as his father had subdued the barons. It was he who made Berlin the capital of Brandenburg, and thus the destined capital of Prussia and of Germany. Thitherto Tangermuende on the Elbe had been the seat of the Margraves of Brandenburg.

POSSESSIONS REUNITED

Frederick died in 1470, without issue, and was succeeded by his brother Albert, under whom the family possessions were thus reunited. This was Albert Achilles, thus surnamed because of his prowess as a soldier. His successor was John Cicero, so called because of his oratorical gifts.

John's successor, the fourth elector, was Joachim Nestor, who was thus dubbed not because of his personal wisdom so much as because of his friendly patronage of learning and his foundation of the University of Frankfort on the Oder. It was his unhappy fate to have to deal with the Reformation and to fail to appreciate its significance. Joachim remained loyal to Rome, though his wife and sons and the great majority of his people became Protestants. He exiled his wife for her change of faith, and also began the German Judenhetze by ordering the expulsion of all Jews from his dominions.

SOME NOTABLE ELECTORS

His son, Joachim II, was surnamed Hector because of his truculent spirit. It is recorded that once, in an after-dinner controversy, he drew his sword upon the famous Duke of Alva. He publicly adopted the Protestant religion, and confiscated the monasteries and other property of the Roman Catholic Church. He was a reckless spendthrift in scattering that wealth abroad. He was succeeded by his son, John George the Economist, who was noted for his thrift and business methods. Also, it may be said, the Economist was the father of twenty-three children, of whom the last was born after John George's death at the age of seventy-three.

Joachim Frederick, the eighth elector, had an uneventful reign. But the ninth, John Sigismund, marked another epoch in two ways. One was his substitution of Calvinism for Lutheranism. The other was his acquisition of the Dukedom of Prussia.

The latter state had been formed under the suzerainty of Poland, and Albert of Hohenzollern of the Nuremberg branch of the family, grand master of the then moribund Order of Teutonic Knights, on the advice of Martin Luther, had made himself its first duke. On his death in 1618, without direct male heir, his kinsman, John Sigismund, who had married Albert's granddaughter, received from Poland recognition of his succession as duke. Under his successor, the weak and vacillating George William, the realm was made the prey of both factions in the Thirty Years' War; and, while George William was ultimately forced by Gustavus Adolphus to declare himself on the Protestant side, his delay gave opportunity for Tilly's sack of Magdeburg.

FOUNDER OF PRUSSIA

Next came the Great Elector, the real founder of the Prussian state, whose monument is one of the landmarks of Berlin. This was George William's son, Frederick William. He signalized his accession by "establishing sovereignty," as he called it. In fact, it was the establishment of absolute autocracy. Also he compelled the Emperor to renounce his suzerainty over Brandenburg, and Poland to recognize the complete independence of Prussia. Thus he consolidated the whole realm under his own personal rule.

Frederick founded the military power of Prussia, developing a standing army, at first for domestic purposes, to impose his will upon the provinces, and afterward to make Prussia respected and feared abroad. As the ally of Sweden in the latter's war with Poland, he captured Praga, in the suburbs of Warsaw; and later, when the Swedes became allied with the French and invaded Brandenburg, he inflicted upon them at Fehrbellin one of the most crushing defeats in history. He also waged maritime war against Spain.

Frederick III, son and successor of the Great Elector, was perhaps the weakest and least worthy of all the line. Yet he did some important things. He founded the University of Halle and the Prussian Academy of Sciences.

Next came his son, Frederick William I, whom Macaulay described as "a prince who must be allowed to have possessed some talents for administration, but whose character was disfigured by odious vices and whose eccentricities were such as had never before been seen out of a madhouse."

FREDERICK THE GREAT

His son, so vilely persecuted and put in peril of death by his inhuman father, was the illustrious Frederick the

Great, who is said to have been acknowledged to be a great man by every one who ever wrote or spoke of him, excepting his own much-loved and highly gifted brother, Prince Henry. The latter was himself one of the very

THE GERMAN CONFEDERATION IN 1815

ablest captains of his age, perhaps second only to Frederick, and was certainly capable of appreciating greatness in others. That he was moved by jealousy of Frederick is scarcely conceivable. On the other hand, Frederick never wearied of expressing appreciation and admiration of his brother.

It was Frederick who placed Prussia among the great powers of Europe and who opened the way for placing her in Austria's old place at the head of the Teutonic world. Then he died, childless, and left the crown to the son of his brother, Augustus William, who, as Frederick William II made of his court a harem, characterized with a flagrant grossness of debauchery seldom rivaled in any civilized capital. For eleven years life in Berlin was an orgy, and the foreign activities of Prussia were either brutal spoliation, as in the partitions of Poland; or disgraceful failures, as in the attack upon the French Revolution.

CRUSHED BY NAPOLEON

The one bright spot in the dark scene was presented by the purity of the domestic life of the Crown Prince and his consort, the beautiful and gifted Louise of Mecklenburg. But when this prince came to the throne as Frederick William III he showed himself as weak a King as he was a good man. Vacillating and hesitant, he at last opposed Napoleon, and was crushed at Jena and sent into long exile at Memel, leaving his Queen to be insulted by Napoleon and to die of a broken heart. Yet he must be credited with the choice of such administrative geniuses as Stein and Hardenberg, and he shared in the achievements of Leipzig and Waterloo. He promised Prussia a constitution, but died with that promise unfulfilled, leaving to his son, Frederick William IV, an absolute despotism.

Frederick William IV also delayed to fulfill that promise of his father's, though urged to it by the multitudinous appeals of the Prussian people. A man of attractive personality, he was pedantic, bigoted, and in politics almost fanatical in his adherence to the doctrine of divine right. So he drifted blindly into the Revolution of 1848, which he suppressed, but to which he was forced to yield so far as to grant the long-delayed constitution. Ten

PRUSSO–GERMAN ACQUISITION, 1866 AND 1871

years later he became paralytic and imbecile, and was replaced by his brother as regent, and on his death three years later as King.

OLD "KAISER WILHELM"

That brother was William I, the grandfather of the present King and Emperor. At his succession he was probably the most hated man in all Prussia. Because of his stern and ruthless policy of suppressing the mob, the Revolution of 1848 raged against him more than against the King, and he was compelled to flee from Berlin in disguise to save his life, passing himself off as "Herr Francis J. Lehman, commercial traveler."

Nor did his early acts as King seem designed to conciliate the people and win their affection. His—or his Minister Bismarck's—cynical and defiant overriding of the constitution which had been won after so long a struggle, increased dislike and distrust. The war for the spoliation of Denmark was intensely unpopular, and so was that against Austria in 1866. But he succeeded. In that was the redeeming feature of his career. Moreover, he was recognized as brave, frank, manly and truthful. And when at last he won the great war against France, and made Prussia the chief state of a new German Empire, of which the Prussian kings were forever to be emperors, he became as much beloved as he had ever been hated; and died in old age the idol of the German people.

VERSAILLES OFFER NOT FIRST

It is interesting to recall that it was not at Versailles, in 1871, that the imperial crown of Germany was first offered to the King of Prussia. It was, as already mentioned, offered to Frederick Wilhelm IV in the strenuous days of 1848, but was refused by him. Why? Because it was offered to him by the German people and his divine right principles would not permit him to accept it from such a source. Had it been offered by the "heaven-ordained" princes he would have accepted it without hesitation! At Versailles, in 1871, the offer of the crown was made to William I by the princes of Germany, and, therefore, he accepted it; being about as great a stickler for "divine right" and having as much contempt for the people as his brother.

After William I came his son, Frederick III, the Noble, for a three-month reign; one of the knightliest figures that ever graced a throne. Latest of all, comes the present King and Emperor, William II.

THE LATEST HOHENZOLLERN

The story of the latest sovereign of the Hohenzollern line is not yet complete. It is being written upon the map of the world in characters of blood and fire and utter devastation. But one salient fact stands out obvious and undisguisable. That is, a paradox comparable with any of those which mark his exemplar, Frederick the Great. For when, in the early years of his reign, everybody was apprehensive lest he should prove an international fire-brand and involve all Europe in war, he sedulously culti-vated and maintained the peace. On the other hand, after twenty-five years of peaceful reign, when people were generally regarding him as one of the great bulwarks of peace, he became involved in and involved nearly all Europe in the greatest war of history.

Twelve electors, nine kings, and three emperors; but, since one was both elector and king, and three both kings and emperors, a total of twenty sovereigns. Such is the record of the house of Hohenzollern. Much more than any other sovereign house now occupying a throne, it has for centuries been intimately and commandingly associated with the greatest military and diplomatic transactions of the European continent, but never before with any approximating the present in importance not only to that family but also to all the world.

AUSTRIA AND THE HAPSBURGS

Those inclined to regard omens might see much significance in the course of Austria during the last generation. The ancient injunction to that land, or to its rulers, the Hapsburgs, was *Bella gerant alii; tu, felix Austria, nube* — let others wage wars; do thou, fortunate Austria, gain thine ends by marriage. In modern years Austria has been making unfortunate marriages, and has vainly sought to gain her ends by means of war. And it is one of the impressive facts of history that scarcely once in her more than eleven centuries of existence has Austria been entirely successful in an aggressive war, unless through the aid of powerful allies, while seldom has she been victorious even in self-defense, even against inferior powers. On the contrary, she has been beaten again and again, by almost every power with which she has come into contact.

CHRONICLES OF DISASTER

When the Hapsburg dukes came into possession of the Eastern Mark, six centuries and a third ago, they extended their domain "by marriage, by purchase and otherwise," but little, if at all, by force of arms, unless those of their allies. The one great Hapsburg victory in battle, the Marchfeld, was won by others than Austrians. The Swiss beat Austria repeatedly, at Morgarten and at Sempach. The Turks beat her, besieging Vienna and compelling the payment of much tribute as the price of her retention of territories beyond the Leith. The Poles beat her in the days of Rudolph II. The French beat her in the days of Ferdinand III and took Alsace from her in the Peace of Westphalia. The Hungarians and Turks beat her badly and again besieged Vienna, and would have taken that capital and conquered all Austria had not John Sobieski and the Poles come to the rescue.

It is true that the famous Prince Eugene did win some notable victories over the Turks, though not solely with Austrian forces; but the fruits of them had to be largely relinquished. Frederick the Great of Prussia beat Austria badly, and she was saved from ruin only by the succor given by the Hungarians and other allies. Again in the Seven Years' War the great Frederick vanquished her. The French revolutionists beat her and drove her out of Lombardy and the Netherlands. Napoleon defeated her, and in 1809 despoiled and humiliated her at will. In the Grand Alliance, at Leipsic and elsewhere, the leadership was given to her for political reasons, and she merely shared in the victories of her allies.

The Venetians beat her in 1848, and though she did recoup that loss she quickly suffered defeat at the hands of the Hungarians, and was saved only by the intervention of Russia. The Sardinians and French overwhelmed her in 1859, and she was saved from far heavier losses than those which she actually suffered only by the perfidy of Louis Napoleon in betraying and selling out his ally. Finally, in 1866, Prussia inflicted upon her one of the most crushing and humiliating defeats in history.

A POLYGLOT AND PATCHWORK REALM

We commonly speak of Austria-Hungary as the "Dual Realm." It is in fact manifold. No other in the world is of so varied and complex formation. Austria alone, not reckoning polyglot Hungary, consists of seventeen states, called "lands." Of these three are kingdoms, namely, Bohemia, Dalmatia, and Galicia and Lodomeria united. The two from which the whole empire takes its name, Upper Austria and Lower Austria, are archduchies. Six are duchies—Bukovina, Carinthia, Carniola, Salzburg, Silesia and Styria. Two, Goerz-Gradisca and Tyrol, are princely countships. Two, Moravia and Istria, are

RACES OF THE AUSTRIAN EMPIRE IN 1915

margraviates. Trieste and its environs form a special crown land, and Vorarlberg is simply a "land."

Each of these seventeen "lands" has its own local legislature, or Diet, ranging in numbers of members from twenty-four in Vorarlberg to 242 in Bohemia. These bodies, elected for six years and meeting yearly, legislate like American state legislatures on all matters not specifically reserved for the Imperial Parliament. They control taxation, education and public works, and in Tyrol and Vorarlberg they have control also of the militia, and their

88

consent is necessary for its employment in any other provinces of the empire.

MANY TRIBES AND TONGUES

As might be supposed, the populations of these various provinces differ greatly in racial composition. The two Austrias (Upper and Lower), Salsburg, Tyrol, Vorarlberg and much of Carinthia and Styria, are occupied chiefly by Germans, who are found also around the edges of Bohemia and in much of Silesia. The rest of Silesia and the greater parts of Bohemia and Moravia are occupied by the Czechs. Western Galicia is Polish, as is also a small part of Silesia. Eastern Galicia and part of Bukovina are the home of the Ruthenians. In Carniola, Goerz-Gradisca, Istria, southern Styria and Trieste the Slovenes predominate, though the Italians and Ladini are also found there and also in Tyrol and the towns of Dalmatia. Serbs and Croats are numerous in Istria and Dalmatia, and Bukovina is largely given up to Roumanians.

The total population of the empire in 1900 was 26,107,304, and at the present time it may be as much as 29,000,000. Estimating it at the latter figure, the Germans may be reckoned at about 9,500,000, the Slavs at 18,500,000, and the Italians and Ladini, with a few Magyars and others, at 1,000,000.

GERMANS DOMINANT

Although the Germans thus form a small minority, they have always been dominant because of their unity and the lack of unity among the Slavs. The Hapsburg dynasty is, of course, purely German. Therefore the court is German, and so is the great mass of the aristocracy. The chief objection of the other Hapsburgs and the court to the Countess Chotek, the wife of the late Archduke Francis Ferdinand, was not merely that she was not of royal blood, but that she was not Austrian, being a member of an ancient Czech family of Bohemia. Until recently, too, the Germans formed a majority of the educated and wealthy classes. Above all, perhaps, they have had the advantage of language. For of all the many tongues of the empire, German is the only one that is of world-wide use and that possesses a literature generally known to the world.

It has long been the aim of the Germans to Germanize the empire. This ambition first was openly manifested in the golden days of Maria Theresa, the greatest of all Austrian sovereigns. She decreed that the German language should be taught in every school and that every one of her subjects should learn it. Her successor, Joseph II, went still further, and made it the official language of the empire.

In spite of all these efforts, however, the Slavs have long been increasing in numbers far more rapidly than the Germans, and have also been increasing their political and other influence.

HUNGARY ALSO COMPOSITE

The Kingdom of Hungary is only a little less composite than the Empire of Austria. With a population of 21,030,000 it comprises 10,050,575 Hungarians or Magyars, 2,037,435 Germans, 1,967,970 Slovaks, 2,949,032 Roumanians, 1,833,162 Croats, and 1,106,471 Serbs. The Slovaks, Croats and Serbs are, of course, Slavs, numbering together 4,907,603. Adding these to the Slavs in Austria, we have a grand total of nearly 23,500,000 Slavs in the realms of a sovereign who began this world strife with a war against Slavs!

90

CHAPTER V

THE STORY OF RUSSIA

Redemption from Czarism in the War — Fall of the German Romanoff Dynasty — The Drama of a Thousand Years — Rurik and the Varangians — Early Designs Upon Constantinople — Battling with the Tartars — Origin of the Romanoff Dynasty — Peter the Great and His "Window Looking on Europe" — Winning Recognition as a European Power — The Struggle for the Sea and the Struggle for Liberty — The Later Czars — Nihilism and Its Crimes — Despotism of the Holy Synod — "Red Sunday" and the Revolution — Establishment of the Duma — Last Struggle of Absolutism — German Intrigues During the War — The Final Uprising of the People — The Russian Republic.

THE RUSSIAN REVOLUTION is thus far the most significant achievement of the war. Doubtless it would have come in time, without the war; but doubtless also the war hastened it. There was an unconscious adumbration of it at the very beginning of the war, effected by the Czar himself. That was when he changed the name of the capital from the German form St. Petersburg to the Russian Petrograd. It would have been well for him and his family if he could at the same time have abolished German influence along with the German name. Himself by ancestry more German than Russian, and his wife almost wholly German, he was unable to get rid of the malign German influences which largely controlled the court, even though he was at war with Germany. In consequence, the people ultimately rose and swept him and the whole Romanoff dynasty, more German than Russian, out of existence. The Russian Republic is the greatest fact in the world's politics thus far in the twentieth century.

It is therefore fitting that we briefly review the drama of more than a thousand years, of which this transcendent achievement is the culmination.

RURIK, OLEG AND IGOR

We must turn back the pages of history more than ten and a half centuries to legendary times; when the great Norse chieftain Rurik and his two brothers invaded Russia with the Varangian crews of many Viking galleys, and founded Veliki Novgorod, the Great New Town, which long disputed with Moscow and Kieff the primacy among Russian cities. Rurik was succeeded by his son Igor, who during his minority was guided by the Regent Oleg, the Charlemagne of the North. It was Oleg who in the year 907 led an army to the very walls of Constantinople and thus first established the Russian design of possessing that city. The Greeks bought him off by making a favorable treaty. But in 941 Igor again attacked the city, with a fleet on the Black Sea and Bosporus said to have included thousands of boats. He was repelled by the use of Greek fire; but returned to still another attack, and then was bought off. Igor met with a fate premonitory of many subsequent tragedies in the Russian Imperial line. Some of his rebellious subjects bent two stout trees together until their top branches touched near the ground, tied his right hand and foot to one tree and his left hand and foot to the other, and then released them. Afterward Igor's widow went to the city of Korosten, now Iskorosk, whose people did this thing, and pretended to wish to make peace. All she asked was that every householder in the city would give her a tame pigeon from his dove-cote. They readily complied with this request, whereupon, at evening, she released all the birds and let

A Russian Cossack Charge in the Carpathians.

Some of the stubbornest and most eagerly contested engagements of the great war took place on the snow covered heights of the Carpathians. This illustration shows a charge of a famous Cossack regiment upon an Austrian battery. The Cossacks are numbered among the finest cavalry organizations in the world and are fearless and relentless fighters. Their horses are

GERMAN ABUSE ·OF THE WHITE FLAG

An incident showing how a company of British soldiers were cut down by an ambushed enemy. The front rank of Germans had been firing from behind a small ridge. In apparent surrender they stood up in a long row and held up the white flag. The British advanced to receive their guns and take them prisoners, when suddenly the entire line

them fly back home, each with a burning firebrand tied to its tail; and thus destroyed the city. Igor begat Sviatoslav, who begat Vladimir, who begat Yaroslav, who begat Vsevolod, who begat Vladimir II, surnamed Monomachus, the first crowned ruler over all the Russian tribes and cities.

DOLGOROUKIS OLDER THAN ROMANOFFS

The youngest of the eight sons of Vladimir Monomachus was Uril of Souzdal, surnamed Dolgorouki, or the Long Armed; founder of the Dolgorouki family which has ever since been conspicuous in Russian affairs. The seventh of his eleven sons was Vsevolod II; the fourth of his eight sons was Yaroslav; and the fourth of his nine sons was that illustrious Alexander who won the surname of Nevski, "of the Neva," by his brilliant victory over the Swedes in 1240. The fourth son of Alexander Nevski was Daniel, the first of the line of Princes of Moscow. Daniel begat Ivan, who begat Ivan II, who begat Dimitry, or Demetrius, who won the surname of Donskoi, "of the Don," by his great victory over the Golden Horde of Tartars at Kulikovo, "the Field of the Woodcocks." A son of Dimitry was Vasili, or Basil, whose first son was another Vasili, called the Darkened, because during his reign he was taken prisoner by some of his hostile cousins and had his eyes burned out with a red hot sword. Vasili the Darkened was the first Russian Prince to be crowned at Moscow. After him came his son Ivan the Great, who was succeeded by his son Vasili III, who in turn was succeeded by the most monstrous figure in all Russian history, Ivan the Terrible, whose atrocities precipitated the extinction of the direct line of Rurik, and so gave opportunity for the ushering in of the Romanoff Dynasty.

ROMAN OF GALICIA

Now let us turn back to Vladimir Monomachus, whose line we have traced through and from his eighth son, Urii of Souzdal. Vladimir's first son was Mstislav, Grand Prince of Kieff, whose first son was Isiaslav, whose first son was Mstislav II. The first son of Mstislav II was Roman, of Galicia and Volhynia, and his first son was Daniel, surnamed Romanovitch and called "King of Galicia," who in his time was one of the most conspicuous and important princes in Eastern Europe and the founder of the Romanovitch branch of the family of Rurik.

Again let us turn back to Ivan, Grand Prince of Moscow, son of Daniel and grandson of Alexander Nevski. We have traced his line through and from his third son, Ivan II, father of Dimitry Donskoi. The first Ivan's first son was Simeon, Grand Prince of Moscow, known as Simeon Ivanovitch, and Simeon the Proud. He was the first to call himself Grand Prince of All the Russias and to proclaim Moscow as the supreme capital. He died of the Black Death in 1353 and was buried at Moscow in the Cathedral of St. Simeon, which he built. To his court at Moscow there came in 1341 from Eastern Prussia one Andrei, or Andrew, Kobyla, a nobleman adventurer, and entered his service. This Prussian became a Russian, prospered greatly, and had a son Feodor, or Theodore, Koschka, who married a princess of the Romanovitch branch of the line of Rurik and became the founder of four great Russian families, of which two, the Scheremetieffs and the Romanoffs, are distinguished to this day. It is a curious coincidence that Nicholas II degraded his brother, the Grand Duke Mikhail, and excluded him from any share in the tercentenary celebration of the Romanoffs, for no other offense than marrying a member

94

of this very Scheremetieff family which sprang from the same source as the Romanoffs themselves. Feodor had a son Ivan, who had a son Sakhariya Ivanovitch, who in turn had a son, Roman Sakhariyavitch. The last named had two children, a son and a daughter. The son, Nikita, married Eudoxia Alexandrovna, a descendant of Andrei, eldest brother of Alexander Nevski, of Rurik's line. The daughter, Anastasia, became the first wife of Ivan the Terrible in 1547.

THE SONS OF IVAN

Ivan the Terrible the first Tsar of Russia, conqueror of Siberia, had numerous wives, and from his domestic infamies proceeded the downfall of his house. Anastasia Romanovna, the daughter of Roman Sakhariyavitch, bore him a son, Dimitry, who died in infancy; a second son, Ivan, whom the Tsar himself murdered; a third son, Feodor, and a daughter, Eudoxia; and then was herself murdered by court conspirators. A year later Ivan married a Tcherkess girl, whom he renamed Maria and who bore him a son, named either Vasili or Dimitry, who died in a few weeks. Maria died in 1569, and three years later Ivan married Martha Sobakin, who died within an hour of the wedding. A few months later he married Anna Koltovskoi, who was childless and whom he accordingly put into a convent so that he might marry another Anna, whom he also presently got rid of. In 1580 he married Maria Nagoi, and the next year planned to dispose of her and to marry Lady Mary Hastings, of England, if he could get her. But in the nick of time Maria Nagoi bore him a son, whom he named Dimitry, and thus saved herself from divorce or death. Happily Ivan himself died in 1584.

The successor to the throne was Feodor, son of Ivan the Terrible and Anastasia Romanovna. He was a weakling and was little more than a puppet in the hands of the Duma of five, of which the dominant members were Boris Godounoff, whose sister Irene was Feodor's wife, and Nikita Romanoff, Feodor's maternal uncle. Nikita died in 1586, however, leaving Boris supreme. Presently the Polish throne fell vacant and Boris put Feodor forward as a candidate for election to it. Feodor could probably have secured it and thus have united Russia and Poland, but for his stubborn refusal to be crowned at Cracow or to recognize the Roman Catholic religion which prevailed in Poland. Thereupon the Poles elected Sigismund Vasa, of Sweden, to be their King and by so doing planted the seeds of great trouble between Poland and Russia. Next arose a conspiracy against Feodor by the Nagoi family, all of whose members had been banished from Moscow to Ouglitch. This was ruthlessly suppressed by Boris and resulted in the sending of the first political exiles to Siberia. A little later, in 1591, the young Prince Dimitry, who had been permitted to remain at Ouglitch was found dead with his throat cut. Suspicion was directed against Boris, but he discreetly had an inquest held by some of the very persons who suspected him, with the result that he was vindicated, the verdict being that Dimitry had killed himself in a fit of epilepsy.

BORIS, THE GREAT BOYAR

Feodor had but one child, a daughter, who died in infancy. In 1598 he himself died, and his widow retired to a convent. Boris Godounoff was thus left supreme and was presently elected Tsar, and for years reigned with skill and justice, winning rank as one of Russia's best sovereigns. He hoped to form a dynasty of his own, however, and thus feared the rivalry of the four sons of his former colleague, Nikita Romanoff. Accordingly he sent the eldest of them, Feodor, into a monastery, and threw the others, Alexander, Vasili and Mikhail, or Michael, into prison. Boris, who was the founder of the system of serfdom and also of the Russian State Church, died on April 13, 1605, supposedly of poisoning, and was succeeded by his fifteen-year-old son, Feodor. But the latter was soon swept away by an adventurer who was put forward by the King of Poland as the son of Ivan and Maria Nagoi; the story being that the youth who was found at Ouglitch with his throat cut was not Dimitry at all but one of his attendants. This impostor, who was probably Gregory Otrepier, an agent of Polish Jesuits, seized the Imperial crown, and threw the boy Tsar, Feodor, and his mother into prison, where they were soon murdered. Then he brought Maria Nagoi back from her convent prison and compelled her to recognize him as her son. Then, considering his place secure, he brought a Polish bride, Marina Mnishek, to Moscow, with a great train of Poles and Cossacks. At this the people of Moscow revolted. Under the lead of Vasili Shouyskie, the man who had conducted the inquest on the body of young Dimitry at Ouglitch, and who was accordingly convinced that the Tsar Dimitry was an impostor, they stormed the palace, threw the pretender from the window, and slew him with their swords. Then Maria Nagoi recanted her recognition and declared that he was not her son.

THE DAYS OF THE PRETENDERS

Vasili Shouyskie, leader of the Tsar-slaying mob, was next proclaimed Tsar, in the spring of 1606, but was not long permitted to enjoy his sovereignty in peace. Pretenders sprang up as if by magic, chiefly on the fertile soil of Poland, whose King, Sigismund Vasa, was intent upon becoming the master of Russia. One story was that the false Dimitry had escaped when the palace was stormed, that the man who was thrown from the window and killed was not he but some one impersonating him, and that Dimitry himself was safe in Poland. Another story related to another person altogether, who was said to be the real Dimitry of Ouglitch. A third pretender called himself Peter, son of Feodor Ivanovitch—who, as already related, had only one child, a daughter, who died in infancy. This pretender raised an army of Don Cossacks, but was defeated and slain. A fourth pretended to be a son of Ivan the Terrible; a fifth, the son of Ivan, the murdered son of Ivan the Terrible; and no fewer than eight more claimed to be sons of Feodor Ivanovitch. Of all this array none proved to be formidable. But in the spring of 1608 still another false Dimitry appeared under Polish patronage, who invaded Russia with a considerable army of Poles and Cossacks, penetrated almost to the environs of Moscow, and established a rival imperial court at Toushin. There Marina Mnishek met him and declared him to be her husband, the original false Dimitry, and many Russian cities swore allegiance to him.

Stubborn resistance was made to him, however, by the city of Rostov, where Feodor Romanoff was Metropolitan Bishop under the name of Philaret. In the end, however, the city fell, and Philaret was captured and let to Dimitry at Toushin, with the expectation of being put to death. Dimitry, thinking thus to strengthen his own position, greeted him in friendly fashion as a beloved kinsman of "our late half-brother," the Tsar Feodor Ivanovitch, and made him Patriarch of Moscow and of All the Russias.

RUSSIA IN ANARCHY

Vasili still held out at Moscow against the pretender at Toushin, and civil war raged. But by 1610 Dimitry's cause waned and was evidently doomed to failure. Thereupon Sigismund of Poland himself invaded Russia and put forward his son Vladislav as a candidate for the throne. Vasili in his desperation committed injudicious acts which provoked Moscow to revolt against him, and in July of that year he was forced to abdicate, and was sent to a monastery. A Duma, or Council of Nobles, was formed to conduct the government until another Tsar could be chosen. This Council hesitated for a time between the latest false Dimitry and Vladislav, but finally offered the crown to the latter, and many swore allegiance to him. At this crisis the Patriarch, Philaret, otherwise Feodor Romanoff, intervened for the salvation of Russia. He led a large delegation of ecclesiastics and nobles from Moscow to meet Sigismund at Smolensk, which city he was besieging, to inquire whether Vladislav, if accepted as Tsar, would adopt for himself the Orthodox Russian religion. The reply given was evasive and unsatisfactory, and the envoys were convinced that Sigismund was seeking the Russian crown for himself and was using his son as a mere mask. Philaret therefore sought to rouse the people of Moscow against the Polish Prince. The nobles, however, betrayed the city into the hands of the Poles and the latter came in and took possession. Philaret was seized and sent as a prisoner to Poland. In Passion Week of 1611 civil war raged in the streets and nearly all of the city was burned, the Poles, however, still holding the citadel. Soon after Sigismund captured Smolensk, while Novgorod gave its allegiance to Karl, the second son of the King of Sweden. The Cossacks at Moscow were inclined to hail as Tsar an infant son of Marina Mnishek, while yet another false Dimitry arose at Ivangorod and established himself at Pskov. Chaos was complete and Russia seemed ruined beyond repair.

SEEKING A SAVIOR

Then at Nijni Novgorod a patriotic uprising began, led by a cattle dealer and butcher named Kozma Minin-Soukhorouk and by Prince Dimitry Pojharskie. The former professed to have had a divine call, like that of Joan of Arc, and thus aroused much religious enthusiasm. A large army was organized, led by Prince Dimitry, and it moved slowly forward toward the capital. It entered into negotiations with the Swedes, and seemed inclined to accept Karl as Tsar if he would adopt the Russian religion. Near Moscow it encountered the Poles and Cossacks, and won a hard battle. Thus warned, on October 24, 1612, the Poles in the Kremlin released a crowd of prisoners whom they had been holding there, including among them Mikhail Feodorovitch Romanoff, the son of Philaret. The next day the Poles surrendered the Kremlin and marched out, and the Russians reoccupied that citadel. This event marked the turning point of the crisis of Russian history. Sigismund, who had been moving toward Moscow, now halted and soon retired to Poland.

Russia thus being freed from serious invasion, the dignitaries of church and state set to work upon the important task of selecting a new Tsar. The direct line of Rurik was extinct, and there was a strong repugnance to the election of any foreign prince. By common consent attention was generally turned toward Mikhail, or Michael, the son of Philaret.

THE FIRST ROMANOFF

In such circumstances and under such considerations the representatives of church and state were soon agreed in supporting the candidacy of the young Romanoff Prince. In "Orthodox Week" of Lent, 1613, the Archbishop of Riazan, with a group of distinguished associates, faced a great conclave of Russian noblemen and clergy in the Red Square of Moscow, and asked who should be Tsar. There was a universal shout of "Mikhail Feodorovitch Romanoff!" On July 11th following he was crowned in the Ouspienskie Cathedral, and the Romanoff dynasty was fully established. For a year he and his associates had hard work to reorganize the disordered finances of the empire and to suppress various rebellions. It was harder still to settle with Sweden and Poland, but he was greatly aided by England in making peace with the former power, and on December 1, 1618, he made peace with Poland, though at the cost of surrendering a number of Russian cities. For this he was repaid, however, by the release of his father, Philaret, who came home in safety and was re-elected to the Patriarchate. With Mikhail at the head of the state and Philaret at the head of the church, the Russian Empire seemed to have emerged from its time of trouble.

The reign of Mikhail, for thirty-two years, in its quietness and moderation presented a striking contrast to the stormy era which had preceded it. It was partly the quietness of national exhaustion and partly that induced by the wisdom and benevolence of the Tsar's father,

101

Philaret, whose name was always joined with that of Mikhail in imperial decrees. The next Tsar, Mikhail's son Alexis, for thirty-one years showed himself an able, broad-minded sovereign, both progressive and aggressive, who codified Russian laws, developed trade, cultivated friendly relations with other countries, incorporated the Ukraine and the whole Cossack country with Russia, and regained the cities which his father had been compelled to relinquish to Poland. The third Romanoff, Feodor II, in half a dozen years did little save to neglect the good works of his predecessors. His chief claim to remembrance is that he destroyed the pedigree books which had long been a prolific source of bickering and wrangling among the nobility.

PETER THE GREAT

Then came another crucial epoch in Russian history. There were two claimants of the throne, Ivan and Peter, sons of Alexis by his first and second wives. The dispute was compromised by letting the two reign jointly under the regency of Sophia, Ivan's elder sister. That arrangement lasted until the death of Ivan seven years later, when Peter sent Sophia to a convent and alone assumed the reins of autocracy. This was that Peter who gave Russia a frontage on the Black Sea and on the Baltic, who built St. Petersburg to be "a window looking on Europe;" who crushed Charles XII of Sweden at Poltava; who suppressed Mazeppa and the Little Russians; who conquered Esthonia, Livonia, Viborg and other Baltic provinces; who created a Russian navy and mercantile marine; who abolished the system of oriental seclusion of women and oriental dress for men, and who well-earned his title of Great.

After his thirty-six years came his widow, Catherine I, who for her two years was content to let the government be conducted by Menshikoff, who had as a boy peddled cakes in the streets until he was taken up, for his good looks, as one of Peter's numerous favorites. He remained all-powerful during Catherine's reign, but soon after the accession of Peter II, son of Alexis, he was deposed and exiled by the Dolgorouki family, who led a reactionary revolution. Peter reigned only three years and at his death Russia fell almost into chaos again, amid the conflicting claims of rival candidates. A secret council of nobles finally selected Anna of Courland, daughter of Ivan, the brother of Peter the Great, as sovereign. This choice was based upon the fact not that her claim was the strongest of all the candidates but that it was the weakest; the idea being that on that account she would be most subservient to the nobles. She indeed signed a document accepting terms which they imposed upon her, making her a mere puppet and vesting all real authority in the High Council. But she soon repudiated that contract and made her favorite lover, Biren, a German Courlander of low birth, supreme. Biren distinguished himself by sending more than 20,000 political exiles to Siberia. Anna died after ten years on the throne and was succeeded by her grand-nephew, Ivan IV. Within the year Biren was expelled from court, Ivan was deposed and sent to prison for life, and Elizabeth, youngest daughter of Peter the Great, succeeded him. During her twenty years' reign Russia became assertive, made much advance in literature and the arts and defeated Frederick the Great of Prussia. She let the government be conducted chiefly by two of her favorites and finally drank herself to death. Her nephew Peter III succeeded her, but as she had brought

him up in seclusion and ignorance he was utterly unfit
for the place. He was a mere puppet in Prussian hands
and gave back to Frederick the Great all that Elizabeth
had taken from him. At that his wife, although herself
a German Princess of Anhalt-Zerbst, repudiated him and
led the Orloffs and other nobles in deposing, imprisoning
and murdering him. He was strangled to death by Alexis
Orloff, who soon after betrayed to her death Princess
Catherine, a daughter of the Empress Elizabeth.

CATHERINE THE GREAT

These tragedies left Catherine, widow of the murdered
Peter, supreme, and for thirty-four years she was one of
the greatest sovereigns Russia ever had, and at the same
time one of the most infamous of women in all the history
of the world. The splendor of her conquests and annexation of territory, of the international prestige which she
had for Russia, and of her law-giving to the Empire was
rivaled only by the monstrosity of her vices and the
depths of moral degradation to which she and her succession of favorites plunged the Russian court. After
her for five years came her son Paul, who began as a saint
and ended as a demon and a lunatic and was assassinated
by his own courtiers just as he was at the point of joining
Napoleon Bonaparte for the conquest of India. His
son, Alexander I, was the Tsar who dealt with Napoleon
at Eylau, Tilsit, Moscow and Leipsic; who added Finland,
Poland, Bessarabia and much of the Caucasus to his
empire; who founded the Holy Alliance and thus provoked the promulgation of the Monroe Doctrine, and
who was driven almost to insanity by fear of assassination
at the hands of the seditious secret societies which then
began to spring up all over Russia. At the end of his

twenty-four years his son Nicholas became Tsar for thirty years; a pronounced reactionary, who defeated and despoiled Persia and Turkey, who crushed the Poles and Hungarians, and who died of a broken heart in the Crimean War. His son, Alexander II, was as liberal and progressive as he had been reactionary, and gained fame as the liberator of the serfs; but perished after twenty-six years as the victim of a Nihilist bomb thrower. His son, Alexander III, peace-loving and domestic, reigned for fourteen years in terror and darkness, for fear of sharing his father's fate, and was thus driven to an untimely grave.

THE LAST OF THE CZARS

His son and successor, Nicholas II, reigned more than twenty-two years and completed three hundred years of the Romanoff Dynasty. Under a strict interpretation of the usual rule of dynastic descent, the Romanoff line would be held to have terminated with the death of the Empress Elizabeth in 1761. For her successor, Peter III, was the son of Elizabeth's sister Anna, whose husband was the Duke of Holstein-Gottorp. As a sovereign is attributed to the house of his father and not of his mother, therefore, Peter III was not a Romanoff but a Holstein-Gottorp, and was the first Tsar of a new dynasty, to which all Russian sovereigns since belonged. The Russian court insisted, however, that the greater family must have precedence over the less. Accordingly, when Anna Romanoff, daughter of Peter the Great, married Charles Frederick of Holstein-Gottorp, the offspring of that union was held to be more Romanoff than Holstein-Gottorp. The Holstein-Gottorp alliance, however, was not ignored, and Peter III and all subsequent sovereigns were credited to the "House of Romanoff-Holstein."

There was thus a certain fitness in the circumstance that this German dynasty which long had tyrannized over Russia should come to an end in a war with Germany, and as one of the results of that war.

In January, 1905, occurred "Red Sunday." A great multitude of workingmen, led by a priest, approached the Winter Palace for the purpose of presenting a petition to the Czar for an increase of civil rights. They were entirely peaceful in their demeanor, and offered no violence whatever. But the troops fired upon them, and hundreds were slain.

CONSTITUTIONAL GOVERNMENT

There followed general disorder throughout the Empire, until in October, 1905, the Czar proclaimed a constitution and the establishment of a Duma, or national Parliament. The latter body met for the first time in April, 1906. It was dissolved on July 8th, having done little or nothing. A second Duma met in March, 1907, and had a stormy and ineffective career. The third met in December, 1907, and became a really authoritative and efficient legislative body. Thereafter there was a persistent fight for extension of parliamentary and popular power, and restriction of the autocratic powers of the Czar.

The outbreak of the great war found government and people apparently united for a vigorous and unrelenting prosecution of the campaign. It was at the beginning of September, 1914, that the Czar by personal decree changed the name of the capital to Petrograd, and that moment marked the zenith of his reign. Soon there began to be perceptible indications of German influence. This was not sufficient to cause Russia's withdrawal from the war. But it did seriously hamper and at times defeat the operations of the armies. German spies continually betrayed Russian military plans to the enemy; and those spies were members of the court circle, if not of the imperial family. Worse than that, supplies of arms and ammunition were withheld from the Russian army, thus dooming it to defeat. The great disasters in Poland were probably chiefly attributable to this cause. The Russian army was without supplies, although there were abundant supplies in the hands of the government.

THE END OF THE CZARS

This treason was fatal to the dynasty, which was not unreasonably held responsible for it. The people were incensed, and, of course, the army was, too. In consequence the army, instead of supporting the throne against the people, as thitherto, became itself the leader in revolutionary aspirations, and manifested a readiness to join with the people in overthrowing a dynasty which was the tool of alien foes. In March, 1917, came the end. There was a wholesale uprising of the people against the Czar. Some violence and loss of life occurred, but the troops in general mutinied and fraternized with the people. The Czar and his family were taken as prisoners of state, and the abdication of Nicholas II in behalf of his brother was exacted. After brief consideration, that brother declined to accept the crown unless he should be elected Czar by the free votes of the Russian people.

A few days later the leaders of the Duma, who were in control of the government, decided not to retain the monarchy, but to organize a republican form of government, and to remove from office all members of the Romanoff or Holstein-Gottorp family, even including the Grand Duke Nicholas who had been so efficient and loyal a leader

of the Russian army. Czarism had partially betrayed
Russia, and Russia was done with Czarism and with all
in any way connected with it. The Russian Empire was
ended; the Russian Republic was begun.

COUNTER-REVOLUTION

It was the purpose of the Provisional Government which
had thus been formed in Russia to remain loyal to the Allies,
and to wage the war against Germany with a vigor and
effectiveness far exceeding the half-hearted efforts of the
half-German imperial régime. Realizing this, the German
government through underground intrigues set about
fomenting a counter-revolution. Through the work of
spies, bribery and mendacious propaganda it succeeded, in
the fall of 1917, in overthrowing the Provisional Republican
government, and substituting in its place a cabal of its own
selection, consisting of the leaders of a faction known as
the Bolsheviki. These worthies promptly established at
Petrograd a reign of loot and terror, stopped all military
operations, ordered the de-mobilization of the army, and
at Brest-Litovsk in December, 1917, made a truce with
Germany and engaged in negotiations for a separate peace,
regardless of the other allies, largely on the basis of the
status quo ante bellum. The immediate effect of this monstrous treachery to the allied cause was to enable Germany
to transfer hundreds of thousands of men from the Russian
front to the Italian and French-Belgian fronts, for great
"drives" there. The action of the Bolsheviki was not
concurred in, of course, by the whole Russian people.

The Cossacks and Ukrainians waged open war against
the Bolsheviki, and presently an independent state of
Ukraine was established under the government of the Rada
of Kieff. Following this, dissolution of the empire pro-

ceeded apace. All the Baltic Provinces, including Lithuania, Courland, Esthonia and Livonia, under German incitement declared their independence. Finland also announced its secession from Russia, and demanded large accessions of territory, so as to give it a frontage on the Arctic Ocean and practical domination of the Russian ports of Kola and Archangel. On March 3, 1918, a treaty of peace was signed, under which Russia relinquished the Baltic Provinces to Germany, and some districts of Caucasia to Turkey. At about the same time Russia recognized the independence of Finland. For a time fighting prevailed in Ukraine between the Bolsheviki and the Germans, but finally Russia was compelled to acquiesce in the separation of that vast region, comprising practically all of the southern part of the empire, and its establishment under German suzerainty.

An earnest contest arose in the late spring of 1918 for the control of Siberia. The Bolsheviki, of course, claimed sovereignty there, but a large part of the population refused to recognize it, while German propaganda was busy, and the Allied powers inclined toward intervention with an international force to save the country from anarchy or from German conquest. Such intervention was, however, withheld because of the unwillingness of the United States government to sanction it. Our government, however, in June, 1918, authorized the recruiting of Russians, Poles and Czecho-Slavs in the United States to fight against not only the Germans but also the Bolsheviki, though at the same time it proposed the sending of a friendly commission to Russia to aid in the rehabilitation of that country.

CHAPTER VI

THE ALLIED POWERS

France and Her Vital Interests in the War — Germany's Former Attempts to Destroy Her and then to Woo Her as an Ally — The Russian Alliance — The *Entente Cordiale* between France and Great Britain — Practically a Triple Entente — Belgium as a Neutral State — Animosity between Great Britain and Germany — Why Great Britain was Compelled to Enter the War — Japan Drawn into Alliance with Her Former Foe — Italy's Anomalous Position in the Triple Alliance — Her Reason for Withdrawing from It and for Entering the War against Her Former Allies — Portugal an Old Ally of Great Britain.

THERE ARE no such things as traditional friends or traditional foes among the nations of the world. That fact is writ clear and large in the alignment of the powers in the great war. There are among the important European belligerents scarcely two enemies which were not formerly allies, and scarcely two allies which were not formerly foes. Observe:

Great Britain and Germany, or in the last analysis England and Prussia, are the bitterest of all foes. Yet never before were they at war with each other, but in the last preceding general European war, which ended at Waterloo, they were allies. Russia and Germany are foes; yet never before did they fight each other, but more than once were allies. Italy is at war with Germany, but it is for the first time, and Prussia was practically Italy's ally in 1866 and 1870.

Great Britain and France are allies; yet they have hitherto fought each other more than any other two powers of Europe. They are both allies of Russia, yet they both fought Russia in the Crimea. Russia and Japan are allies; yet only a few years ago they were foes in a mighty war. Germany and Austria are allies; but they were foes in 1866.

GERMANY'S DRIVE AT FRANCE

Of all the warring powers, France had at the beginning perhaps the most vital interest in the war. It was to her a matter of life or death. The ancient quarrel, dating from the time of Charlemagne's sons, between her and Germany, was revived in 1870 by Germany on the strength of a falsified dispatch, deliberately falsified by Otto von Bismarck in order to drag France into war. As a result of that war France was robbed of two provinces and of a cash indemnity so vast that it was supposed she would be unable to pay it, or that in paying it she would be hopelessly impoverished and ruined. To the chagrin of Germany, she paid it promptly and regained more than her old prosperity; whereupon a few years later Germany sought to force another war upon her with the confessed intention of "bleeding her white." The diplomatic intervention of Great Britain balked this scheme of Germany's, and thus planted the seeds of that hatred of Great Britain which Germany has ever since cherished. Then Germany devoted herself to the incitement of enmity between France and Great Britain and also to efforts to induce France to join her in war against the "modern Carthage," as German statesmen called the United Kingdom.

France spurned these German overtures, and instead entered at first into an entente and then into a complete alliance with Russia. Under the diplomatic influence of Edward VII of England the irritation and estrangement which had for some time existed between France and Great Britain, largely through German marplotry, were allayed and an *entente cordiale* was established, which under George V became practically an alliance. And at the same time France was the means of bringing Russia and Great Britain into friendly relations and into something like an entente. All this intensified the wrath of Germany against France, and the result was that when the German Emperor decided to begin his long cherished war for the conquest of the world he aimed his first blow at France. Knowing that she was unprepared, he hoped to crush her completely before any other powers could come to her aid. Having done that, he could turn his triumphant armies against the next foe that appeared.

NEUTRAL BELGIUM

The chief blow at France was struck through Belgium, and it was thus that Belgium was brought into the war. The direct frontier between Germany and France was so strongly fortified by the French that a rapid invasion in that quarter was impossible. But the invasion to be successful must be rapid, so rapid as to assure the capture of Paris before the French army could be put on a war footing or British or Russian armies be brought into the field. The French frontier abutting upon Belgium was unfortified, and invasion there would be easy, if only Belgium would give passage to the German army.

This, of course, Belgium refused to do. The German Government strove to get Belgian consent, at first with bribes and blandishments and later with menaces. But Belgium was inflexible in her refusal; for a reason which the German imperial and official mind seemed unable to understand. That was, good faith and honor. Belgium was a neutral state. Her neutrality and the inviolability of her territory had been guaranteed by the powers, Germany among them, in solemn treaties. She therefore felt herself bound by honor and good faith to maintain the neutrality of her territory and not let it be used as a basis or avenue of attack by one power upon another. The history of human heroism contains no finer record than that of little Belgium standing alone against the overwhelming might of Germany, and suffering martyrdom rather than regard a solemn treaty as a "scrap of paper." The neutrality of Belgium, it may be recalled, was guaranteed by treaties in 1831, 1839 and 1870, to all of which Germany, or Prussia, was a party, and by the treaty of The Hague, to which the United States also was a party.

ANGLO-GERMAN ANIMOSITY

A long train of incidents led to Great Britain's participation in the war. In 1870 Prussia was angry at Great Britain because the latter, in pursuance of neutral principles, sold munitions of war to France as freely as to Germany. This anger was increased when Great Britain practically forbade Germany to attack France again and to "bleed her white." When this proceeded to the making of intrigues with other powers against Great Britain, resentment arose in the latter country, and for a number of years before the war there was an estrangement between the two countries amounting almost to antagonism.

The actual causes of British participation in the war, however, were chiefly two. One was, the British obligation to vindicate the neutrality of Belgium. Great Britain had participated in the establishment of Belgium as an independent kingdom, in 1830, and was a party to the various treaties which not merely recognized Belgium as an independent and neutral state but also pledged the signatories to protect and maintain her in that status. Great

Britain therefore conceived it to be her moral and legal duty to intervene to protect Belgium from invasion and violation of her neutrality; or to redeem her from the outrage which was inflicted upon her.

The second specific cause was found in the entente or alliance between Great Britain and France, under the terms of which each nation was pledged to aid the other in certain contingencies. It was to keep faith with France, too, therefore, that Great Britain entered the war. It may be added that these reasons, like Belgium's, were apparently quite unappreciated by Germany. Instead, the German Government seemed to take it as a grievance that Great Britain did not break faith with Belgium and France, regard her treaties with them as "scraps of paper," and stand idly by while Germany ravaged them. For this cause Germany began singing her national "Hymn of Hate," and using as her watchword, in church, in the army and everywhere, "God punish England!" Also, she expressed profound and sneering disregard for England's "contemptible little army."

JAPAN RUSSIA'S ALLY

Japan was drawn into the war at an early date. For some years she had been the ally of Great Britain. But ten years before she had been engaged in a gigantic war with Russia; and Russia and Great Britain were now allies. She was therefore placed in the dilemma of either abandoning her ally or allying herself with her former foe. The latter course was adopted without hesitation, and Japan entered the war as the ally of both Great Britain and Russia.

This was effected easily and without repugnance, for several reasons. One was the fact that the former enmity and cause of enmity between Japan and Russia had disappeared, and both nations had for some time been drawing together, feeling that the welfare of both demanded friendly co-operation in Chinese affairs. Another was the fact that Japan had long felt bitter resentment against Germany, and particularly against the Emperor. That was for three major reasons. One was, Germany's intervention twenty years before to prevent Japan from securing the advantages which she had fairly won in her war with China. Another was, the German Emperor's flamboyant efforts, years before, to arouse a European crusade against Japan in order to avert what he called the "Yellow Peril." The third was, Germany's seizure of extensive Chinese territory and her occupation of various islands in the Asian seas, which Japan regarded as a menace to herself.

ITALY'S ANOMALOUS POSITION

The position of Italy at the beginning of the war was strangely anomalous. Indeed, her position as a member of the Triple Alliance had for years been anomalous; for she was thus leagued with the power, Austria, which had for generations been her cruel oppressor and despoiler, with which she had repeatedly been at war, and which was still holding several provinces which properly belonged to Italy—the "Italia Irredenta," which it was Italy's national ambition, and the personal ambition of every Italian citizen, to redeem. In that incongruous alliance, Italy had been victimized for the benefit of the others, and especially of Germany. She had been compelled to spend more money than she could well afford for military preparations, and had been hampered in her own legitimate aspirations.

It was therefore with sentiments of relief and exultation that Italy saw in this war an opportunity to release herself from the hated bonds of the Triple Alliance, and to regain her provinces from her old-time foe. This door of opportunity was opened to her by Austria herself. That power had only a year before acted in a manner grossly inimical to Italian interests in the matter of the disposition of Albania at the end of the Balkan war; so that Italy would then, on that ground, have been justified in withdrawing from the Triple Alliance. But worse remained to be done. In all the controversy with Serbia, before and after the tragedy at Sarajevo, Austria ignored Italy, while she was in constant and most intimate conference with Germany; being guided and controlled by orders from Berlin. In thus conducting negotiations of the gravest character in international affairs, which might involve the Triple Alliance, without consulting or even informing Italy, Austria violated the spirit and intent of the Triple Alliance and gave Italy the fullest moral and legal release from her obligations under that instrument. Long before the actual declaration of war, the people of Italy were clamorous for it, and when at last it came they entered into the conflict with passionate eagerness.

PORTUGAL ENGLAND'S OLD ALLY

The position of Portugal was interesting. In Europe she did not come into territorial contact with any of the belligerents, and her interests were little affected. But in Africa her colonies did come into contact with those of both Germany and Great Britain, and her interest in their fate was considerable. As an ally of either she could make herself an important factor in the war.

Of her choice of allies there was never a moment's doubt

for the reason that she was and long had been an ally of Great Britain. According to their treaty of alliance, each power was bound to assist the other in case of invasion, with men, arms and ammunition, and also to help to protect the other's colonies, with ships of war and troops. In assisting Great Britain in Africa, therefore, Portugal acted in accordance with her treaty pledges. Portugal did not declare war against Germany, but merely began to aid England in Africa. Thereupon, on March 10, 1916, Germany declared war against Portugal, and the latter power then extended her military operations to Europe.

ROUMANIA'S ENTRY

The sympathies of the Roumanian people and their leaders were from the beginning with the Allies, and there was much eagerness on the part of many to enter the war, in order that in the final victory Roumania might reclaim Transylvania, which was chiefly peopled by Roumanians but which was held by Hungary. Two things restrained the government, however, from taking such a step. One was the personal influence of the King and Queen, who were both Germans, the King being a member of the Hohenzollern family, related distantly to the German Emperor. King Charles died on October 10, 1914, a few weeks after the outbreak of the war, and was succeeded by his nephew, Ferdinand, a son of Prince Leopold of Hohenzollern-Sigmaringen. The new Queen, Marie, was a princess of Saxe-Coburg and Gotha.

The other restraining fact was the lack of arms. A year before the war Roumania had shipped most of her artillery to Germany, to be rebored and otherwise improved, and at the outbreak of the war it had not been returned to her. It was necessary, therefore, to wait until

117

she could get another equipment, by way of Russia. At last, in August, 1916, Roumania declared war against Austria, and invaded Hungary. At once the Central Powers concentrated all possible forces against her, and half of her territory was overrun by the enemy.

REVOLUTION IN GREECE

The King of Greece was hesitant in his policy, though, being a Dane, he was naturally inclined toward the Allies. But the Queen was the stronger and more positive character of the two, and she was the sister of the German Emperor. She succeeded in preventing the government from joining the Allies, though she was unable to get it to cast in its lot with the Central Powers. The sentiment of the people was strongly in favor of the Allies.

Eleutherios Venizelos, the foremost statesman of Greece and the most popular leader, openly rebelled against the attitude of the King and his subservient ministry, and established a rival ministry at Salonika, under the protection of the Allies; to which the majority of the Greek people gave their allegiance. On June 12, 1917, King Constantine abdicated the throne and was succeeded by his second son, Alexander; on June 25th Venizelos became Prime Minister, and four days later Greece entered the war on the side of the Allies.

All other European countries, to wit, Spain, Switzerland, Holland, Denmark, Sweden and Norway, remained and remain neutral, though all suffered much from the war. Their popular sympathy inclined toward the Allies.

Chapter VII

WAR POWERS OF EUROPE IN 1914

The Vast Burden of Militarism — Europe a "Weary Titan" — Size of the Various Armies on Peace Footing and on War Footing — The People Burdened Almost beyond Endurance — Origin of Prussian Militarism — The Model for All the Continent — France's Heroic Efforts to Keep the Pace — The Fortresses of Belgium — Brialmont's Work in Roumania — British Dependence Upon Sea Power — Lord Roberts' Warnings and Pleas Disregarded — All Nations Unprepared Except Germany.

THE GREAT powers of Europe in 1914 groaned under the burden of militarism. They were almost crushed by it, yet they could not cast it off, nor prevent its steady increase. They were like Arnold's "Weary Titan"—

> The Weary Titan, with deaf
> Ears, and labor-dimmed eyes,
> Regarding neither to right
> Nor left, goes passively by,
> Staggering on to her goal,
> Bearing on shoulders immense,
> Atlantean, the load
> Well nigh not to be borne,
> Of the too vast orb of her fate.

Year by year the competition between potential rivals compelled an increase of the burden; until some said there would soon have to be war, to bring relief from the load, while others declared that the armaments had become so colossal and so potentially destructive that no nation would dare to go to war. Indeed, the military situation in continental Europe was in 1914 almost beyond the

119

possibility of popular comprehension. Mention of the magnitude of the armaments was like mention of the extent of the interstellar spaces. The human mind could scarcely grasp such numbers.

THE RUSSIAN LEGIONS

Russia, for example. Her military increase that year was perhaps the most sensational of all. With her new scheme of keeping the fourth class with the colors for three months longer than formerly, she swelled her peace establishment—her standing army in time of peace, to the quite unprecedented numbers of more than 1,700,000. Legislation then provided that that establishment should be kept up to 1,760,000 the year around, while during three or four winter months it would be above 2,000,000.

Russian authorities estimated that as a result of the new legislation the war force of the empire would be

Fully trained men	3,500,000
Partly trained men	800,000
Total	4,300,000

That was a big showing. But the German General, Blume, who was one of the best informed authorities in all Europe concerning all armies but the German, declared that those figures were far too small. The real size of the Russian army, he insisted, would be in time of war something like this:

Regular war footing	6,665,000
Levy en masse	1,433,000
Total	8,098,000

On the basis of these figures, there is no room for wonderment at the increase of the Russian military budget from $275,000,000 in 1908, to $445,000,000 in 1914.

This was called Russia's answer to the new German army law. Let us see what that measure was, which so aroused the martial rivalry of Russia.

GERMANY'S GROWING ARMY

The German rule had always thitherto been to keep the peace strength of the army at about one per cent of the population, and the various army laws provided for increases from time to time, according to the increases of population shown by the census. The size of the army on a peace footing was thus as follows under the successive acts of the Reichstag:

	MEN
1871–1880	401,659
1881–1887	427,274
1887–1890	468,409
1890–1893	486,983
1894–1898	557,000
1899–1904	574,000
1905–1911	585,000
1911–1912	595,000

At the same ratio the numbers for 1912–13 would have been 626,000, and those for 1913–14 would have been 661,000. But the new law made the former no less than 723,000 and the latter 870,000 all told. That was more than one per cent of the population. It was about 1.35 per cent, while the Russian percentage was only about 1.25 and that of France, as we shall see, was no less than 1.47. This new law imposed upon the German people the greatest military burden they had ever borne in time of peace, and was considered by many to be the limit of their endurance. They were bearing it with apparent patience, but they would have welcomed relief from it with general joy.

THE FRENCH ESTABLISHMENT

France made no response, in numbers, to Germany's increases in 1911 and 1912. In 1905 she made a law under which at the beginning of 1913 she had only 567,000 men. That was 303,000 fewer than Germany had; a tremendous disparity. She then turned to the three years' service plan, and under it swelled her peace strength to 673,000, all told, or 197,000 less than that of Germany.

THE OTHER ARMIES

Italy was credited with a peace army of 306,300, and a war force of from 750,000 to 1,100,000, of first and second lines only. Austria-Hungary had a peace army of 425,881, which in time of war would be increased to 810,000 in first and second lines, and to 2,000,000 when the reserves were included.

Great Britain had what the German Emperor slightingly called a "contemptible little army," of only 275,000 on a war footing; her reliance having long been placed upon her unequaled fleet.

THE PEOPLE'S BURDEN

It was no wonder that statesmen were beginning to wonder where it would all end. Here were armies on a peace footing of nearly seven million men, which in time of war would be swelled to fifteen millions. The burden of taxation imposed upon the people was appalling. Here is the European army budget of the six great powers for 1913–14; the last year before the war:

122

Russia..................................	$445,000,000
Germany................................	300,000,000
France.................................	183,000,000
Austria-Hungary........................	111,000,000
Italy..................................	84,000,000
Great Britain..........................	140,000,000
	$1,263,000,000

Here were more than a billion and a quarter dollars spent in a year of profound peace upon the armies of the powers, beside what was spent upon their navies.

PRUSSIAN MILITARISM

There can be no exaggeration nor injustice in charging this state of affairs chiefly against Germany, or, in the last analysis, Prussia. From the earliest times Prussia has been essentially a military state. Its growth in territory has been achieved by a succession of wars, waged for that express purpose. Under Frederick the Great, the "Drill Master of Europe," it was decidedly the most efficient military power on the continent. After his death it fell into less competent hands. But after it had been crushed by Napoleon, in its preparation for the War of Liberation, it adopted what was a device of its own military statesmen and what has been developed into the military system of that and other European countries today. That is, the system of enforced universal military service. Under that system every young man is compelled to serve for several years with the colors, and to serve in the reserve for a number of years afterward, the result being that every able-bodied man in the country is a trained soldier.

For many years the other nations of Europe did not seem fully to realize what this meant. But after the

123

astounding victories of Prussia over Austria in 1866, and of Prussia and her German allies over France in 1870–71, the eyes of all Europe were opened, and the powers, with the exception of Great Britain, generally adopted the same or a similar system.

FRANCE'S HEAVY BURDEN

Upon France the burden was greatest of all. She felt that it was necessary for her to maintain a military establishment about equal to that of Germany, in order to protect herself against the renewed attack by that power which had been threatened and which she regarded as inevitable. But it became every year more difficult to do this, because of her practically stationary population as compared with Germany's rapidly increasing census roll. For the last half century the birth-rate in France has scarcely if at all exceeded the death-rate. In Germany, on the other hand, there has been a considerable surplus of births over deaths. So the population of Germany has been steadily and even rapidly increasing over that of France, until at the outbreak of the war it exceeded it by fifty per cent.

This, of course, meant that if France was to maintain a standing army as large as Germany's, there would be serving with the colors a much larger percentage of her sons than of Germany's. It also meant that she could not possibly have as many reserves as Germany, and that her total strength, in a mass levy, would be considerably less than Germany's. A nation of 42,000,000 cannot put into the field as large an army as a nation of 65,000,000.

THE WORK OF BRIALMONT

In addition to the armies, there were the fortresses. France constructed a chain of them along her German

124

frontier, such as Belfort and Verdun. But the most powerful of all were supposed to be in two of the smaller states, Belgium and Roumania. The fortifications of those countries were the chief life-work of Brialmont, the famous Belgian military engineer. He designed and constructed the forts at Liege, Namur and Antwerp, in Belgium, and at Bucharest, in Roumania; the latter city being considered the most powerfully fortified in the world.

When it was done Brialmont's work was probably the best of its kind in the world. His forts were dome-shaped structures of steel and concrete, the latter being several feet in thickness and supposed to be proof against any artillery. But at that time the stupendous 42-centimetre siege guns of the German army had not yet come into existence. These monster weapons quickly smashed the concrete and reduced Brialmont's best forts to ruins.

THE BRITISH NAVY

Great Britain was the one considerable power which did not adopt the Prussian military system. That was for two major reasons. The one was traditional. Great Britain had never been a military country; it had never had conscription; wherefore with the characteristic conservatism of the race, it was disinclined to adopt it. The other reason was, that British dependence was placed upon the fleet. Being an insular nation, the United Kingdom could be attacked only by sea, and if its fleet could be maintained at a sufficient strength to keep control of the sea, no army would be needed. Since Trafalgar the power of England at sea had been unchallenged.

Of course, the potential military power of the British Empire on land was enormous. The United Kingdom alone could provide an army of millions. The colonies of Canada, Australasia and South Africa could send powerful contingents. Then there were the myriads of India, especially the Sikhs and Ghoorkas and other warrior races, to whom the breath of battle was as the breath of life, and who were eager to serve in the armies of their Kaiser-I-Hind.

NATIONS BEHIND THE ARMIES

Behind these armies were nations of varying strength and resources. The British Empire, with the smallest army though by far the largest fleet, had the greatest wealth and the greatest industry. France also had enormous wealth, and had perhaps more varied resources than any other continental power. Germany had far less wealth, but a larger population, and her industrial capacity was stupendous. Russia, on the other hand, with an enormous population, was poor in money and was meagerly equipped with industries, so that she would have to depend upon other nations for her supplies of munitions of war.

In the matter of preparedness for war there was a great contrast. Germany was fully prepared; as completely prepared as France was said to be, but was not, in 1870, "to the last shoe-button." Rifles and artillery, immense stores of ammunition, and in brief everything that could be wanted in a strenuous campaign, were ready for the German legions; in stores so vast that it was confidently expected that they would be sufficient for the entire war. They would have been thus adequate had the first German drive at Paris succeeded; as it would have succeeded had not the stubborn forts at Liege delayed the German advance a few days.

But no other nation was ready. In fact, all others

were if possible more than ordinarily unready. Great Britain particularly was quite unprepared, excepting in her fleet. Not long before her greatest soldier, Lord Roberts, had argued, pleaded, exhorted, for an increase of military strength, to meet the war which in prophetic vision he saw in the not distant future. The only answer that he got was abuse and threats that unless he ceased his alarmist talk he might be deprived of his pension! It was a bitter reflection to the British Government and nation, when the storm broke, that they were unprepared because they had thus scorned his warnings.

CHAPTER VIII

THE OUTBREAK OF THE WAR

The Mysterious Tragedy of Sarajevo — Who Killed the Archduke Ferdinand and His Wife, and Why?—Did the Slavs Conspire to Kill a Man Whom They Loved, or the Germans to Kill One Whom They Hated and Feared? — Significant Antecedents, Circumstances and Sequels of the Tragedy — Austria's Demands Upon Serbia — Dictation from Berlin — Refusal to Seek a Peaceful Settlement — War Declared on the Basis of a Falsehood — Successive Declarations by Many Governments — International Law Ignored — A Treaty as a "Scrap of Paper" — Proclamations of Neutrality — Attitude of the United States.

ON JUNE 28, 1914, occurred the tragedy of Sarajevo. The city is the capital of Bosnia, one of the Serbian provinces illegally seized by Austria a few years before the war. Thither on the date named went Archduke Francis Ferdinand, heir presumptive to the Austro-Hungarian thrones, and his morganatic wife, Sophia Chotek, Duchess of Hohenberg. In the morning they drove through the streets, and a bomb was thrown at them, without serious effect. In the afternoon they again drove through the streets, and were killed with pistol shots by Gavrilo Princip, a Bosnian youth, an Austrian subject, said by Austrians to be of Serbian ancestry but by Serbians to be a renegade Jew. Such is the brief record of one of the most mysterious crimes in the world's history, and one with the most tremendous and disastrous sequel. If it was not the cause, it was at any rate the pretext for the war of the nations.

As a mystery, it ranks with two other unexplained tragedies in royal and imperial life in the same quarter of the continent, namely, the death of the Austrian heir

HAULING BIG GUNS BY TRACTOR

Thousands of these caterpillar tractors, made in the United States, were used in France to transport heavy guns to the front-line positions.

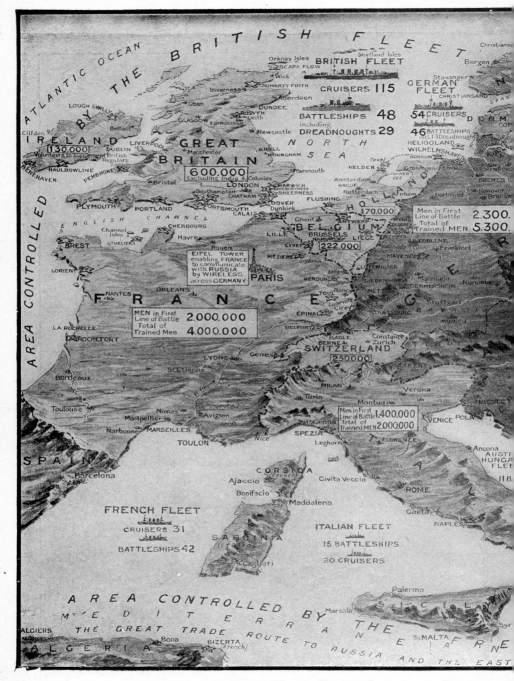

RELIEF MAP OF EUROPE, SHOWING THE TREMENDOUS

All the estimates are given in round numbers for graph
figures to

Men in First Line **2,000,000**
Can be increased later to **4,000,000**
Total of Trained MEN **5,500,000**

Men in First Line of Battle **1,200,000**
Total of Trained MEN **2,000,000**

550,000

240,000

500,000

MONTENEGRO
40,000

300,000

700,000

AREA
CONTROLLED
BY
RUSSIAN
FLEET
17 BATTLESHIPS
14 CRUISERS
(PART in BALTIC)

NOTE FORTRESSES, FORTIFIED DOCKYARDS & NAVAL HARBOURS shown thus

IN LAND AND SEA OPERATIONS AT THE BEGINNING

and also because of the difficulty of reducing official
minator.

British Official Photograph. Copyright by Underwood & Underwood, N. Y.

MONSTER BRITISH TANK POISED ON THE EDGE OF A GERMAN TRENCH

One of the latest and largest tanks plunging forward on its irresistible way to carry terror and destruction to the Hun. It was the work of tanks like this that contributed largely to the British victory at Cambrai.

apparent, Rudolph, and his mistress, at Meyerling, and the butchery of King Alexander and Queen Draga of Serbia at Belgrade. Neither of these has ever been explained, while each was invested with circumstances which seem to suggest some relationship with the crime at Sarajevo.

HOW DID THE ARCHDUKE DIE?

The Austrian Government insisted that the murder of Francis Ferdinand was the result of a criminal conspiracy formed by Serbs and promoted and directed from Serbia, perhaps by the Serbian Government itself. In support of this theory it pointed to the fact that there had been anti-Austrian agitations in Serbia ever since the Austrian rape of the provinces of Bosnia and Herzegovina. The Serbian Government denied that such was the case. The best informed Serbs in private did not hesitate to ascribe the crime to entirely different sources. They pointed out that the murdered Archduke had been beloved by the Serbs, because he had married a Slav and was believed to regard their national aspirations with favor; while he was hated by the Germans of Austria, even by the old Emperor Francis Joseph himself. There was thus no reason why the Serbs should wish to get rid of him, while there were reasons why his removal would be welcome to the Germans, particularly if the responsibility for it could be made to seem to rest upon the Serbs.

The Serbs therefore insisted that the crime was planned and directed by Austrians, probably by members of the Austrian court. Some thought that it was not intended to kill him, but merely to wound him, and thus provide a pretext for a quarrel with and conquest of Serbia. Others, the majority, however, held that it was meant to kill both him and his wife, and that the German Government at Berlin was privy to the crime. In support of these astounding theories the Serbs were able to point to several well-established facts, showing the devious ways of Austrian "provocative agents."

FORMER AUSTRIAN PLOTS

Some weeks before the tragedy at Sarajevo the "*Reichspost*" of Vienna, a sort of court organ, printed several articles which hinted that something serious was likely to happen soon in Bosnia. In the same paper a year before there had been similar hints at coming events in Croatia. The sequels to those former hints were the alleged discovery of bombs intended for criminal purposes, and a series of trials at Agram for treason felony. But it was afterward revealed that the bombs which were there used or "found," and which served as the basis of prosecutions for treason felony, had been in fact manufactured for the purpose in one of the government arsenals. They were carried by a government agent from Austria into Montenegro, thence to be transferred to Croatia. At an appointed place and time this agent passed the bag containing them to another person, who was to be the scapegoat, and the latter was presently arrested with the bombs in his possession. Of course, he was surreptitiously set at liberty, while a number of innocent persons were accused of complicity in the plot.

THE BELGRADE BUTCHERY

It has come to be pretty well known, too, that the butchery of the Serbian sovereigns, Alexander and Draga, at Belgrade, was incited and directed by Austria. The affair was not intended to be a tragedy at all, but merely a kidnapping and compulsory abdication, such as had been successfully forced upon Alexander of Bulgaria many years before. But in attempting to execute that design, passions rose higher than had been expected and got quite out of hand, and the gruesome butchery was the result. So it was meant that the Archduke at Sarajevo should merely be made to appear to have been in deadly peril. That would throw suspicion upon Serbia and rouse Austrian anger against her, and provoke a breach between the crown prince and the Serbs, with whom he was growing too friendly to please the Hapsburg "Ring."

THE ARCHDUKE'S POLITICS

It is also to be taken into account that the Archduke, despite his former anti-Magyar proclivities, which had won for him the hatred of the ruling caste in Hungary, had entered into sympathetic relations with the so-called Hungarian Independence party; precisely, it is suggestively recalled, as Archduke Rudolph did just before the mysterious tragedy at Meyerling. By his attitude at that time toward the Hungarians, Rudolph incurred the bitter animosity and resentment of the Hapsburg "Ring," and the unexplained tragedy which overcame him has by many been regarded as having had a political origin.

The fact is that Francis Ferdinand, having recovered from the madness of the days in which he was a follower of the notorious Jew-baiting Dr. Lueger in his "Christian Socialist Anti-Semite Party," and his almost equally venomous anti-Magyar propaganda, had adopted the momentous design of recasting the Dual Realm and of transforming it into a Federal Empire on a basis resembling that of Germany. He meant that when he became Emperor there should be a number of sovereign states. Austria should have the hegemony of them, as Prussia does in Germany. But there should be several other ostensible independent and equal states, such as Hungary, Bohemia, Croatia, and perhaps Moravia and Transylvania.

This design was intensely offensive to the old Emperor and the entire Austrian court, and also to the ruling castes in Austria and Hungary. It was equally offensive to the German Emperor at Berlin, who was cherishing the design, after the death of Francis Joseph, of subordinating Austria-Hungary more than ever to German domination.

On the other hand the Serbs, both in the empire and in Serbia itself, looked upon his plans as on the whole favorable to them. The creation of a strong Serb state of the empire, comprising Croatia, Slavonia, Bosnia and Herzegovina, would be for the immediate advantage of its inhabitants and would greatly strengthen their hands for the ultimate revolt against Austrian domination and the recreation of the great Serbian Empire. It was also welcome to them because of the dissension which it would create between Francis Ferdinand and the rest of the Hapsburgs.

CIRCUMSTANCES OF THE CRIME

So much for motives and lack of motives for the crime of Sarajevo. Certain indisputable circumstances were strangely suggestive. One was the course which was taken by the driver of the car in which the Archduke and his wife were riding. Instead of proceeding along the chief street of the city, which was simply lined from end to end with police, he suddenly, and without orders, turned the car into another narrower and comparatively obscure street, running parallel with the main street, on which there were few if any police.

132

Copyright by Underwood & Underwood, N. Y.

GERMAN PRISONERS IN AN AMERICAN CAMP IN FRANCE.

American soldiers keeping a watchful eye on their captives. The "Boches" are useful as laborers in American Training Camps behind the lines and as a rule are very glad to exchange the life of the trenches for the safe, if monotonous life, of a prisoner.

AMERICAN HOWITZER IN ACTION

One of the many hastily constructed gun pits, camouflaged and protected by sandbags, where huge howitzers belched forth death on the Kaiser's legions before Château Thierry.

It was on this side street that the tragedy occurred. Why that course was taken is a question which has not been and probably never will be satisfactorily answered, but which inevitably provokes grave speculations and suspicions. Nor has it been explained why, just before the murderous attack was made, the driver, without orders, slowed down the car, as if to facilitate the assault. It is said, it is true, that this change in the route was made because of the bomb-throwing in the main street shortly before. But that convinces nobody. The very fact that the bomb-throwing did occur on the main street, and that in consequence all the police of the city had been massed there, is regarded as the very best reason why the second trip should have been made along the same thoroughfare.

It is also pointed out that the murders were committed by a youth who knew something which down to that time had supposedly been known by nobody outside of the imperial household. That was that the Archduke wore a bullet-proof waistcoat, for which reason the assassin shot at his head instead of his breast. How did the assassin get that knowledge?

HOW THE NEWS WAS RECEIVED

The news of the tragedy was instantly transmitted to Vienna, and it was an extraordinary circumstance that practically every important personage of the court, save only the Emperor, was there to hear it, though it was Sunday, and usually they all went out of town on Saturday in summer. No grief, but rather satisfaction, if not exultation, was expressed. The news was sent to the old Emperor at Ischl, and his only comment was, "What impertinence of those Bosnians!" The police of Sarajevo were never reprimanded for not guarding the Archduke

133

better, but, on the contrary, the heads of the force were promoted.

The coffins containing the bodies of the Archduke and his wife were brought to Trieste by sea, handled as so much freight. When they were being unloaded from the steamer the sailors let one of them drop upon the quay, and let it lie there until they had got rested from carrying it. The funeral was conducted in third-class style, with not even sufficient candles for the chapel ardente. At Arstatten a violent storm drove the funeral party to shelter in a tavern, where most of the party got drunk. There were tales in Vienna of the coffins being placed on chairs and then tumbled off upon the floor. On the whole, the late heir to the throne was buried with less respect than would have been shown to some hired lackey of the court. All of which gives poignancy to the fearful speculation, Who murdered the Archduke?

AUSTRIA'S DEMANDS UPON SERBIA

Following the tragedy at Sarajevo diplomatic communications were conducted between the Austro-Hungarian and Serbian governments, the latter earnestly striving to ameliorate the situation and to reach an amicable settlement, but the former almost undisguisedly seeking to force an open quarrel. At the same time intercourse between Vienna and Berlin was such as to indicate that the policy of the Austrian Government was being dictated by the German.

Finally, at six o'clock on the evening of July 23d, Austria presented an ultimatum to Serbia, an answer to which was required within forty-eight hours, or before six o'clock on the evening of July 25th. This contained eleven categorical demands, which with the Serbian replies may be summarized as follows:

SERBIA'S REPLIES

1. That the Serbian Government give formal assurance of its condemnation of Serb propaganda against Austria. To this Serbia unhesitatingly assented.

2. That a declaration to this effect be published in the next Sunday's issue of the Serbian "Official Journal." To this Serbia also assented.

3. That this declaration express regret that Serbian officers had participated in the propaganda. To this Serbia assented, despite the fact that no proof of such participation was offered.

4. That the Serbian Government promise to proceed rigorously against all guilty of such machinations. To this Serbia assented.

5. That this declaration be at once communicated by the King of Serbia to his army and published in the official bulletin as an order of the day. To this Serbia assented.

6. That all anti-Austrian publications in Serbia be suppressed. To this Serbia assented.

7. That the Serbian political party known as the National Union be suppressed and its means of propaganda be confiscated. To this, too, Serbia assented.

8. That all anti-Austrian teaching in Serbian schools be suppressed. To this Serbia assented.

THREE EXTRAORDINARY DEMANDS

9. That all officers, civil and military, who might be designated by Austria as guilty of anti-Austrian propaganda, be dismissed by the Serbian Government. Extraordinary as was this demand, for Austrian proscription of Serbian officials, so eager was the Serbian Government for peace and friendship that it assented to it; merely stipulating

that the Austrian Government should offer some proof of the guilt of the proscribed officers.

10. That Austrian agents should be permitted to enter Serbia to co-operate with the Serbian Government in suppressing all anti-Austrian propaganda, and to take part in the judicial proceedings conducted in Serbia against those charged with complicity in the crime at Sarajevo. This astounding demand, which was in effect that Austrian agents should control the police and courts of Serbia, it was impossible for Serbia to accept without abrogating her sovereignty. She did not, however, unconditionally reject it, but asked that it be the subject of further discussion, or be referred to arbitration.

11. That Serbia explain to Austria the meaning of anti-Austrian utterances of Serbian officials at home and abroad, since the crime of Sarajevo. This was assented to, on condition that if the explanations given were not satisfactory, the matter be submitted to mediation or arbitration.

GERMANY DICTATES REJECTION

Thus Serbia granted ten of Austria's demands, and did not altogether reject the eleventh, although it was obvious that its acceptance would mean the end of Serbian liberty and independence. It is probable that the Austrian Government, left to itself, would have accepted the replies, or at any rate would have continued diplomatic negotiations. It must have done so, had it been sincere in its profession of desire merely to obtain reparation for the tragedy.

But the German Emperor apparently deemed the moment fitting for the launching of a long contemplated war of conquest against the rest of Europe. His army, navy and entire empire were in a state of the most perfect readiness for instant action, while not one of his potential antagonists was in even the usual condition of preparedness. And his will was scarcely less supreme at Vienna than at Berlin. Therefore the Austrian Government summarily rejected the Serbian replies as wholly unsatisfactory, and the Austrian minister quitted Belgrade.

EFFORTS TO KEEP THE PEACE

That was on the evening of July 25th. Instantly the news was flashed over the world, and various governments interested themselves in efforts to prevent this breach of relations from leading to war. Russia intimated that she could not with indifference see Serbia oppressed. Great Britain urged that Germany, France, Italy and Great Britain hold a conference for mediation or arbitration. This was exactly in accord with the policy to which all the powers had pledged themselves in the treaty of The Hague. It was an eminently fair proposal, since it excluded Russia and Austria-Hungary, as prejudiced parties, and included only four powers which might reasonably be supposed to be impartial. If they had any predilections, Germany and Italy were Austria's partners in the Triple Alliance, while Great Britain and France were Russia's friends in the Triple Entente. The proposal was promptly accepted by France and Italy, but was summarily rejected by Germany.

That was on July 27th. The next day Austria-Hungary declared war against Serbia. Russia declared that, on the day on which Austrian troops invaded Serbia, there would be a mobilization of Russian troops, in order to prepare for further contingencies. Thereupon Germany took the initiative and the aggressive. She proclaimed that she would not permit any interference by anybody between Austria and Serbia, but that Austria must be left free to work her will, whatever it might be, upon her little neighbor. She ordered Russia to stop mobilization proceedings and to dismiss whatever troops had already been mobilized; and she demanded of France an immediate and categorical statement of what that country would do in case of a war between Germany and Russia.

More arbitrary and insolent utterances were probably never made by any power. They were obviously intended to mean either universal European subjection to Prussian autocracy, or war. In fact they meant war.

FALSEHOODS AND SCRAPS OF PAPER

Germany declared war upon Russia on August 1st, because Russia would not refrain from mobilizing her army at Germany's demand. Austria meantime three days before had bombarded the Serbian capital. On August 2d German troops invaded Luxembourg and Belgium, thus regarding as "scraps of paper" Germany's solemn treaty pledges to respect and to defend the inviolability of those neutral states. At the same time German troops violated the French frontier, without any declaration of war.

The next day Germany declared that France had begun war against her, by sending hostile aeroplanes across the frontier to bombard German towns and railroads. It has since been officially acknowledged in Germany that these charges against France had no foundation in fact; so that war was really declared by Germany against France on the basis of a German falsehood.

BELGIUM'S APPEAL ANSWERED

The Belgian Government made appeal to Great Britain, as one of the guarantors of Belgian neutrality, for protection against the invading German army. The British Government therefore at once demanded of Germany withdrawal of the invaders and respect for the neutrality of Belgium. The reply was a flat rejection of the demand and an attack by the German army upon the Belgian city of Liege. Thereupon, at eleven o'clock on the evening of August 4th, the British Government declared that a state of war with Germany existed.

The United States Government, through the President, at once made the customary proclamation of neutrality, on the same conditions that had prevailed in other foreign wars to which this country was not a party; and other neutral nations generally did the same. Italy, though an ally of Germany and Austria in the Triple Alliance, also made a proclamation of neutrality, informing Germany as she did so that she considered that the circumstances of the declaration of an aggressive war by Germany and Austria released her from all obligations under her treaty with those powers. Thus the issues were joined, and the world's greatest war was begun.

CHAPTER IX

THE WAR IN FRANCE AND FLANDERS

Three Epochs of a Stupendous Campaign — The Invasion of Belgium — Brialmont's Work — Liege the Savior of Europe — Unspeakable Atrocities of the Germans — Northern France Overrun — The Drive at Paris — Battles of the Marne and Aisne — Ypres and Loos — Beginning of Trench Warfare — The Second Epoch of the Campaign — The German Drive at Verdun — "They Shall Not Pass" — Beginning of the Third Epoch — The Campaign on the Somme River — Bapaume and Peronne the Impregnable — The Great British and French Drive from Switzerland to the Sea — Breaking of the "Hindenburg Line" and Steady Retreat of the German Armies — New German Drives — The War in Italy.

THE WAR in western Europe, before American participation, saw three major stages, or epochs, in which three nations successively held the center of the stage. The first was very short, measured in weeks, or perhaps only days; when the handful of Belgians were holding back the multitudinous German legions until France, taken all unawares, could rally her forces for the defense of Paris. The second lasted a year and a half, when France, putting forth efforts which would have seemed incredible had they been predicted in advance, held the Germans in check until a British army could be created out of raw material and be put into the field. The third was marked by the tremendous aggressiveness of the British army in co-operation with its French allies. Let us very briefly review these three epochs; briefly, because this is not a complete and detailed history of the war, but merely such an account of it as will make clear the chief happenings before the United States was dragged into the fray.

Photo by Trans-Atlantic News Service Co.

KING ALBERT OF BELGIUM AT THE HEAD OF HIS ARMY

The splendid defense put up by the Belgians against the German invaders astonished all the military authorities and gave time for the armies of France to come to their assistance.

Photo by Paul Thompson.

King George at Aldershot

King George V of England is a splendid equestrian, and, in addition to deriving much pleasure from this exercise, carries himself

LIEGE THE IMMORTAL

August 3, 1914. Like the Egyptian plague of locusts, devouring the land, the German armies rushed forward to devour France. They were four in number. One struck through central Belgium, the second through Luxembourg, the third between Metz and Nancy, and the fourth between the Vosges and the Swiss frontier. We have to do with the first named, by far the most formidable of all. Admitting that invasion of Belgium would be gross violation of law and treatment of a neutrality treaty as a "scrap of paper," the German Government had tried to seduce Belgium into consenting to the deed. Since Belgium would not be seduced, but held out for faith and honor, Germany went in with force. The frontier was crossed on August 3d, [and on the next day the invaders reached and began to attack the first of the Belgian fortified cities, Liege.

Brialmont, the great military engineer, had made it as he supposed impregnable. But that was before the days of the 42-centimeter guns. These stupendous engines soon pounded Brialmont's steel and masonry forts into ruin. But it took them three days to do it. Indeed, the last of the Liege forts was not reduced until August 18th. And by causing that delay to the German advance, Liege was the savior of Europe. Had it not been for that delay, and the time it gave France to mobilize her troops, Paris surely would have fallen. On August 20th Brussels was occupied without resistance. On the following three days the first great battle was fought at Namur, Mons and Charleroi, as a result of which the Belgians, French and British were driven back and the German rush toward Paris began.

THE MARTYRDOM OF BELGIUM

Meantime the Germans instituted such a reign of atrocities in Belgium as the world had not known since the days of Tilly and Pappenheim, or perhaps of Timur Leng and Genghis Khan. This campaign of "frightfulness" was ordered from Berlin, partly in the hope of terrifying the nations into submission, and partly in vindictive spite against Belgium for having dared to resist the will of the Kaiser. Almost every principle of international law was violated. Unfortified and undefended cities and towns were sacked and burned. Unoffending civilians were murdered by hundreds, and by other hundreds were put to death wholesale by the military authorities on various lying pretences. Vast tributes were exacted from municipalities, under threat of destruction of the towns and massacre of the inhabitants. Private houses and shops were looted. The university library of Louvain, one of the most precious in the world, was wantonly burned. Churches were looted and their altars used as latrines Men, women and children were tortured to death, by crucifixion, by burning alive, and by hideous mutilations. Women, from girls scarcely in their teens to venerable granddames, were ravished by hundreds, generally in public where their children, parents or husbands were compelled to witness the infamy; many of them being thus abused by many soldiers until they died under the torture. Living or dead, they were often obscenely mutilated, and then their mangled bodies were "pegged out" upon the ground with bayonets or stakes driven through them. Babes were snatched from their mothers' arms and tossed about on bayonet points. Whole families, after indescribable ill treatment, were fastened in their houses and the houses burned. All through

142

Belgium and northern France, wherever the German armies went, there was such an orgy of lust, loot and murder as the civilized world had not seen for centuries.

SALVATION OF THE MARNE

Meanwhile, reinforced by armies which had pushed through Luxembourg, the Germans swept on toward

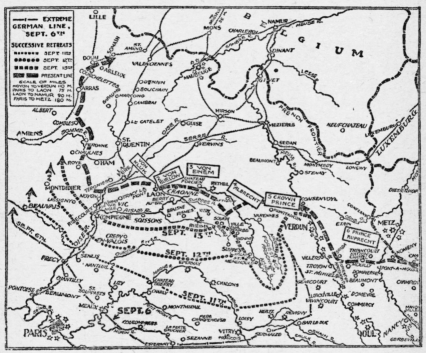

POSITION OF THE WESTERN ARMIES ON OCTOBER 1, 1914

Paris. By September 3d the French and their allies had been driven to the line of the Seine, Marne and Verdun, and the French Government fled from Paris to Bordeaux. But the French army, with a small British contingent, halted there to give battle. "We stop the Germans here,"

143

said the French commander, "or here we all die." For three days the contest, one of the world's decisive battles, raged; the allied lines held firm; by September 9th the entire German army was in retreat; and Paris was saved.

The allies followed the retreating foe as far as the River Aisne, where the Germans turned and gave battle. In magnitude the battle was greater than that at the Marne had been, but its results were less decisive. The Germans held their ground, and established themselves in the systems of trenches which were thereafter so striking a feature of the war on the western front. By the middle of September the Germans were thus established along a line from near Verdun to Bapaume which, with minor changes, they continued to hold for two years.

THE WAR IN FLANDERS

From Bapaume northward desperate struggles continued for some time. The Belgians and British, who chiefly represented the allies there, at first hoped to hold a line running from Bapaume through Lille, Ghent and Antwerp. But from October 9th to 12th the three places last named were taken by the Belgians. There was desperate fighting at Ypres and at Loos, in which two-thirds of the British army was destroyed or disabled, but the surviving remnant stubbornly held on. The little Belgian army also inflicted heavy losses upon the Germans on the Yser, and with the aid of floods caused by cutting the dikes prevented further advance of the invaders. The year ended with the Germans in possession of all of Belgium save a small triangle at the extreme southwest corner of the kingdom.

On the lines thus established, the armies remained for two years, waiting for the British Government to recruit, train and equip an army of several millions. And just as the Belgians held the Germans in check for a few days until the French could get ready to fight for Paris on the Marne, so during all this longer time it fell chiefly to the French to hold the Germans back until the British could come to their aid. Meantime the Germans did all the damage they could to the parts of France which they were occupying, taking especial pleasure in mutilating or destroying priceless works of art and historic buildings. Thus they nearly destroyed and hopelessly damaged the cathedral of Rheims, one of the noblest churches and most interesting historic landmarks in the world.

THE SECOND STAGE

There followed more than a year and a half of trench fighting, with few important gains for either side and no decision of the whole campaign. The Germans were paying chief attention to the war against Russia on the eastern front, and the French were simply holding their own until the millions of soldiers in the British training camps could be prepared to take the field, and until artillery and munitions superior to that of the Germans could be provided. There was a fierce renewal of the German drive toward Calais, in April, 1915, which was repulsed by the allies.

In September of that year the allies launched a general drive against the German lines along nearly the whole front. In Picardy and Artois the British fought a series of bloody battles, aiming toward Lille and centering around Loos, while the French in Champagne won some considerable successes. Following these operations, an attempt was made at both points to break through the German line. But by this time hundreds of thousands of German troops had been hurried across from Poland, and the allies were not only repulsed but were also once more placed upon the defensive.

"THEY SHALL NOT PASS"

The third stage of the western war began in the last week of February, 1916, and for four months was marked with a persistent ferocity never before witnessed in this or any war. It began with a German attack upon the French fortress town of Verdun. The German Crown Prince was in command, and at his disposal were hundreds of thousands of the very flower of the German army. His orders from his father were, that he must capture Verdun, at any cost. Upon that achievement depended his promotion to the rank of Field Marshal, which he coveted and which the Emperor felt it a reproach for him not to have.

The first German attacks were successful, and at the northeast the French were driven back upon the city. Two forts close to Verdun were captured by the Germans, Douaumont on May 24th and Vaux on June 6th. But that was their high-water mark. From the beginning the French commander had grimly declared, "They shall not pass!" They did not pass. Worn with their furious onset the Germans halted, weakened, and faltered. The French rallied and assumed the aggressive. The drive at Verdun had failed.

THE THIRD STAGE

June, 1916, marked the turning of the tide of war on the western battle front. At the beginning of July came a general forward movement of the Allies in the valley of the Somme. All through July and August the Germans were inch by inch driven back toward Bapaume and

Peronne, on a frontage of fifteen miles. In September the fighting grew still more bitter, and a new element was introduced, the British "tanks" or armored automobiles, which created great consternation among the enemy.

In mid-November the severity of the weather compelled a slackening of the campaign. But in January the British gained further advantages, while the German Crown Prince made another attack upon Verdun. In March the Allies began a "spring drive," and soon forced the Germans out of Bapaume and Peronne. This advance continued with steadily increasing force. The progress of the Allies was measured by miles rather than, as before, by yards. But it failed to reach Cambrai, which had been aimed at, or to break the Hindenburg Line.

In March, 1918, the Germans resumed the offensive, with a fierce rush toward Amiens, advancing 35 miles and taking 90,000 prisoners and 1,300 guns. So desperate was the Allies' plight that every available soldier of the American army which had then begun to arrive in the war zone, was hurried to the front, and from that time dates American participation in the fighting in the trenches. That drive was stopped short of Amiens. Three weeks later a second was aimed at Ypres, but was stopped within a dozen miles. A third came at the end of May, and gained 32 miles in Champagne, with 65,000 prisoners. That was a drive at Paris. The fourth, in the early part of June, 1918, was also aimed at Paris, but was stopped after making six miles. In all these drives the German losses were far greater than those of the Allies. In them all American troops effectively aided the Allies.

THE ITALIAN FRONTIER

Immediately after declaring war against Austria, on May 23, 1915, Italy sent two armies against her foe. One invaded the Trentino and advanced toward Trent. A counter invasion of Italy in that region was made by Austria, but was repelled. The second and larger Italian army proceeded toward Trieste, by way of the Isonzo River and Gorizia. Much fighting was done, including some extraordinary operations on the slopes and summits of lofty Alpine peaks and ridges, but comparatively little was achieved in the way of conquest. Gorizia was captured by the Italians on August 8, 1916, but no further progress was made toward Trieste, save in an occasional aeroplane raid.

As soon, however, as the Bolsheviki treachery in Russia stopped the military operations of that country, German and Austrian troops were rushed thence to the Italian frontier. German spies and propaganda also corrupted some of the Italian forces. A Teutonic drive at the end of October, 1917, retook Gorizia and all other territory which the Italians had taken, and invaded Italy as far as the suburbs of Venice. British and French aid was sent, and a desperate rally enabled the Italians to check the invaders on the line of the Piave River. In June, 1918, an army of a million Austrians began a grand drive toward Venice, in concert with the German drives in France. But the Italians had recovered their morale and not only offered effective resistance but also assumed the offensive. The Austrian army was routed with appalling losses. In these operations a number of American aviators participated, and before the end of June several detachments of American troops were landed in Italy and united with the Italians and other Allies at the front.

148

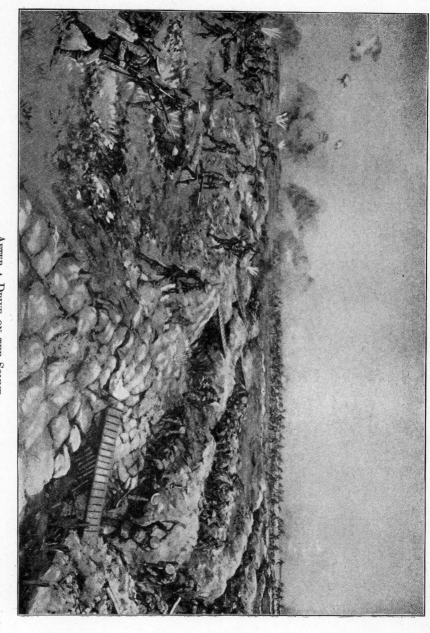

AFTER A DRIVE ON THE SOMME

British advancing over the captured German trenches, after heavy artillery fire had reduced them to tangled ruins and crushed their powers of resistance.

PIGEON SERVICE AT THE FRONT

American officers of a division of infantry before the headquarters dugout sending a message by carrier pigeon.

CHAPTER X

THE WAR IN THE EAST

Serbia's Successful Defense — Russia's Invasion of East Prussia — The Disaster of the Masurian Lakes — Secrets of Russia's Weakness — The Conquest of Galicia — Tremendous Counterstrokes by Hindenburg and Von Mackensen — Przemysl and Lemberg — The German Invasion of Poland and the Baltic Provinces — Riga and Petrograd Threatened — The War in the Balkans — Conquest of Serbia — The Dardanelles and the Gallipoli Campaign — Greece and Salonika — The Struggle at the Head of the Red Sea — Armenia and Mesopotamia.

THE FIRST shots of the war were fired on the eastern frontier when Austrian artillery bombarded the Serbian capital, Belgrade, from across the Danube. This action was not important, and was soon followed by a far more successful counter attack by Serbians and Montenegrins upon Austria. An Austrian regiment which attempted to cross the Danube east of Belgrade was annihilated. On August 12th the Serbs and Montenegrins crossed the border into Bosnia and swept irresistibly toward Sarajevo. Heavy fighting occurred at Shabatz and on the Save River, in which the Serbs were on the whole successful. The Austrian invasion of Serbia was foiled, and the Serbian invasion of Bosnia was maintained.

Meantime a far greater campaign was undertaken at the other side of the Austro-Hungarian Empire. The Russian army was mobilized in three grand divisions. The center was in Russian Poland. The left wing, under the Grand Duke Nicholas, one of Russia's greatest generals, began on August 11th an invasion of Galicia, or Austrian Poland; while the right wing a week later crossed the border into East Prussia.

149

THE GALICIAN DRIVE

The Russian left wing was at first highly successful. After seven days of incessant fighting it completely over-

SCENE OF WAR IN THE NEAR EAST

whelmed the Austrians on September 2d, and the next day occupied the important city of Lemberg. The next day Halicz was taken; on September 9th the Austrians were vanquished in a hard battle at Rawaruska; on September 22d Jaroslav was captured, and five days later Russian troops were in the Carpathian mountain passes, and crossing the Hungarian frontier. The great fortress of Przemysl, the last Austrian stronghold left in Galicia, was invested and besieged all that fall and winter, but was not captured by the Russians until March 22d. Its fall cleared the way for a Russian advance into Hungary, or would have done so had not something happened elsewhere to bring the Russian plans to naught.

IN EAST PRUSSIA

The Russian advance at the right was at first equally successful. East Prussia was invaded, and on August 26th Insterburg and on August 27th Tilsit were captured. An important victory was won at Gumbinnen, and the main Prussian army was apparently shut up in Königsberg. A detachment of the Russian army moved forward into the region of the Masurian Lakes, to clear the way for an advance on the lower Vistula.

That gloomy and forbidding region was, however, destined to be the scene of disaster for the Russians. Germany's greatest General, Hindenburg, known as the "Old Man of the Masurian Lakes," advanced to the attack upon them, with a superior force and with infinitely superior knowledge of the "lay of the land." The Russians were trapped among the lakes and almost interminable marshes, in places where it was impossible for supplies of munitions to reach them. For three days a tremendous conflict raged at Tannenburg and Allenstein, which resulted

THE RUSSO-GERMAN THEATER OF WAR

in the complete defeat of the Russian troops, with enormous losses. A retreat back into Russia followed, after which the initiative remained with the Germans, who presently began an invasion of Russia from Posen.

POLAND INVADED

Meantime the Germans and Austrians sought a diversion of the war at the two wings by means of a vigorous attack in the center. Hindenburg moved against Warsaw from the northwest, while an Austrian army moved toward the same city from the southwest. The Russian resistance was feeble, and by mid-October the Germans were within a short distance of Warsaw. This emergency compelled the Russians to withdraw troops from the Galician campaign to protect their center; which they did effectively. Within a week the Germans began to be driven back and before the end of the month they were cleared out of Poland. The Russians followed up their advantage, crossing the frontier into Posen on November 8th, and a week later resuming the Galician drive and advancing to within twenty miles of Cracow.

Then the see-saw was repeated. Hindenburg struck furiously at Poland again, and again penetrated to the neighborhood of Warsaw. This compelled a withdrawal of Russians from Galicia and suspension of operations toward Cracow. The Germans were again driven back from Warsaw, and at the end of the year there was a renewal of the Russian aggressive all along the front. A third time, in February Hindenburg took the aggressive, this time at the Russian right, and succeeded in driving the Russians out of East Prussia. But the Russian center held firm, and at the left an important invasion of Hungary seemed imminent.

RUSSIAN DISASTERS

Then the tide turned. The Russian army had exhausted its supplies of ammunition, and further supplies were not forthcoming. There is reason to believe that plenty of munitions were at hand, but were purposely withheld from the troops through the machinations of German intriguers in Russia. At any rate, the Russians were left without ammunition, to meet the onset of a furious German offensive.

The German army under Von Mackensen set out from Cracow on April 29, 1915, with an amplitude and completeness of equipment as notable as was the Russian lack thereof. The advance was bewilderingly rapid. On May 6th Tarnow and Gorlice were taken, on June 3d the great fortress of Przemysl was reoccupied, and Lemberg was entered on June 22d. For fifty-two days the Germans advanced at the average rate of four miles a day. The reason was that they were moving against practically unarmed men. The Russian cannons were chiefly silent, and the men, with no cartridges, were fighting with clubbed rifles, knives and even with stones and bludgeons.

THE CONQUEST OF POLAND

Having swept the unarmed Russians out of Galicia, the Germans turned northward for the conquest of Russian Poland. Three powerful armies, from north, west and south, simultaneously converged upon Warsaw. Still destitute of proper supplies, the Russians could do nothing but retire, and it was a wonderful achievement that there, as in Galicia, they were able to retire without being thrown into confusion and rout and without losing such equipment as they had. Never did a defeated army retire in better order. But it did retire. Kovno was abandoned on August 17th, Brest-Litovsk on August 26th, and Grodno on September 3d. The German conquest of Poland was then practically complete.

Meantime German armies at the extreme left were driving the Russian right before them, through Courland, until they were close to Riga and were planning to menace Petrograd itself. But from the fall of 1915 to the early summer of 1916 the lines remained practically unchanged. The Germans were being kept busy on the western front, and the Russians were preparing themselves for a renewal of their campaign under happier auspices.

ANOTHER RUSSIAN DRIVE

Early in June, 1916, the Russian armies were ready for action. Under the command of General Brussiloff they struck, with their left, against the German and Austrian right, in Galicia and Bukowina, with tremendous effect. The movement began on June 5th. Four days later Czernowitz was taken, and by the end of the month Kolomea was also captured. Stanislau fell on August 9th, and a few days later Lemberg was threatened. Then, unfortunately, a diversion was caused by the German invasion of Roumania, and it was necessary to stop the Galician advance in order to send troops thither.

During 1917 German counter drives retook all that

155

Brussiloff had gained, captured Riga, and threatened Petrograd. Then, as told elsewhere, the Bolsheviki treason in Russia abandoned the war on that front, leaving the Germans in possession of all they had gained, and permitting the transfer of most of their troops to the other fronts.

THE WAR AT THE STRAITS

Turkey entered the war at the end of October, 1914, but it was not until four months afterward that it became

involved in serious operations. It was in the latter part of February, 1915, that the Allies undertook the formidable task of capturing Constantinople. This movement had two major objects. One was, to gain control of the Dardanelles and the Bosporus, so that supplies could be sent to Russia by that short and direct route. It was, indeed, the only route that could be used to aid Russia, for her northern ports were ice-locked. The harbor of Archangel, where supplies had been received, was now closed, as it always is from the end of September to June. The other object that the Allies had when they undertook to get through the Dardanelles was to cut the line of communication between

LORD KITCHENER INSIDE A TURKISH FORT

An inspecting trip to one of the captured Turkish fortifications on the Gallipoli peninsula in company with Colonel Sir Henry McMahon and a French General, during the ill-fated attempt to force the Dardanelles.

The Historic Landing from the "River Clyde," at Seddul Bahr, Gallipoli, April 25, 1915

Germany and Asia Minor, so that the Central Powers could draw no further supplies from that source.

An attempt was at first made to force the passage of the Dardanelles with the allied fleet. Some of the forts at the entrance were bombarded and silenced, and allied vessels proceeded for some distance up the strait. But Germany had sent submarines overland to Constantinople, where they were placed in the Bosporus and thence went down to the Dardanelles, and the waters were thickly sown with mines. After the loss of several vessels from these causes the allies abandoned the attempt to force the passage with ships alone, and an army was sent to cooperate with the fleet.

THE GALLIPOLI CAMPAIGN

The ensuing campaign was one of the most gallant but most fruitless of the war. The almost unprecedented feat was performed of safely landing a considerable army on the Gallipoli Peninsula, in the face of a hostile force much superior in numbers and powerfully entrenched. This was done on April 25th, and was repeated in the landing of a second army in June, further up the peninsula at Suvla Bay. Numerous minor engagements were fought, and the allies made some progress during the early part of the summer. Early in August a great battle was fought, lasting five days, in which the allies aimed to drive the Turks from the lower part of the peninsula. In this they failed, and the battle terminated indecisively.

In one respect, however, it was decisive. It convinced the British military authorities of the folly of attempting to pursue the campaign further. They held their ground for some time longer, however, until the entrance of Bulgaria into the war enabled the sending of German troops and supplies to Constantinople, and a succession of phenomenal storms and floods almost swept the camps out of existence. At the middle of December Suvla Bay was abandoned, and on January 9, 1916, the last position of the allies on the peninsula was evacuated.

THE RAPE OF SERBIA

Bulgaria's entrance into the war, on October 6th, was the signal for a concerted attack upon Serbia, for the

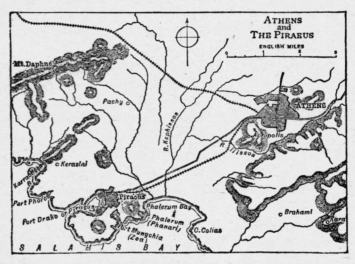

purpose of eliminating that nation from the map of Europe. Bulgaria armies, reinforced by Turks, poured into Serbia from the east, while a German and Austrian army, under German command, crossed the frontier at the north. The purpose was not alone to destroy Serbia but to compel Greece to join the Central Powers or else share the fate of Belgium, and thus to give the Central Powers possession of the entire Balkan Peninsula, with a great frontage on the Mediterranean.

Disregarding Greek neutrality, or with the permission of the ministry, the allies began rushing troops to Salonika, to be sent to the defense of Serbia. But it was too late. The Serbians earlier in the war had been able to hold the Austrians in check, but they were unable to stand against a German army, while a Bulgar-Turkish force was attacking their flank. The German and Bulgarian armies met and joined forces at the end of October, and a few days later captured the important Serbian city of Nish. Before the end of the year every foot of Serbian soil had been conquered, and a large part of the Serbian people had been massacred.

For nearly a year the Teuton-Bulgar forces had undisturbed possession of Serbia, looting it and desolating it at will, while a polyglot army of allies, British, French, Serbian, Italian and Russian, stood at bay at Salonika. At last, however, the allies moved northward through Macedonia, and succeeded in redeeming a small part of Serbia, the Serbs reoccupying their city of Monastir, or what was left of it, on November 19, 1916.

THE ROUMANIAN BLUNDER

Early in the war agitation arose in Roumania for entry into the conflict. But lack of preparedness, and realization of the futility of the fortifications of Bucharest against modern artillery, restrained the government from taking that step until the latter part of August, 1916—more than two years after the outbreak of the war. Immediately after the declaration the Roumanian army invaded Transylvania through several narrow mountain passes, which they strangely neglected to guard after their passage. The result was that the passes were seized by the Germans behind them, and they were all but annihilated.

159

By the middle of October the blundering Roumanians were all killed, captured, or scattered, and in a few weeks more than half of the kingdom was occupied by the enemy, the capital, Bucharest, falling on December 6th. The advance of a considerable Russian army finally checked the invaders at the River Sereth. Immense supplies of foodstuffs and oil fell into the hands of the Germans, and the net result of the entry of Roumania into the war was a decided advantage for the Central Powers

SUEZ CANAL.

The Bolshevist treason in Russia left Roumania helpless, and in March, 1918, that country was compelled by force to make a treaty of peace, under which it surrendered much of its territory, abolished its army, and placed its material resources at the disposal of Germany.

THE WAR IN ASIA

Three separate campaigns have been waged in Asia. One has been in Arabia and on the Egyptian frontier, where Turks and Germans made vigorous attempts to seize the Suez Canal and to incite an insurrection against British rule in Egypt. There the British were successful in defeating their foe . In addition, practically the whole of Arabia, including the Holy Cities of El Medina and Mecca, revolted against Turkey and established its independence.

THE DESOLATION OF ARMENIA

Russia undertook at the beginning of the war a campaign through the Caucasus into Armenia and Asia Minor. It was marked with blundering and came to naught. In return, the Turks invaded the Transcaucasian provinces of Russia, and then began, under German direction, the extermination of the Armenian nation. The German atrocities in Belgium were emulated by the Turks and their Kurd levies, on a gigantic scale. Certainly several hundred thousand and probably nearly or quite a million non-combatant Armenians, men, women and children, were put to death with every refinement of cruelty—rape, mutilation, flaying burning, drowning and starvation.

At last the Russian Grand Duke Nicholas, the conqueror of Galicia, was put in command in the Caucasus, and in February, 1916, he swept into the Turkish Empire in Asia, capturing Erzeroum, Bitlis, Trebizond and Erzingan. He was too late to save Armenia, but he was able to co-operate efficiently with a British army which was moving up Mesopotamia.

The collapse of Russia, and the Bolshevist treaty of peace, practically sealed the fate of what was left of Armenia, all of which was surrendered to the Turks; even including the part which for many years had been in Russian possession.

THE BAGDAD CAMPAIGNS

Twice the British essayed to reach Bagdad from the Persian Gulf. The first attempt was made in the fall of 1915, and the expedition was successful in penetrating to within less than twenty miles of the ancient city. It was animated with more valor than discretion, however, being too small and not sufficiently supported along its

11

161

lines of communication and supply at the rear. The result was that it had to fall back to Kut-el-Amara, where it was besieged for several months and at last was compelled by starvation to surrender, on April 28, 1916.

The second British expedition up the Tigris and Euphrates valley was better planned and was more successful; having also the advantage of the co-operation of the Russians at the north. It captured Kut-el-Amara on February 26, 1917, and on March 11th occupied Bagdad, eighty miles further on. A junction was then effected with the Russian forces moving down from Erzeroum.

"JERUSALEM DELIVERED"

Late in December, 1917, the forces of the British General Allenby, moving eastward and northward from Egypt and the Sinaitic Peninsula, achieved the conquest of all Southern Palestine, from the coast to beyond the Jordan, including Bethlehem, Jerusalem, and practically the entire ancient kingdom of Judea. The capture of Jerusalem, for the first time since the Crusades, was happily effected without bombardment or any action which would damage the sacred shrines, and the only injury done was the looting of the Church of the Holy Sepulchre by the Germans before their flight from the city.

Following this, and in accord with a pledge by the British government that the Jews should come to their own, a Jewish Legion was organized in America to assist in completing the conquest of Palestine for a restoration of the Jewish Commonwealth.

CHAPTER XI

COLONIAL CONQUESTS

Origin and Extent of Germany's Colonial Empire — Her Ambition to Rival Great Britain — Dreams of a German South Africa — Loss of Sea Power Fatal to Her Outlying Possessions — Japan's Seizure of Kiao Chao — Australia and the German Islands — Other Groups in the Pacific — Togoland and the Kamerun Territory — The Boer-British Conquest of German South Africa "the Most Unkindest Cut of All" — German East Africa the Last to Fall.

THE GERMAN Colonial Empire vanished. That was one of the first definite results of the war, and one of the most significant. The development of a world-wide colonial empire, rivaling that of Great Britain, had long been the dream and the ambition of the Kaiser and his lieutenants. The colonial policy had been devised and founded by Bismarck himself, just thirty years before this war undid it all, and it had been consistently and earnestly promoted by all his successors. At the outbreak of the war the German Colonial Empire existed in Africa, in Asia, in the Indies, and in Polynesia. It had a total land area nearly five times as great as that of Germany itself, and a population one-fifth as great. Most of the German colonies were in Africa, and it was the dream of Germany to dominate that continent, north, central and south. Togoland and the Kamerun territory were among her earliest possessions, and she planned to extend the latter so as to include most if not all of the Congo State. It was thus a part of her scheme in attacking Belgium at the beginning of this war to acquire, through the conquest of that little kingdom, the Congo State which belonged to it. The following were

163

the various German possessions as enumerated in "The Statesman's Year Book," all of them being Crown Colonies, under the absolute rule of imperial governors:

THE GERMAN COLONIES

	Date of Acquisition	Estimated Area, Sq. Miles	Estimated Population
In Africa:			
Togoland............................	1884	33,700	1,000,000
Kamerun.............................	1884	191,130	3,500,000
German Southwest Africa.............	1884–90	322,450	200,000
German East Africa..................	1885–90	384,180	7,000,000
Total African possessions...........	1884–90	931,460	11,700,000
In Asia:			
Kiauchau Bay........................	1897	200[1]	30,000[1]
In the Pacific:			
German New Guinea:			
Kaiser Wilhelm's Land..............	1885–86	70,000	} 300,000
Bismarck Archipelago...............	1885	20,000	
Caroline Islands...................	1899	} 560	
Palau or Pelew Islands.............	1899		}
Marianne Islands...................	1899	250	
Solomon Islands....................	1886	4,200	} 56,000
Marshall Islands, etc..............	1886	150	
Samoan Islands:			
Savaii.............................	1899	660	} 33,000
Upolu..............................	1899	340	
Total Pacific possessions...........	1884–99	96,160	389,000
Total Foreign dependencies..........	1884–99	1,027,820	12,119,000

[1] Exclusive of the Bay with an area of about 200 square miles, and the neutral zone with an area of about 2,500 square miles, and population of 1,200,000.

AFRICAN AMBITIONS

In North Africa she began intriguing for control of Morocco years ago, coveting its strategical position, com-

FLEET OF HYDRO-AEROPLANES, AUXILIARY TO BRITISH NAVY

Among Britain's force of heavier-than-air and gas-buoyed airships, none are capable of rendering more vital service to the fleet than

SCENE AT AN AVIATION CAMP SOMEWHERE IN FRANCE.

On the right is a sergeant of the R. F. C., wearing the new badge of a propeller on his arm. He is saluting two aviation officers, one dressed for flying, the other wearing the flying certificate badge. On the right is an army B. E. biplane, with its four-bladed propeller and two seats for pilot and observer. This type, it is stated, is becoming more and more the standard pattern of machine for use by the R. F. C. On the left is

manding one shore of the strait between the Mediterranean and the Atlantic. Her intrigues there led to the serious controversy with France which brought those countries near the verge of war and which was at last settled, very

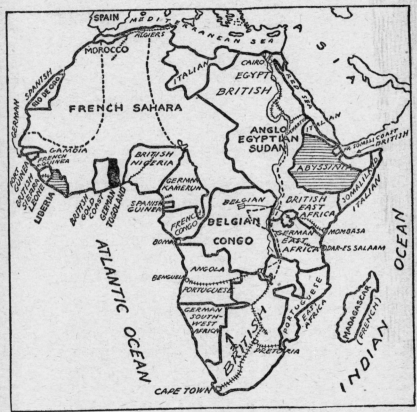

POSSESSIONS IN AFRICA AT THE OUTBREAK OF THE WAR

unsatisfactorily to Germany, at the Algeciras Conference of 1906. Indeed, it was probably his diplomatic defeat in that affair that determined the Kaiser to proceed with the world-war which he provoked eight years later.

165

THE SOUTH AFRICAN DRAMA

Most notable of all, however, was the empire-drama of South Africa. It was there, that the German Colonial Empire was founded, when in 1883–84 Prince Bismarck sent Frederick Luederitz to Angra Pequena to organize the colony of German Southwest Africa. It was a costly job, for it brought on the Hottentot war, which cost nearly $80,000,000 and the lives of several thousand Germans, while about 30,000 natives were exterminated. The next step was the acquisition of German East Africa, which extended inland to the boundary of the Congo and thus prevented any connection between British East Africa and British South Africa.

When trouble began to brew in South Africa between the Boers and British, the German opportunity seemed to have come. The Kaiser sent his famous message of sympathy and encouragement to Paul Kruger, on the Jameson Raid, and tried to make the Boers feel that Germany was their friend, and that they had an ally on the spot in German Southwest Africa. Again when the Boer-British War came on, neutrality was grossly violated by the Germans in Southwest Africa in aid of the Boers, who were permitted to cross the frontier at will when pursued by the British, and then to return to the war. There were secret negotiations between the Boers and the Germans for a compact between them, to the effect that if the Boers succeeded in expelling the British from South Africa, all the colonies there should be put under German protection and be allied with the German colonies at the west and northeast of them, making practically a great German empire occupying the whole of South Africa.

THE SCHEME DEFEATED

The leader of the Boers at that time, and the foremost advocate of that scheme, was Louis Botha, probably the ablest man the Boer race has ever produced. He was defeated in that war by Roberts and Kitchener, however, and he accepted the result loyally, and later became the Prime Minister of the British Union of South Africa. As soon as the present war was started, German agents approached him with plans for a revolution. He was to lead the revolution, throw off British government, and declare the union of the former British colonies with the German colonies, in a German South Africa extending from the Cape to the Congo.

But Botha said, No. He had accepted the results of the Boer war in good faith, and had sworn allegiance to the British crown, and he meant to keep his word. A few of his former comrades were seduced by the German tempters, and a small insurrection was started. Louis Botha thereupon took the field against them and suppressed them. He then organized the Boers into an army and set forth to conquer German Southwest Africa for the British crown; and did it! There have been few more striking incidents in history than that, in which the very men who were expected by the Germans to betray British South Africa to Germany, instead conquered German Southwest Africa for Great Britain.

OTHER AFRICAN COLONIES

Togoland was easily taken by the British early in the war. The Kamerun territory fell later, British, French, Belgians and Portuguese participating in the campaign. German East Africa was the last to fall in that continent. The German half of New Guinea, Kaiser Wilhelm's

Land and the Bismarck Archipelago, were promptly taken by Australia, near the shores of which they lie. Other islands scattered about the Pacific Ocean were seized by the British and by the Japanese.

One of the first to be taken was Kiao-Chao, the German colony in the Province of Shan-Tung, China, which had been seized by the Kaiser's personal orders in 1897, and which was intended to be made the basis of a German partitioning of the Chinese Empire. Japan laid siege to the place and after a blockade lasting from August 27 to November 6, 1914, the Japanese troops, aided by a small British contingent, captured the place.

In such fashion the German Colonial Empire was removed from the map of the world.

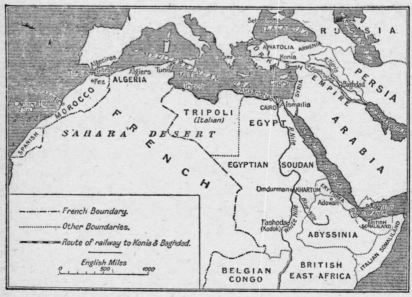

EUROPEAN INTERESTS IN NORTH AFRICA

Chapter XII

THE WAR AT SEA

Great Britain's Sea Power Quickly Manifested — Her Fleet in Control of the Ocean — Disappearance of German Commerce from the High Seas — Many Vessels Interned in Neutral Ports — The German War Fleet Held Under Shelter at the Kiel Canal — Hundreds of Vessels of Millions of Tons Seized or Destroyed — Many Naval Vessels Also the Victims of War — Daring Raids of German Cruisers — Admiral Tirpitz and the Policy of Frightfulness — The Submarine Boat Campaign — Rules of International Law Disregarded — Destruction of American Vessels — The Tragedy of the Lusitania — The Battle off Jutland — Renewal of the Submarine Campaign — Enormous Destruction of Commerce, Including American, in the Weeks Before Our Declaration of War.

THREE HUNDRED merchant vessels of about two-thirds of a million tons burden destroyed in seven weeks, six of them being American vessels. That was the record of the German U-boat campaign of frightfulness, immediately before our declaration of war.

That, however, was only a small part of the operations at sea during the great war, and a comparatively minor part; since great as were the losses to the commerce of the allies and of neutral nations, they were not sufficient to affect materially the carrying trade of the world, while they did not in the least degree affect the steel barrier of blockade which the allies maintained along the German coast.

BRITISH SEA POWER

At the very beginning of the war the sea power of Great Britain was triumphantly manifested. The German Emperor sneered at what he called that country's "contemptible little army," but he had a wholesome respect for its fleet and made no serious attempt to cope with it. His armies were mobilized and rushed irresistibly into France and Russia. But his mighty war fleet remained within the shelter of inland waters, chiefly at the Kiel Canal, while the mercantile marine of Germany, which had been the second largest in the world, disappeared utterly from the high seas. All vessels that could ran into home waters for safety. Many which were in American and other neutral waters remained there, interned for the duration of the war. Many were captured or destroyed by the navies of the allies. Meantime, despite many losses inflicted by a few daring German cruisers, the sea power of Great Britain enabled the commerce of the allies to continue substantially as in time of peace.

THE COMMERCE OF THE NATIONS

At the outbreak of the war the chief maritime nations had the following mercantile fleets:

Nations.	Vessels.	Tonnage.
British Empire	11,353	21,274,064
Germany	2,166	4,706,027
United States	2,589	3,522,913
Norway	2,174	2,529,188
France	1,539	2,285,728
Japan	1,155	1,826,029
Italy	1,177	1,736,545
Sweden	1,462	1,122,883
Russia	1,256	1,054,762
Holland	809	1,522,547
Austria-Hungary	433	1,018,210
Spain	642	899,204
Denmark	835	854,966
Belgium	105	181,687

These figures suggest how comparatively slight was the loss to the British Empire of the nearly 2,000,000 tons of shipping destroyed during the war by the German U-boats and a few cruisers. It amounts to less than ten per cent of the whole; and in fact was nearly compensated for by the building and purchasing of new ships and the capture of German vessels.

THE NAVIES OF THE WORLD

Statistics of the navies of the various powers cannot be given quite so completely as of the mercantile fleets, the tonnage being lacking. The following table gives, however, the numbers of ships of various classes in the navies of the chief eight powers just before the outbreak of the war. The numbers include those built and in commission and also those actually in process of construction. Under "Battleships" are included dreadnoughts, pre-dreadnoughts and super-dreadnoughts. The eight powers, the names of which are abbreviated in the table, are the United Kingdom, France, Russia, Italy, Japan, Germany, Austria-Hungary, and the United States. They are thus given, not in the order of their strength, but according to their grouping in the early part of the war; the first five being the allied powers, the next two the central empires, and the last being the then neutral United States:

Vessels.	U. K.	Fr.	Rus.	It.	Jap.	Ger.	A.-H.	U. S.
Battleships	72	31	15	14	19	41	16	36
Coast Defense	0	0	0	0	0	0	0	10
Battle Cruisers	10	0	4	0	4	7	0	0
Armored Cruisers	47	24	12	9	15	9	2	17
Light Cruisers	85	8	10	18	19	49	12	18
Destroyers	237	87	140	46	53	145	18	53
Torpedo Boats	106	153	25	95	33	80	85	33
Submarines	96	76	43	20	15	38	11	47

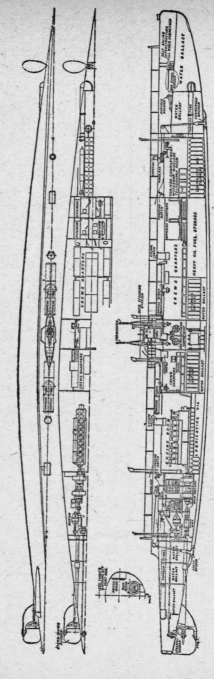

SECTIONAL PLAN OF A SUBMARINE

Upper View—Top of vessel showing deck torpedo tubes and fore and aft diving rudders.

Center View—Section showing the upper half of the submarine with engine room, crew and officers' quarters, and one of the bow torpedo tubes with a torpedo ready to be loaded.

Lower View—Plan of submarine showing arrangement of torpedo tubes, engines, motors, batteries, tanks and crew quarters.

A typical submarine measures 120 feet in length, has a beam of $12\frac{1}{2}$ feet and a draught of 12 feet, 5 inches. The displacement is $225\frac{1}{2}$ tons, and when submerged, $280\frac{1}{2}$. The motive power consists of two Diesel heavy oil engines of 200–220 horsepower, with two electric motors developing a total of 250 horsepower for running under water. The conning tower in the deck is used when running on the surface, and when submerged the boat is operated by the periscopes and controls in the central operating compartment.

TORPEDO DEFENCE

Warships at anchor surround themselves with nets rigged out on spars to catch torpedoes.

Courtesy of Joseph A. Steinmetz, Phila.

ENCOUNTER BETWEEN A SUBMARINE AND A PATROL BOAT

Thousands of small fast motor boats were built in America for Coast duty and to send abroad. They were the submarine's deadliest foe. They were so shallow that a torpedo would not reach them, swift, inexpensive and armed with a gun capable of sinking the

MERCHANT VESSELS DESTROYED

In the early part of the war enormous ravages were caused in both the mercantile and military fleets, chiefly by submarines and by cruisers. Several German cruisers for a long time evaded the pursuit of British ships, and cruised about the world destroying many British vessels. But by far the greater part of the destruction on both sides was done by submarines. The losses of the various countries, belligerent and neutral, in the first seventeen months of the war, were as follows:

Countries.	No. of Vessels.	Tonnage.
British Empire	602	1,192,551
Germany	65	161,888
Norway	77	103,023
France	54	125,978
Denmark	29	33,293
Sweden	35	32,667
Holland	21	36,843
Russia	31	34,193
Italy	25	60,217
Turkey	18	18,150
Belgium	6	12,211
Austria-Hungary	6	13,240
Spain	3	5,223
Japan	3	16,015
Greece	9	18,424
United States	7	14,087

Nearly half of the British ships were fishing smacks, trawlers and other small craft of from 100 to 300 tons. There were, however, fifty merchant steamers of more than 5,000 tons each. The German losses were at first chiefly inflicted by British cruisers which were ranging the seas in quest of the German raiders, but later they were caused by submarines. The heavy losses of Norway were caused chiefly by mines in the North Sea. The American losses in that stage of the war were caused by mines, with the exception of one vessel, the William P. Frye, which was destroyed by a German cruiser under the pretence that she was carrying contraband.

HEAVY NAVAL LOSSES

The naval losses were heavy on both sides, and were pretty evenly balanced between Great Britain and Germany, down to the beginning of the year 1917. Only one important sea battle had been fought, and two or three minor engagements, and the losses were therefore inflicted chiefly by mines and torpedoes discharged by submarines. Down to the date named Great Britain lost 9 battleships; 3 battle cruisers, all of which were in the battle of Jutland; 12 armored cruisers; 7 light cruisers; 2 torpedo gunboats; 17 destroyers; 4 torpedo boats; 12 submarines; and 3 mine sweepers.

During the same period Germany lost 4 battleships, all dreadnoughts and all in the battle of Jutland; 3 battle cruisers, of which two were in that same battle; 1 pre-dreadnought, also in that battle; 6 armored cruisers; 20 light cruisers; 1 unprotected cruiser; 4 gunboats; 13 (probably many more) destroyers; 1 mine-layer; and a large number of submarines.

Thus the British lost 69 vessels of all types, and Germany lost 53, besides an unknown number of submarines and probably some more destroyers. The British vessels lost, omitting submarines, mine-sweepers, etc., aggregated 381,105 tons. The known German losses, omitting submarines and an unknown number of destroyers, aggregated 331,336 tons. The German losses were therefore nearly equal to the British in actual tonnage, and were much greater than the British in proportion to the entire navy.

GERMAN CRUISER RAIDS

A few German war vessels at the beginning of the war were unable to gain shelter with the rest of the navy at the Kiel Canal. The Goeben, a powerful battle cruiser, and the Breslau, a smaller cruiser, were in the Mediterranean, and fled to Constantinople, where they were purchased by Turkey, and afterward did service in the Black Sea. The swift cruiser Emden was in the Pacific. There and in the Indian Ocean she cruised for three months, destroying twenty-five or more merchant steamers worth $10,000,000, before she was overhauled and destroyed at Cocos Island by an Australian cruiser. Another, the

The Environs of KIEL

Königsberg, also in the Pacific, destroyed a dozen ships and then was caught hiding in the mouth of a river in East Africa. A third, the Karlsruhe, made a long and destructive raid in the Atlantic.

Other daring and destructive raiders were the Moewe, the Prinz Eitel Friedrich, and Kronprinz Wilhelm, the last two of which ultimately sought refuge and were interned at Newport News, Va., while the first-named returned in safety to a home port. The only submarine raider to cross the Atlantic paid an unexpected and friendly visit to Newport, R. I., in the fall of 1916, and the next day sank several British and neutral ships within sight of our coast.

NAVAL BATTLES

The first naval battle of the war, in which several ships were engaged, was on August 28, 1914, when a British

MAP SHOWING THE SCENE OF THE GREAT NAVAL BATTLE OF JUTLAND

squadron dashed into the Bight of Heligoland and sank three armored cruisers and two destroyers. The second

occurred on November 1st following, when the German
Far East squadron, of five powerful cruisers, heavily
armed, met four much weaker British vessels off the coast
of Chili and quickly destroyed two of them, the other
two making their escape. On December 8th a stronger
British squadron came up with the Germans and destroyed
them all.

After several raids upon the British coast, in which a
few unfortified coast villages were bombarded and some
women and children were killed, a powerful fleet of German
battle cruisers attempted a dash across the North Sea.
They were intercepted by a British squadron, one of the best
of them was sunk, and the rest were driven back to port.

Finally, at the end of May, 1916, a large part of the
German battle fleet came out from behind Heligoland
and steamed northward. A much weaker squadron of
British battle cruisers promptly engaged it, suffering heavy
loss but inflicting still greater, until the main fleet could
come up, when the surviving German vessels fled back
to port in disaster. This so-called battle of Jutland was
by far the most important of the war, and while at first
announced as a German victory, was in fact a crushing
defeat for the Germans and a clean-cut victory for the
British navy.

TIRPITZ AND FRIGHTFULNESS

The chief operations of the Germans at sea were in
submarine boats. This campaign was devised and prosecuted under the direction of Admiral Von Tirpitz, whose
policy was one of "frightfulness." He meant to disregard
the international laws of naval warfare, and to destroy
ruthlessly and without warning every British vessel he
could find and also every neutral vessel that did not obey

German dictation. The rules that merchant vessels must be visited and searched before they are condemned and destroyed, and that the passengers and crews must have warning and a chance for escape to safety, were quite ignored.

We speak elsewhere of the destruction of American ships by the submarines, and of the destruction of American lives on ships of other nationalities; particularly in the infamous sinking of the Lusitania. It was this policy of frightfulness that led to America's chief controversy with Germany, and to the ultimate declaration of war. We have already referred to the destructiveness of the German submarines during the recrudescence of their campaign in the weeks immediately preceding the declaration of war by our government. This was the record in detail, from February 1 to March 22, 1917:

TOLL OF THE U-BOATS

In the fifty days there were destroyed by German submarines the following named vessels, of the nationalities and tonnage indicated:

Nationality.	Number.	Tonnage
American	6	20,746
British	191	378,142
French	9	30,906
Russian	4	8,238
Italian	8	12,394
Spanish	8	16,435
Norwegian	37	65,014
Swedish	2	3,759
Dutch	13	49,066
Greek	9	16,226
Miscellaneous	12	19,193
	299	620,119

FAILURE OF FRIGHTFULNESS

Tremendous as was the damage done, the campaign of frightfulness was a failure. The boast of Von Tirpitz had been that a million tons a month would be destroyed. In the eighteen days of February he destroyed only 245,140 tons, or 13,619 tons a day—little more than one-third of his boast. In the fifty days of February and March, already noted, he destroyed an average of only 12,402 tons a day.

U-BOAT WAR AGAINST NEUTRALS

The magnitude, however, of German's submarine war against the neutral commerce of the world has been appalling. The following table tells the story of the destruction of neutral shipping down to the time of our entry into the war, in April, 1917:

Nationality of Ships.	Mined.	Tor-pedoed.	Total Ships Sunk.	Total Ascertained Tonnage.
Dutch............	41	35	76	148,921
Swedish..........	30	71	101	99,628
Norwegian........	54	382	436	987,816
Danish...........	20	94	114	123,385
Spanish..........	2	33	35	75,769
American.........	4	16	20	59,256
Brazilian.........	—	2	2	6,719
Greek............	1	59	60	147,923
Argentine.........	—	1	1	281
Peruvian.........	—	1	1	1,419
Uruguayan.......	—	1	1	2,537
Totals........	152	697	849	1,653,654

THE BALANCE SHEET OF SHIPPING

To offset this destruction the Allied nations, particularly Great Britain and the United States, have been building new shipping at a rate never before approximated or dreamed of, until by the summer of 1918 they were producing more than the U-boats destroyed.

The total loss in shipping from submarine attacks and mines since the beginning of the war amounts to this:

	1914	Tonnage.
August and September		399,947
Fourth quarter		281,416
	1915	
First quarter		320,447
Second quarter		380,419
Third quarter		529,481
Fourth quarter		494,373
	1916	
First quarter		524,195
Second quarter		522,289
Third quarter		592,039
Fourth quarter		1,159,343
	1917	
First quarter		1,619,373
Second quarter		2,236,934
Third quarter		1,494,473
Fourth quarter		1,272,843
	TOTALS	
United Kingdom		7,079,492
Other nations		4,748,080
Grand total		11,827,572

The total production, excluding that of enemy countries, during the same period was this:

	Tonnage.
1914–1915, August to August	1,012,000
1915–1916, August to August	1,202,000
1916–1917, August to August	1,688,000
1917–1918, August to June	2,704,275
Total new construction	6,606,275
Enemy tonnage seized and utilized	3,589,000
Grand total	10,195,275
RECAPITULATION:	
Total loss, 1914–1918	11,827,572
Total gain, 1914–1918	10,195,275
Net loss	1,632,297

The First Camp of United States Marines in France

These "dog tents" were but the temporary quarters of our "soldiers of the sea," and were soon replaced by well-built barracks.

RAMMING A SUBMARINE

A merchant vessel, attacked by a submarine, sometimes can ram and sink her enemy before the fatal torpedo is fired home. The artist has revealed the result.

NAVAL CONSTRUCTION

The building of fighting ships has also proceeded during the war, apart from submarines, at a greater rate than the destruction of them. Omitting submarines, destroyers, etc., the following additions have been made to the British navy, of vessels of the dreadnought or "all big gun" type, the years named being those of the completion of the ships:

Year.	Name.	Tons.	Guns.	Knots.
1914	Queen Elizabeth	27,500		25.0
1914	Warspite	27,500		25.0
1915	Barham	27,500	8 15-inch	25.0
1915.	Valiant	27,500		25.0
1915.	Malaya	27,500		25.0
1915.	Royal Sovereign	25,750		22.0
1915.	Royal Oak	25,750		22.0
1916.	Ramillies	25,750	8 15-incn	22.0
1916.	Resolution	25,750		22.0
1916.	Revenge	25,750		22.0
1917.	One Ship	27,500	8 15-inch	25.0
1917.	Renown	25,750		
1917.	Repulse	25,750	8 15-inch	22.0
1917.	Resistance	25,750		

The German shipbuilding programme is not as well known as that of Great Britain, but is believed to have been as follows:

Year.	Name.	Tons.	Guns.	Knots.
1914.	Grosser Kurfürst	25,388		22.0
1914.	Markgraf	25,388		22.0
1914.	König	25,388	10 12-inch	22.0
1915.	Kronprinz	25,388		22.0
1916.	"T"	28,500		23.0
1916.	Ersatz Wörth	28,500	8 15-inch	23.0
1917.	Ersatz Friedrich III	28,500		23.0

Germany has also built four big battle cruisers, two of which were lost in the battle of Jutland, together with one older one. As she lost four battleships also in that engagement, it will be seen that her increase of naval strength during the war had been less than the British. For Germany has built seven and lost four battleships, a net gain of three, while Great Britain has built fourteen and lost nine, a net gain of five.

SCIENCE AGAINST SUBMARINES

English experts, says a Swedish writer who is a high authority on technical information, have now so highly perfected the use of the submarine microphone on shipboard that they are now able to bear automatically down on the submarine, while formerly they were unable to locate a vessel beneath the surface. The microphones are placed below the water, close to the keel of the vessel, and answer the same purpose as the microphones of a telephone. By listening to the beat of the submarine's propeller they can determine the exact location of the enemy and attack him before he has the slightest idea of what is happening.

The detection instruments used with the microphones are very complex. One of them shows the distance of the submarine on a graduated scale, the indicator responding electrically to the sound from the submarine's propellers. The variations of distance are shown with marvelous accuracy. Another device shows whether the enemy is on the port or starboard side. The electro-magnet hand moves to the side on which the sound is loudest and the ship is guided accordingly.

When the proper spot is reached bombs are dropped. Their under-water force is so great that they can destroy a submarine 150 feet from the point of explosion.

CHAPTER XIII

THE WAR IN THE AIR

Literal Realization of the Poet's Dream of Two Generations Ago — Early Use of Balloons in War Time — For Observation in Our Civil War — Gambetta's Escape from Paris in 1870 — Aeroplanes Used in the Balkan War and by the Italians in Tripoli — Extensive Employment of Various Kinds of Air Craft in the Great War — Captive Balloons for Observation — Aeroplanes for Scouting and Signaling — For Bombardment on Land and for Detecting Submarines at Sea — Aeroplanes Fighting in Mid-air Singly and in Squadrons—Zeppelins and Other Dirigible Balloons — Their Futile Efforts to Invade Great Britain — Universal Recognition of Air Craft as an Essential Arm of War on Land and Sea.

THREE-QUARTERS of a century ago one of the world's greatest poets, in one of his loftiest flights of sheer imagination, wrote that he—

". . . dipt into the future, far as human eye could see,
Saw the Vision of the world, and all the wonder that would be;

Saw the heavens fill with commerce, argosies of magic sails,
Pilots of the purple twilight, dropping down with costly bales;

Heard the heavens fill with shouting, and there rain'd a ghastly dew
From the nations' airy navies grappling in the central blue;

Far along the world-wide whisper of the south-wind rushing warm,
With the standards of the people plunging thro' the thunder-storm;

Till the war-drum throbb'd no longer, and the battle-flags were furl'd
In the Parliament of man, the Federation of the world."

It was a dream, the world declared; regardless of the fact that while—

> "Some dreams we have are nothing else but dreams,
> Unnatural, and full of contradictions;
> Yet others of our most romantic schemes
> Are something more than fictions."

Three-quarters of a century; and now is the most graphic and most amazing feature of the bard's fancy fulfilled to the very letter; leaving us amid our wonderment to speculate, pleasingly and hopefully, upon the possible fulfilment in equal measure of the remainder of the splendid vision.

EARLY USE OF WAR BALLOONS

Some use of balloons was indeed made in war at a very early date. Scarcely a dozen years after Montgolfier's invention there was formed in 1794 at Meudon, near Paris, an aeronautical institute for the purpose of training men to make military observations from balloons, and such observations were actually made, with valuable effect, at the battle of Fleurus, near Charleroi, in June, 1794. It is probable that those aerial observations materially contributed to the winning of that crowning victory of the French Revolutionary army over the Austrians.

Balloons were also used for similar purposes in the Austro-Italian War in 1859, and during our own Civil War. In the Suakin campaign in March, 1885, observation balloons were first used by the British army. These were all, of course, captive balloons, held fast with ropes, and served no other purpose than that of giving an extremely elevated point of view. The most important use of moving balloons was made at Paris in 1870–71, during the siege. It was in such a vehicle that Leon Gambetta left that city, to organize government outside its walls; and in such fashion millions of letters were sent out from the beleaguered capital before its surrender.

184

AEROPLANE DEVELOPMENT

All this, however, was very far from anything like "airy navies grappling in the central blue," and down to the beginning of the present century there was little thought, except among dreamers and inventors, of the practical use of air craft as fighting machines. It was supposed, however, that it might be possible to drop explosives and incendiary devices from balloons upon armies, camps and cities, and accordingly at the congress at The Hague

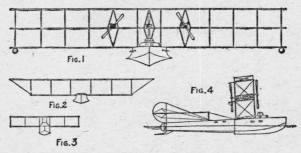

COMPARISON OF THE CURTISS TRIPLANE FLYING BOAT (FIG. 1) OF 133-FOOT SPAN, WITH THE "AMERICA" (FIG. 2) OF 72-FOOT SPAN, AND A STANDARD HYDRO-AEROPLANE (FIG. 3), 35-FOOT SPAN. FIG. 4 IS SIDE VIEW OF FIG. 1

in 1899 there was adopted a rule—to which, however, the United States and Great Britain alone of all the powers declined to subscribe—prohibiting such use of balloons for bombardment, for a period of five years from that date. At the same time, it may be added, a rule was adopted forbidding the use of poisonous or asphyxiating gases in warfare.

The inventions and practical demonstrations of Langley and the Wright brothers in America presently revealed to the world the extraordinary possibilities of an entirely different type of air craft. This was the aeroplane; a true flying machine. It was heavier than air, containing

185

no reservoir of buoyant gas, but depending for levitation upon the form of its wings or planes and upon the action of an engine-driven propeller. The development of the first crude models into air craft capable of soaring several

WRIGHT BIPLANE

miles above the earth and rushing through space at the rate of a hundred or a hundred and fifty miles an hour, with singular nicety and certainty of guidance and completeness of control, must be accounted one of the most remarkable achievements of inventive science in human history.

At the same time the balloon, or "lighter than air" craft, was not abandoned, but more or less successful attempts were made to make it dirigible and self-propelling.

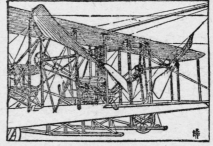

WRIGHT BIPLANE (rear)

Count Zeppelin, in Germany, was most successful in this direction, constructing vast ships, hundreds of feet in length, capable of carrying each a score or more of men with artillery and heavy stores of explosives, and of making well-directed voyages of hundreds of miles without descending. With such vessels it was hoped effectively to invade England.

AERIAL EQUIPMENT OF THE POWERS

At the beginning of the war France easily led the world in aeroplanes. Her army had 1,200 such machines, besides

26 dirigible balloons, of which 12 were nearly 400 feet in length. Germany had only 600 military aeroplanes, with 35 dirigible balloons of the Zeppelin and other types, many of them as much as 490 feet long. Russia had 800 aeroplanes and 16 small dirigibles; Great Britain 500 aeroplanes and 15 dirigibles; Austria 100 aeroplanes and 10 dirigibles; Belgium 40 aeroplanes and 2 dirigibles; and Serbia 40 aeroplanes.

The chief powers immediately began the purchase and manufacture of air craft on an enormous scale, and inventors busied themselves with devising all sorts of improvements upon them for military purposes. In Germany both aeroplanes and gigantic dirigibles of the Zeppelin type were constructed, while the other powers gave their attention almost exclusively to aeroplanes. The latter were made to carry one or two men, and were armed with rifles and machine guns, for fighting other aeroplanes and also for attacking the huge Zeppelins after the fashion of torpedo boats attacking a dreadnought. They were used as adjuncts to the army, to observe the position and movements of the foe and to direct the artillery fire upon vulnerable points. They were also used in connection with the fleet, especially to spy out submarines and to give warning of their approach; a submarine forty feet below the surface being clearly visible from an aeroplane cruising overhead.

In order to repel attacks by aeroplanes and dirigibles, and to destroy them, both land forces and vessels were equipped with guns specially designed for shooting high into the air, and these were often used with much effect, especially against the giant Zeppelins.

THE WAR IN THE AIR

As the war proceeded the number of air craft multiplied until the aeroplanes on each side along the western battle

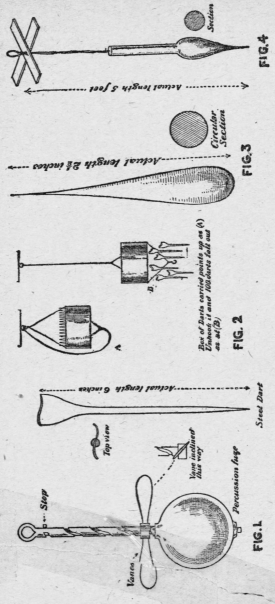

TYPES OF AIR-CRAFT WEAPONS

Fig. 1.—An aeroplane bomb containing 12 pounds of tetranitranilin, with a screw stem up which the vanes travel in flight, and thus "arm", the fuse. Fig. 2.—Steel dart and boxes of darts used by Taube aeroplanes over Paris, showing how they are inverted and released. Fig. 3.—A French "arrow bullet"; very light, but able to kill a man from a height of 1,800 feet. Fig. 4.—A French aerial torpedo used by aeroplanes against Zeppelins, exploding when it has pierced an air-ship's envelope and is suddenly arrested by the wooden cross.

A MORTAL BATTLE IN THE AIR

A fast-flying German "Taube"—so-called because of its resemblance to a dove—trying to escape from a French aeroplane which is equipped with a rapid-fire machine gun. This is an unusual photo of an encounter between air scouts above the battlefield of Arras.

SUBMARINE HUNTING.

A small naval dirigible used for scouting by the British Navy. Under the cigar-shaped balloon is swung an aeroplane chassis equipped with powerful motors and steering apparatus, together with a light gun.

front were to be counted by thousands. Many of the aviators did most of their work singly, in mid-air duels, and there were those who had records of having brought down twenty, thirty or more aeroplanes of the enemy. Some of the most daring and most efficient on the French side were American volunteers, who were indeed so numerous that an American squadron of aviators was formed.

Much of the fighting was also done in squadrons, and there were days when from a single point on the battle front hundreds of aeroplanes were visible, soaring, circling, signaling and fighting. Of the immense value of these craft there was never a moment's doubt.

THE FAILURE OF THE ZEPPELINS

The gigantic Zeppelins, as the dirigible balloons were called after their inventor, were on the contrary a costly failure. So far as the most careful investigation can determine, not one of those vessels made a single raid with results at all commensurate with its cost, while almost every one that undertook an important exploit came to disaster and ruin. Some were wrecked in storms, some had trouble with their engines or gas tanks and exploded, but most of them were shot down by terrestrial artillery or by the swift and agile aeroplanes which whirled about them like tiny kingbirds attacking crows.

Many of them did fly over England, and by dropping explosive and incendiary bombs upon residential villages destroyed some houses and churches and killed many non-combatant people, chiefly women and children. Some even raided parts of London and did a little damage there, though their chief effects were to afford exciting spectacles to the populace, and to exasperate the people into enlisting more numerously for military service. In forty-four

189

raids they killed 431 persons. But scarcely one of them returned to Germany to tell the tale. Several were shot down, and plunged to English earth, blazing wrecks, while others were pursued, overtaken and destroyed at sea by the vengeful bird men of the British aeroplane service.

FALSE TALES OF DESTRUCTION

The only important achievements of the Zeppelins were performed in the imaginations of German officials and newspaper writers. There were some lurid tales of

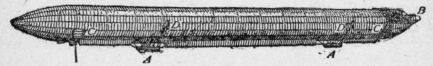

AIRSHIP ZEPPELIN III
a a, engines; *b*, rudder; *c c*, dipping-planes; *d d*, propellers.

destructive raids which had laid England under a reign of terror, every word of which was false. Thus on February 1, 1916, the German Naval Staff officially reported that airships had thrown bombs upon Liverpool and Birkenhead with important results, including heavy explosions and great fires. The German Embassy at Washington added that a large number of bridges had been damaged so that they could not be used, several ships were damaged, docks, dry docks, engine works, boiler works and a powder factory were destroyed, and in all over two hundred houses were destroyed by bombs and fires.

Now, says Mr. S. S. McClure, the well-known American publicist, who visited Liverpool shortly after that date, "As soon as I reached Liverpool I was eager to see for myself what had happened. I saw nothing, for nothing had happened. No Zeppelin had ever come near Liverpool, Birkenhead or Manchester." ("Obstacles to Peace," page 158.)

Accurate figures now available show that of fifty-three Zeppelins put into commission since 1914, thirty-five have been totally destroyed; two have been badly damaged and put permanently out of commission; two are missing and probably destroyed; one badly damaged was temporarily out of commission in December, 1917; thirteen remain in service, eight of which are detailed to the North Sea, two to the Baltic and three as experimental or school ships.

THE FUNCTION OF THE AIRSHIP

The net conclusion thus far attained, as the result of nearly three years of war, is that the gigantic dirigible balloon is of little practical value for military operations; not at all commensurate with its cost and its perils. The aeroplane, on the contrary, both of the small one-man type and of the large two-men or three-men type, is of immense and practically indispensable value.

Its use hitherto has been chiefly as an adjunct to the army and navy, for observation, scouting and signaling purposes, and the occasional dropping of bombs upon vulnerable points.

OUR AERIAL ARMY AND NAVY

The Aviation Corps, indeed, promises to be the most striking feature of the American army abroad. An appropriation of $720,000,000 was made for its uses early in the summer of 1917, and an Aircraft Production Board was appointed to promote the work of manufacturing aeroplanes by thousands and perhaps tens of thousands. The initial programme called, indeed, for the construction of 23,000 aircraft of all types, and 49,000 engines for them, at a cost of $337,500,000. Most of the remainder of the appropriation was for the creation of training camps and schools, and the employment and instruction of an aerial army of 100,000 men, a larger force than our entire standing army before the war.

There was some delay, incidental to the creation of so vast a plant and the perfection of the machinery needed. But in June, 1918, it was announced that all difficulties had been overcome and that production of aircraft, equipped with "Liberty" motors, was beginning on a great scale. Meantime, numerous American aviators, using foreign-made planes, were increasingly active and effective on the battle front, in Flanders, France and Italy. It was then seriously suggested that American-made planes, instead of being carried as cargo on steamships, should fly across the Atlantic, via Newfoundland, the Azores and Portugal. This was believed to be entirely practicable.

Aviation training camps have been established at Mineola, N. Y.; Mount Clemens, Mich.; Fairfield, Ohio; Rantoul, Ill.; East St. Louis, Mo.; Ashburn, Ill.; San Diego, Cal.; San Antonio, Tex.; Belleville, Ill.; Essington, Pa.; Fort Sill, Okla.; Hampton, Va., and Omaha, Neb., the last named being a balloon school.

There are Schools of Military Aeronautics at the Massachusetts Institute of Technology, Boston; Cornell University, Ithaca, N. Y.; Ohio State University; the University of Illinois; the University of Texas; the University of California; the Georgia School of Technology, and Princeton University, Princeton, N. J.

CHAPTER XIV

THE SINEWS OF WAR

The World's Costliest War — Finances of the European Belligerents — Their Huge Debts Before the War — Enormous Credits Voted — Astonishing Response of the People — Figures that Stagger the Imagination — Throwing the Almost Inexhaustible Wealth of America Into the Scale — Seven Billions Voted in a Single Lump — A Huge Loan to Our Allies — The Problem of Supplies of Food and Munitions of War — Importance of Sea Power — Nations Haunted by the Spectre of Famine — Historic Instances of Starvation in War.

THIS WAR costs billions where other wars cost millions. It is incomparably the most expensive war, in dollars and cents, that the world has ever known. That is not only because of its magnitude in geographical extent and in the number of nations and men involved. It is also because the advanced scientific methods of waging war are far more costly than the old ways. A single dreadnought now costs more than the whole British navy did in Nelson's day. When the shells which are fired from cannon cost hundreds of dollars each, and are fired by hundreds of thousands, the ammunition bill "staggers the imagination." The result is that the belligerents are incurring indebtedness almost beyond the power of the average human mind to appreciate.

Before the war began the European powers were heavily burdened with debts, which had, as we have seen, been largely incurred through military preparations and the maintenance of huge armaments.

DEBTS BEFORE THE WAR

The public debts of the belligerent nations just before the war, expressed in United States money, were as follows:

Austria-Hungary	$3,709,534,000
Belgium and Congo	795,785,000
Bulgaria	135,300,000
France and Colonies	6,469,894,000
Germany, States and Colonies	4,945,314,000
Great Britain, India and Colonies	8,307,442,000
Italy	2,669,748,000
Japan	1,271,745,000
Portugal	968,324,000
Roumania	294,061,000
Russia and Finland	4,639,305,000
Serbia	128,078,000
Turkey	554,441,000
United States	1,027,575,000

In this table Austria-Hungary is charged with the joint debt of the two countries and with the separate debt of each; Germany is charged with the imperial debt, the various state debts, and the colonial debt; Great Britain alone bore much less than half the debt charged to her with India and the colonies; the United States is charged with only the national debt and not with any of the state debts.

DEBTS CAUSED BY THE WAR

The principal European belligerents promptly voted enormous credits for carrying on the war, to which the people responded with a readiness far beyond normal anticipation. Loans were generally far over-subscribed, though they amounted to billions each. Down to July 1, 1918, the increased indebtedness of the nations on account of this war was in round numbers as follows:

The British Empire.....................	$33,000,000,000
Russia...............................	22,000,000,000
France...............................	20,000,000,000
The United States....................	12,000,000,000
Italy................................	6,000,000,000
Belgium..............................	750,000,000
Serbia...............................	500,000,000
Roumania............................	400,000,000
Total for chief Allies...............	$94,650,000,000
Germany.............................	$32,000,000,000
Austria Hungary......................	17,500,000,000
Bulgaria and Turkey..................	3,000,000,000
Total for Central Powers............	$52,500,000,000
Grand total for belligerents........	$147,150,000,000

To these tremendous figures must be added large sums for other belligerents, such as Portugal and Japan, and the Central and South American nations which have declared war against Germany, and also for Holland, Switzerland and the three Scandinavian countries which have been put to much expense for the maintenance of neutrality. It will be no exaggeration thus to estimate the public indebtedness now borne directly on account of the war at not less than $150,000,000,000; while the direct cost of the war to all the nations concerned is $150,000,000 a day, or nearly $54,000,000,000 a year. These figures so vastly exceed the aggregate of expenses of all preceding wars in the last two centuries as to be quite out of comparison. Thus the largest figures of the United States public debt at the close of the Civil War were less than $2,700,000,000, or less than one-fourth of what has already been incurred for this war. All the campaigns of Marlborough added less than $190,000,000 to the British debt; and in the twenty-three years of the Napoleonic wars the indebtedness was increased only a little more than $3,000,000,000.

LOANS AND TAXES

The figures of indebtedness given do not, of course, represent the whole cost of the war, but only that part of it that is met with borrowed money. Another considerable part is being met directly with increased revenue from taxation, and in a much larger part than had been supposed possible. Thus from August 1, 1914, to March 15, 1917, the British Government borrowed $15,328,000,000, while at the same time it raised $5,205,000,000 through taxation. Thus it met more than 25 per cent of the war expenses through taxation, without borrowing or increasing its indebtedness, an extraordinarily large proportion. In France the war had cost on June 30, 1917, the sum of $16,580,000,000, of which $2,420,000,000 had come from taxation, or about 14.5 per cent.

Germany, on the other hand, at first made no increase in taxation, but depended exclusively upon loans. The theory of this system was, that Germany would conquer the allies and compel them to pay indemnities sufficient to redeem all her war loans. All that was necessary, therefore, was to borrow money until the end of the war, and then make the conquered nations pay the debts. Germany also extorted—in plain English, stole—enormous sums from Belgium, which she added to her war chest. She also had the advantage of keeping all her money at home. The blockade of her coasts prevented her from purchasing supplies abroad, and so no money was sent out of the empire, save comparatively small amounts to Denmark, Holland and Turkey. By the spring of 1917, however, Germany had incurred indebtedness the interest upon

196

THE PANAMA CANAL

A bird's-eye view of the great canal, which was planned as a short cut for the
fleet of the United States from one ocean to the other.

THROUGH THE PANAMA CANAL

The U. S. battleship "Ohio" in the east chamber of the Pedro Miguel Locks. On the left is seen one of the four electric locomotives used in taking a vessel through a lock.

which was $747,000,000 a year. Now the entire revenue of the empire before the war was only $634,000,000 from taxation and $260,000,000 from railroads, posts and telegraphs; wherefore a considerable increase in taxation was necessitated, to meet the interest charges on the debt.

AMERICAN SUPPLIES FOR THE ALLIES

The allied powers have from the first been looking to the United States for a great part of their supplies, both of muuitions of war and of foodstuffs. The result has been an enormous increase in the foreign trade of the nation. Our exports had ranged from $2,170,000,000 in the fiscal year ending June 30, 1912, to $2,716,000,000 in that ending June 30, 1915; but in the next year, the first full fiscal year of the war, ending June 30, 1916, they increased to $4,272,000,000; an increase of 57 per cent. In the calendar year 1917 they exceeded $6,000,000,000.

Still more significant was the destination of this trade. Our exports to the Central Powers of Europe practically ceased, while those to the allies enormously increased. Thus before the war we had sold $335,000,000 worth yearly to Germany, but in 1916 that amount shrunk to only $288,851. On the other hand, our exports to France rose from $146,000,000 in 1913 to $630,000,000 in 1916; those to Italy from $76,000,000 to $270,000,000; to Russia from $26,000,000 to $313,000,000; and to Great Britain from $597,000,000 to $1,518,000,000. There was also a great increase, for a time, to certain neutral countries: To Denmark from $18,000,000 to $55,000,000; to Norway from $8,000,000 to $53,000,000; and to Sweden from $12,000,000 to $51,000,000. It was quite obvious that this increase could not be required to supply the needs of those countries, but, as they were in close commercial intercourse with Germany, that the enormous surplus above their own requirements was being transshipped to the latter country. It was on that perfectly logical and just ground that the allies interfered with that trade and prevented unlimited imports into neutral lands having trade relations with Germany.

EXPORTS OF MUNITIONS OF WAR

Significant, too, was the character of our trade. Thus animals, chiefly horses and mules, rose from $7,000,000 in 1913 to $99,000,000 in 1916; brass and brass ware from $8,000,000 to $164,000,000; vehicles from $54,000,000 to $167,000,000; chemicals from $26,000,000 to $124,000,000; explosives from $5,000,000 to $467,000,000; iron and steel from $304,000,000 to $621,000,000; leather from $63,000,000 to $146,000,000; woolen goods from $4,000,000 to $53,000,000; and zinc from $406,000 to $48,000,000. These changes could have only one possible meaning. The United States was supplying the allied powers with a large proportion of their munitions of war.

There was also a large increase in our exports of foodstuffs of various kinds, though this was not so marked as the increase of munitions because the surplus above our own needs was limited. But so much was sent abroad as to cause an enormous rise in the domestic prices of food. Never before in our history did prices rise so high as in the spring of 1917. The gold prices of wheat and potatoes then were considerably higher than they had been in depreciated paper currency during the Civil War. The highest price of wheat in depreciated paper scrip in the Civil War was about $2.85 a bushel; in April, 1917, it rose to $3.10 in gold.

THE SPECTRE OF FAMINE

From an early date in the war the grim spectre of potential famine haunted the European belligerents; and by the second year of the war all the peoples were placed upon a siege diet. The governments took possession and control of all food supplies, and fixed the prices and determined the amounts that should be distributed to the people. First attention was paid to the wants of the armies, it being essential that the physical strength of the soldiers should be maintained. After that, the non-combatant population fared but meagrely, especially in the blockaded Central Empires. Still, at the worst, they did not approximate the famine-pangs which others had endured in other wars.

There has, for example, been in Germany no such privations as those which German armies a generation ago imposed upon beleaguered Paris. In that City of Light in the war of the Terrible Year the market price of eggs rose to 45 cents apiece. A box of sardines cost $3 and a cauliflower the same. Potatoes were $10 a bushel. Fresh butter was $12 a pound. A head of cabbage cost $2.50, while a single carrot was valued at 45 cents. Preserved beef was $3 a pound and ham was $7 a pound. A fowl cost $14, a hare $15 and a rabbit $12.

So much for legitimate food supplies. But in the horrors of that siege Parisians eagerly devoured that which at other times would have caused their gorge to rise as filthy and obscene. Cats were eaten, by those who could pay $3 apiece for them; crows were delicacies at $1 each, and even rats were not disdained at 50 cents. As for bread, there was a loathsome composition, consisting largely of sawdust, but containing other ingredients which cannot decently be named, and this was doled out daily at the rate of a third of a pound to each person.

HORRORS OF ANCIENT SIEGES

One of the most appalling examples of siege starvation the world has known was in the last siege of Jerusalem, when parents slew and devoured their own children. But some cases, in comparatively recent times, were scarcely less gruesome. One was that tremendous siege of Londonderry, in which the defenders of the city gathered in the cathedral and, before the altar, vowed and decreed the death of a traitor to any one who should so much as utter the word "surrender." There are tales of cannibalism during that fearful struggle, while it is related that one prominent citizen whose corpulence strangely enough was not materially diminished by the famine seldom ventured to show himself in public because of the hungry and wolfish looks which were cast upon him by his starving neighbors. For a time, before the relief of the city, the rations of each fighting man were half a pound of tallow and three-quarters of a pound of salted hide. These were given to the men whose strength must be kept up so that they might fight. As for the rest of the populace, pity forbids speculation upon the scantness and the horrors of their fare.

THE HEROES OF LEYDEN

Still more appalling was the plight of the defenders of Leyden in the last grim struggle of the Netherlanders against the might of Spain. For weeks, before the succor of the northwest hurricane, famine in its most hideous forms held sway over the devoted city. "Bread, malt cake and horse-flesh had entirely disappeared; dogs, cats, rats and other vermin were esteemed luxuries. A small number of cows, kept as long as possible for their milk, still remained; but a few were killed from day to day

200

and distributed in minute portions hardly enough to support life among the famishing population. Starving men swarmed daily around the shambles where these cattle were slaughtered, contending for any morsel which might fall, and lapping eagerly the blood as it ran along the pavement; while the hides, chopped and boiled, were greedily devoured. Women and children, all day long, were seen searching gutters and dunghills for morsels of food, which they disputed fiercely with the famishing dogs. The green leaves were stripped from the trees, every living herb was converted into human food, but these expedients could not avert starvation."

The dying parents sent their dead children to the Burgomaster in protest against his resolution not to surrender, but these moved not his iron will. Indeed, he came out before them, bearing in his body the marks of as great privations and suffering as any of them had endured, and bade them kill him and eat his flesh for food rather than expect him to surrender the city to a fate far worse than death. Thus were they heartened again, so that they flocked to the crumbling battlements of the city wall and shrieked defiance at their merciless besiegers. "Ye call us rat eaters and dog eaters," they cried, "and it is true. So long, then, as ye hear dog bark or cat mew within its walls, ye may know that the city holds out. And when all has perished but ourselves, be sure that we will each devour our left arms, retaining our right to defend our women, our liberty and our religion against the foreign tyrant."

Against such resolution what could avail the might of Spain? At last came the spring tide and the northern hurricane, sweeping through the broken dikes and returning the land to the sea; upon the van a fleet of ships thronged with the wild Zealanders, more wild than the gale, more raging than the tide, sweeping on through flooded meadow land and orchards, the men bearing their ships upon their shoulders over the bars and shallows, hurling themselves in more than Berserk fury upon their countrymen's besiegers, spitting Spanish cavaliers upon their whale harpoons or dragging them with barbed boat-hooks to within reach of their deadly flenching knives. And the Spanish fled when they thus saw the sea "devouring the earth beneath their feet, while on the waves rode a flotilla manned by a determined race whose courage and ferocity were known throughout the world."

THE PRESENT SCARCITY

We shall look for no such starvation in this war, though beyond doubt the present scarcity is painful. Before the war Germany was the greatest importer of food supplies in all the world, in both gross and net. Her imports of food amounted to $1,640,000,000, and her exports to only $398,000,000, leaving net imports of $1,242,000,000—a colossal volume, the loss of which could scarcely fail to cause speedy and desperate distress. The second importer was Great Britain, with $1,403,000,000 imports and $163,000,000 exports, or net imports of food, drink and tobacco of $1,240,000,000. France was much more nearly self-sustaining, but even she imported $340,000,000 and exported $170,000,000, making her net imports of food $170,000,000. In Russia the balance was on the other side. Her imports of foodstuffs were set down at only $67,067,000, while her exports were $494,273,000, making her net exports $427,206,000. Russia could therefore easily get along without foreign supplies, and France could also do so; while for either Germany or Great Britain complete blockade would mean starvation.

CHAPTER XV

GERMAN RELATIONS WITH AMERICA

Colonial Days — Attitude of Frederick the Great in the Revolution — Employment of Hessians and Other German Troops by the British Government — The Era of German Migration to America — German Unfriendliness in the Spanish War — Its Animus — The Perilous Episode at Manila — Prince Henry and the German Propaganda — German Professors — Denial of the Monroe Doctrine — Germany Warned Out of Venezuela — Anti-American Intrigues at Panama — Meddling in the Danish Islands.

RELATIONS BETWEEN the United States and Germany began at a later date than those with Great Britain, France or Spain. That was because Germany was not one of the colonizing powers in North America, and because down to the time of and during our Revolution the affairs of Europe engaged German attention to the exclusion of everything on this side of the sea. The German settlers in the thirteen colonies, while of a substantial character, were not sufficiently numerous to affect the course of public affairs. Among the patriot leaders of that time the great majority were of English origin. There were also some, including some of the foremost, of Scottish, Irish, Welsh, Dutch and French extraction. Germans were conspicuous by their absence.

FREDERICK THE GREAT

Germany's first interest in America, if interest it may be called, was at the beginning of the Revolution. Because British soldiers sympathized with the Americans and refused to fight against them, the German King of England

203

was constrained to look elsewhere for mercenary troops. His first application was made to Russia, and his second to Holland. He failed to get troops there, from the one because Catherine the Great could not well spare them, and from the other because the Dutch would not fight against a people struggling for their liberty. The next application was made to various German states, among them Prussia. Now Prussia, under Frederick the Great, had only a few years before risen into prominence as a great military power, and a detachment of its army would have been of great service to George III. But Frederick refused to hire him any troops; probably for three reasons. One doubtless was, that he felt aggrieved at England for what he regarded as her desertion of him in a former war. Another was, that in the unstable equilibrium which then existed among the powers of Europe he did not deem it prudent to separate himself from soldiers whom he might himself need at any time.

The third reason, which has been ascribed to him was that, as he is reported to have said, he was not willing that his soldiers should fight against people who were seeking their freedom. It is entirely possible and not improbable that he, with his strange, contradictory, enigmatic character, did feel and express that sentiment. That his sympathy with America went any further does not, however, appear. We know that he persistently refused to receive or to have any dealings with the American envoy who was sent to his court, and while he doubtless felt and may have expressed admiration for the military genius of Washington, there is no indication that the story of his sending of a sword to him with the message, "From the Oldest General to the Greatest," is anything more than a picturesque fiction.

THE HESSIANS

Other and minor German princes were more compliant with the wish of George III, and in Hesse and elsewhere thousands of soldiers were procured, who formed the majority of the British army all through that war. These soldiers did not, of course, enter the service voluntarily. They were sold by their rulers, like so many cattle, at so many dollars a head. Nor did their rulers thus sell them because of any anti-American feeling. It was simply a sordid matter of business. Many of the soldiers were reluctant to come hither, and some of them deserted at their first opportunity. Most of those who were taken prisoners preferred at the close of the war to remain here rather than be repatriated, and many of them became excellent American citizens.

It must be remembered, however, that the Germans who fought through that war under the British flag were as a rule characterized by brutality and lack of humanity. Most of the excesses and outrages against non-combatants were committed by them—such as the murder of the wife of Caldwell, the pastor of the church at Springfield, New Jersey, who, because of that atrocity rushed into his church and brought out hymn-books for the patriot troops to use for gun wadding. Indeed, because of the tragic deeds of those days the name "Hessian" has ever since been in this country a synonym for lawlessness and brutality.

STEUBEN AND DE KALB

Occasional attempts have been made in recent years to attribute to Germany great helpfulness to the American cause, on account of the services of Steuben and De Kalb. There is no question of the splendid value of their services to the American army, or of their whole-hearted devotion to this country. But they are not to be credited to Germany.

Steuben, for whom no praise could easily be too high, was a Prussian, and was one of the most brilliant of the great Frederick's lieutenants. But he came to this country from France, where he had been living, and at the urging of a Frenchman, the Count St. Germain; and by so doing he incurred the displeasure of the Prussian King to such an extent that at the end of the war he deemed it best not to return to Germany, but to become an American citizen and remain here, which he did.

De Kalb was also a brave and efficient soldier. He was a Bavarian, whose entire military career before coming hither had been in the French army, largely fighting against Prussia, and he came to America as a French officer, in company with Lafayette.

Excepting, therefore, for the accident of their place of birth, America was not indebted to Germany for either of these fine soldiers, but directly and solely to France.

GERMAN IMMIGRATION

German immigration to America may be said to have begun in the decade from 1831 to 1840. Before that time it was a negligible quantity, as was all immigration but that from the United Kingdom. Thus in the preceding eleven years, 1820 to 1830, more than 75,000 came hither from the British Isles and only 6,761 from Germany, and fewer than 100,000 from all the world. But in 1831–40 the number from all Europe rose to nearly 500,000. More than half of them were from the United Kingdom, chiefly from Ireland, but no fewer than 152,454 came from Germany. Then in the next decade, the revolutionary era on the continent, there came nearly 1,600,000, of whom two-thirds were from the United Kingdom and 434,600 from Germany. Finally, in the next decade, that just preceding our Civil War, immigration from Europe totaled nearly 2,500,000, more than half being from the British Isles, and 951,667 from Germany.

Since that time the influx of Germans has not been large; in late years it has been almost nil. But the multitudes of that nationality who came hither before the Civil War have formed with their descendants an important element of the American nation, and have contributed much to our statesmanship, scholarship and business and industrial progress. They have generally been regarded as forming one of the most substantial and valuable elements of the body politic.

GERMAN IMPERIAL UNFRIENDLINESS

Because of this great influx of Germans and their generally excellent character, strong ties of sympathy arose between this country and Germany. American sympathy was with Prussia against Austria in 1866, and it was also largely with Germany in 1870. Indeed, it was practically altogether with Germany at first, until after the fall of Louis Napoleon, and even after that it was given to the new German Empire no less than to the French Republic; and thenceforward for many years the relations between the two countries were of the most amiable description. There was a little friction in Samoa, but it caused no ill will toward Germany as a whole.

But in 1898 the German Government suddenly assumed an attitude of decided unfriendliness toward the United States. Just before the declaration of war with Spain, it formed a cabal of the great powers, to seek mediation of some description. That was a most offensive impertinence, since for two-thirds of a century we had made it clear that we considered our relations with Spain in respect to Cuba as a matter of concern to no other power; but the gentle forbearance and tact of President McKinley passed it over without the sharp rebuke which it really deserved. This course was taken by the President because Germany had persuaded the British Ambassador, under a plausible pretext, to act as the spokesman of the cabal, in order that the odium might fall upon Great Britain and cause bad blood between the United States and that country. The complete failure of the scheme, either to secure mediation and thus let European powers meddle in purely American affairs, or to cause trouble between us and Great Britain, so angered the Kaiser that he presently recalled his luckless Ambassador in disgrace.

SPANISH WAR MEDDLING

The Kaiser at that time began to broach the arrogant principle that no important international business should be transacted anywhere in the world without taking him into consultation. His displeasure with the United States therefore waxed hot. The press of Germany, taking its cue from the Wilhelmstrasse, raged against the "Yankee Pigs" more savagely than that of Spain itself. Anticipating our seizure of the Philippines, the Kaiser sought to avert it by himself occupying them first. So he rushed a fleet thither, and great was his wrath to find that Dewey had got there first and had destroyed the Spanish fleet. In his anger he ordered the commander of his fleet to ignore Dewey's authority. He violated international custom and courtesy by sending thither a much stronger fleet than ours, and in having it not only disregard Dewey's authority but also actually give aid and comfort to the besieged Spanish garrison. Two German vessels went to a neighboring port and materially assisted the Spanish by firing upon Filipino troops which were co-operating with the Americans.

The climax came when the German ships committed a particularly flagrant breach of Dewey's orders, and Dewey curtly informed the German Admiral that if he wanted war he could have it, there and then. The German thereupon consulted the British commander, Admiral Chichester, and strove to inveigle him into concerted action against the Americans. The Englishman's reply was, that he was acting under orders the purport of which were known to only himself and Dewey, and he thereupon moved the British squadron to a position between the German and American ships, so that the German Admiral, with his superior force, could not attack Dewey without firing over the British vessels. There is no doubt that Chichester's orders from the British Government were, in case of a clash between the German and American fleets, to place himself and his ships at Dewey's command.

PRINCE HENRY'S PROPAGANDA

Thus foiled, the Kaiser tried new tactics. He sent his brother, Prince Henry, to America, ostensibly on a mission of courtesy and friendship, but in fact to found and promote a German propaganda in the United States. A vast German-American League was formed, with semi-military organization, the chief objects of which were to keep alive devotion to the Fatherland, to prevent Germans here from becoming Americanized, and to remind them that under the anomalous laws of Germany they were still German subjects despite the fact that they had formally renounced allegiance to the Kaiser and had sworn allegiance to the United States. That system of "dual allegiance" was purely a German device, recognized by no other country.

A system of exchange of professors between German and American universities was also arranged, and several active German propagandists secured election as permanent professors in American universities, where they busied themselves with the insidious extension of German principles and interests to the utmost possible degree.

AGAINST THE MONROE DOCTRINE

With the development of the German Colonial Empire and the vast extension of German commerce, the need of some German possessions in America was felt. The acquisition of such a holding was barred by the Monroe Doctrine, and therefore German opposition to and denial of that American principle were incessant. While other European governments either tacitly or in terms recognized and respected it, Germany alone persistently refused to do so in any way, but habitually referred to it with contempt.

During the administration of President Roosevelt three attempts were made by Germany to discredit the Monroe Doctrine and to injure the interests of this country. One was in connection with Venezuela. Germany put forward certain claims against that country, and purposed to send a naval and military expedition thither to invade the country and seize upon a part of it at least until the claims should be satisfied. Our government had not objected to the collection of just claims by proper methods, but to this, which savored of conquest for the satisfaction of probably spurious claims, it did object. The President therefore informed the German Ambassador that when the German expedition reached Venezuelan waters, it would find waiting for it the American line of battle fleet, under command of Admiral Dewey. The German expedition was not sent.

MEDDLING AT PANAMA

Another attempt to thwart American policy and to impair American interests was made by Germany at Panama. When negotiations were undertaken by our government for a treaty with Colombia, giving us the right to construct the Isthmian Canal, German influences prevailed upon the Colombian Minister, Mr. Concha, to refuse to make the treaty; and he finally quitted his post at Washington, and went to Germany, rather than complete the negotiations. His successor, Dr. Herran, did negotiate a treaty, but German influence at Bogota was directed against it, and ultimately prevented its ratification. Meantime efforts were made to persuade Colombia to grant a canal concession to a German company.

It was during that same administration that a treaty was made with Denmark for our purchase of the Danish West India Islands. It was ratified by our Senate, and by the Lower House of the Danish Parliament; but it was defeated in the Upper House, notoriously through German influences and intrigues.

Chapter XVI

THE TRIBULATIONS OF A NEUTRAL POWER

America's Attitude toward the War, and the Attitude of the Belligerents toward America — German Disregard of Treaties — American Insistence upon International Law — Questions of Contraband and Blockade — Restraints of Neutral Trade — The Use of Neutral Flags by Belligerents — Germany's Submarine Warfare in Violation of International Law — The Lusitania Infamy — German Perjuries — "Strict Accountability" — The Sussex Case — American Warnings to Germany — The Falaba, Cushing, Gulflight, Nebraskan, Arabic and Other Vessels — German Evasions — American Patience Exhausted — The Arming of Merchant Ships — Severance of Diplomatic Relations — Declaration of War.

"THE UNITED STATES," said President Wilson in his neutrality note to the Senate on August 14, 1914, "must be neutral in fact as well as in name." It was. But its neutrality did not save it from serious and distressing tribulations at the hands of belligerents who had no regard for neutrality, who reckoned good faith a weakness, and to whom treaties and international law were mere scraps of paper.

The Secretary of State on August 6 caused inquiries to be made of all belligerents whether the Declaration of London, of 1909, would be respected as the law of naval warfare. Germany and Austria-Hungary replied in the affirmative, but Great Britain, France and Russia submitted certain modifications, enlarging the list of contraband and reconstructing the rules for prize courts. In view of this disagreement of the belligerents, the United States then announced that it would insist upon the rights of this country and its citizens as defined by international law and treaties, regardless of the Declaration of London. Great Britain

212

on August 5th and 13th issued lists of contraband articles, which it would not permit to be carried into German ports; practically all "conditional" contraband being thus made absolute. Similar lists of contraband were issued by the other belligerents.

Early in the war some controversy arose with Germany over the treatment of armed merchant vessels, our government holding that they should be treated as merchant vessels so long as the arms were for defense only, and Germany insisting that they should be treated as warships. The dispute was left for the time unsettled. Some controversy also arose with Great Britain over her interference with our commerce, in the course of which the British Government pointed out that it was following the rules laid down by our own government during the Civil War.

GERMANY'S SUBMARINE WAR

The abandonment of international law in naval warfare was announced by Germany on February 6, 1915. The German Government then proclaimed that the high seas surrounding the British Isles, including the whole of the English Channel, were a war zone, and that on and after February 18th every enemy merchant ship found therein would be destroyed without regard for the safety of passengers and crews. That meant that the long-established rule providing for visit and search before seizure of destruction was to be ignored, and that vessels were to be torpedoed on sight, even without warning, without any attempt to ascertain their real character or that of their cargoes. It was also stated that neutral ships would be in danger of the same treatment, since it would not be possible in all cases to discriminate between them and enemy vessels.

The reason for this astounding proclamation of piracy

was simple. Germany's navy dared not come out and face the British fleet, and all maritime operations had therefore to be conducted by submarines. But submarines were so vulnerable that they dared not show themselves above water in the vicinity of possibly hostile vessels. They dared not, therefore, employ the usual and legal methods of visit and search, but purposed to attack and destroy suspected ships without any such formalities.

THE AMERICAN PROTEST

Against this monstrous policy the United States protested. In a note of February 10, 1915, it declared that if in pursuance of this policy Germany should "destroy on the high seas an American vessel or the lives of American citizens, it would be difficult for the United States to view the act in any other light than as an indefensible violation of neutral rights which it would be very hard indeed to reconcile with the friendly relation subsisting between the two governments." In the same note our State Department continued with the memorable words:

"If such a deplorable situation should arise, the Imperial German Government can readily appreciate that the Government of the United States would be constrained to hold the Imperial German Government to a strict accountability for such acts of their naval authorities and to take any steps it might be necessary to take to safeguard American lives and property and to secure to American citizens the full enjoyment of their acknowledged rights on the high seas."

GERMANY ON THE BLOCKADE

The German Government replied on February 16th that it had been driven to the adoption of this policy by

"England's murderous method of conducting maritime war." The "murderous method" was nothing in the world but the long-established and universally recognized system of blockade, by means of which contraband goods were excluded from the ports of the enemy—precisely such as the United States maintained along its Southern coast during the Civil War. This, of course, excluded foodstuffs, and thus threatened Germany with famine. But in railing against this as "murderous" and "contrary to law of war and every dictate of humanity," Germany strangely ignored the fact that in her war against France in 1870–71 she had pursued precisely the same course, excluding foodstuffs from the cities of Strasburg, Metz and Paris until the civilian population died by thousands of sheer starvation and the places were forced for that reason alone to surrender. She ignored the fact that when, on those occasions, the women and children and other helpless non-combatants sought to depart from the beleaguered cities, leaving the fighting men to bear the brunt of famine, they were forced back into the cities at the point of the bayonet and were even fired upon.

In further communications the German Government refused to admit the right of merchant ships to be armed, even for purposes of defense, and insisted upon the free admission of food supplies into Germany to meet the wants of the civilian population. The pretense that imports of food were thus sought solely for civilians, and that such food should not be considered contraband, was of course a quibble, since the civilians would have had enough food without importing any if their supplies had not been taken from them for the army. The new supplies which were demanded were therefore intended to meet a deficit caused by military uses, and were thus obviously contraband.

TRAFFIC IN MUNITIONS OF WAR

The German Government in April, 1915, accused the United States Government of violation of neutrality and of taking an unfair attitude toward Germany, because it did not prohibit the export of munitions of war to the allied powers. This was grossly disingenuous, to say the least. The German Government must have known that it was not in the power of the Administration, but required an act of Congress, to place such an embargo on commerce. It certainly knew that in selling arms the United States was merely maintaining the policy which had prevailed since the foundation of the government, and the policy which other nations, Germany herself conspicuously included, consistently followed. Germany had provided Spain with all the munitions of war she needed in the Spanish-American War of 1898, and the United States had never thought of objecting or remonstrating.

Of course in the present war there was no unfairness to Germany. American manufacturers would have been just as ready to sell munitions to Germany as to the allies. But Germany, because of the disappearance of her commercial marine from the high seas, was unable to purchase our goods; or if she did purchase any, was unable to get them transported to her shores. Her claim was, therefore, the absurdly illogical and unreasonable one, that because she did not want or could not carry home our goods, we should refuse them to those who did want them and were able to take them. To this preposterous demand the American Government fittingly replied that "the placing of an embargo on the trade in arms would be a direct violation of the neutrality of the United States," inasmuch as it would be a change of policy calculated to help one belligerent and to injure another.

216

GERMAN ORDERS TO AMERICAN CITIZENS

There then occurred an incident unique in diplomatic history, involving one of the grossest affronts that one government ever offered to another. The United States, as already related, had insisted upon the right of its citizens

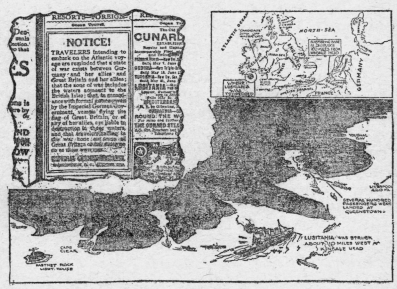

GERMANY'S OFFICIAL PAID ADVERTISEMENT FOREWARNING AMERICANS AGAINST DISASTER; MAP SHOWING WHERE IT TOOK PLACE

This advertisement was wired to forty American newspapers by Count von Bernstorff, German Ambassador at Washington. It was ordered inserted on the morning of the day the Lusitania sailed.

to travel unmolested upon the high seas, and had said that it would hold to "strict accountability" anyone who interfered with that right. Now the German Imperial Government, through its embassy at Washington, issued a proclamation to the people of the United States, by means of advertisements in the leading newspapers. In that proclamation it warned them that they would thus travel at peril of their lives, unless they complied with the commands of the German Government as to the routes which they should take, the time of their journeys, and the vessels on which they traveled. It practically told American citizens that if they wanted to travel in safety they must not trust to the protection of their own government, but must obey the directions and trust to the protection of Germany.

In any other country of the civilized world the publication of so astounding an impertinence would probably have resulted in the instantaneous dismissal and expulsion of the Ambassador who had dared to utter it, if not also severance of relations with his government. But our government patiently endured the outrage, merely referring to its "surprising irregularity" and saying that no such warning could be accepted as an excuse for or palliation of an unlawful act.

THE LUSITANIA

There swiftly followed fulfilment of the German menace. On May 7, 1915, the British steamer Lusitania, an unarmed merchantman, bound on her regular voyage from New York to Liverpool, was torpedoed without warning by a German submarine. Of her passengers and crew numbering 1,959, no fewer than 1,198 were lost, including 124 Americans, a large proportion of them being women and children. This unparalleled atrocity, which was regarded with horror by all the rest of the world, was greeted with delirious outbursts of joy throughout Germany, and by the German and pro-German element in the United States. When the news of it reached New York, the walls of German restaurants, theatres and beer gardens literally quivered under the stress of the exultant cheers. In Germany the government issued medals commemorative of the event, on which was a grim representation of the slaughter of women and children.

Our government patiently contented itself with a diplomatic note, declaring it to be "wise and desirable" that the American and German governments should "come to a clear understanding as to the grave situation." There followed much diplomatic controversy. Germany at first insisted that the Lusitania was armed, and not merely for defense but for attack, so that she was in fact a ship of war. An agent of the German Government was produced, who swore that he had seen cannon placed aboard the ship. This was utterly false, and it was afterward admitted that the German agent had deliberately and purposely committed perjury. There were intimations that the German Government might be willing to pay an indemnity of so much a head for the Americans who had been murdered, but it would not disavow the crime; and in the end the controversy lapsed without result, and crime remained unatoned.

OTHER VESSELS DESTROYED

The Falaba, a British vessel, was destroyed by a German submarine on March 28, 1915, and one American life was lost. The Cushing, an American vessel, was on the same day attacked by a German aeroplane. The Gulflight, an American vessel, was destroyed on May 1st, with the loss of one American life. These all preceded the Lusitania. The attacks on the Cushing and Gulflight were explained by Germany as "mistakes," and an offer was made of such reparation as the facts in the case might warrant. Similar disposition was made of the case of the American steamer Nebraskan, which was attacked by a submarine on May 25th; of the Leelanaw, an American ship, which was destroyed on July 27th; and of the English steamer Orduna, on July 9th.

The British steamer Arabic, with a number of Americans aboard, was sunk by a submarine on August 19th, and an attempt was made to excuse the act on the lying pretense that the Arabic had attacked the submarine. But on October 5th Germany disavowed the act, offered to pay indemnities for the American lives lost, and stated that strict orders had been given which would prevent any more such occurrences. This was received by our government with expressions of gratification.

In January, 1916, the United States proposed to the allied belligerents a set of rules for the regulation of naval warfare, providing that no merchant vessel should be armed; that no vessel should be attacked without warning or without being ordered to stop and be searched; and that all should thus submit to search. The powers declined, however, to accept these rules on the mere strength of a non-guaranteed German promise that if they complied with them the German atrocities would cease.

THE CASE OF THE SUSSEX

The British passenger steamer Sussex was sunk by a submarine in the English Channel on March 24, 1916, with several Americans among its company. The German Government at first tried to pretend that the Sussex was mistaken for a mine-layer, and then that she had been sunk by a British mine. Our government promptly proved, however, that she was an unarmed passenger vessel; that she had been sunk without warning, by a German torpedo; and that eighty of her passengers, non-combatants, including many women and children, and including several American citizens, had perished. In its note to Germany on the case the American Government said:

"It has become painfully evident that the use of sub-

The "Lusitania" and Her Pygmy Destroyer

This sectional view shows where the great ocean liner was struck by the deadly missile which sent her to the bottom with many of her crew and non-combatant passengers.

DAMAGE CAUSED BY A TORPEDO

This photograph shows the bow of a steamer in drydock after being struck by a torpedo on the port side. The explosion blew numerous fragments of wreckage through the plates on the starboard side.

marines for the destruction of an enemy's commerce is of necessity because of the very character of the vessels employed and the very methods of attack which their employment of course involves, utterly incompatible with the principles of humanity, the long-established and incontrovertible rights of neutrals, and the sacred immunities of non-combatants. . . ," and threatened to sever diplomatic relations.

In response the German Government declared that it could not dispense with the use of submarines, but that it would make certain concessions to the rights of neutrals and modifications of the under-sea warfare which it believed would be satisfactory to the United States. This assurance was accepted by the United States and the matter was considered settled.

THE BREACH OF RELATIONS

There followed some futile correspondence between this country and the powers on both sides concerning peace, and then, at the end of January, 1917, came the beginning of the end. On January 31st the German Ambassador at Washington handed to the American Secretary of State a note withdrawing the pledges which had been made in settlement of the Sussex case, to the effect that merchant ships should be warned before being sunk and that neutral lives and property should be protected. It was official notice that the war zone around the British Isles was to be still further extended and that a most ruthless campaign of destruction was to be waged against all vessels entering it. It was condescendingly stated that one American ship a week would be permitted to visit a certain English port, provided that it would comply with various fantastic German requirements.

This exhausted the patience of the American Government. On February 3d President Wilson directed that passports be given to the German Ambassador and that the American Ambassador be recalled from Berlin, thus severing diplomatic relations between the two countries. This, as the President made clear in a convincing address to Congress, was in fulfilment of the warning which had been given, as hitherto quoted, in the Sussex case. A few days later Germany, through Switzerland as an intermediary, sought to parley over the matter, but the President declined to receive the overtures which were offered.

ARMED NEUTRALITY

The next step was that of armed neutrality. We were not at war with Germany, and it was still hoped by some that we should be able to avoid war. But Germany was putting into effect her threats of a resumption and intensification of the submarine campaign, and had sunk not only many British vessels but also two American vessels, the Housatonic and the Lyman M. Law. Accordingly on February 26th the President asked Congress for permission to supply defensive arms to merchant ships at his discretion.

The German press, by permission of the imperial censor and thus presumably with the approval of the Imperial Government, printed conspicuous articles, declaring that the submarines would thereafter destroy all vessels found within the war zone, regardless of their character or nationality. In fulfilment of that threat the armed American merchant steamer Aztec was attacked and sunk. This was on April 1st, off the French coast, near Brest. Eleven of the crew were reported lost.

The next day, April 2d, the President asked Congress to declare war.

222

CHAPTER XVII

FUTILE EFFORTS FOR PEACE

Germany's Cynical Overtures — Their Rejection by the Allied Powers — Their
Purposes Disclosed — President Wilson's Peace Note — His Conception of the
Objects of the Belligerents — The Interests of the United States Involved — Seeking
Acceptable Terms — Equivocal Acceptance by Germany — Rejection by the
Allies — The President's Peace Message to the Senate — Proposing the Principles
of the Monroe Doctrine for All the World.

WE TRIED peace first. That fact must be remembered,
and it will be well to turn back a moment and recall the
various overtures which were made for peace only a little
while before Germany forced America into this monstrous
war. Germany and her allies themselves suggested peace,
in characteristic fashion. On December 12, 1916, they
issued an identic note to the United States and other
neutral powers, for transmission to the opposing belligerents,
proposing a peace conference. They said:

"The four allied powers (Germany, Austria-Hungary,
Bulgaria and Turkey) have been obliged to take up arms
to defend justice and the liberty of national evolution.
. . . The spiritual and material progress which were
the pride of Europe are threatened with ruin. . . . If,
in spite of this offer of peace and reconciliation, the struggle
should go on, the four allied powers are resolved to continue to a victorious end, but they disclaim responsibility
for this before humanity and history."

REJECTED BY THE ALLIES

This cynically insincere proposal, with its unblushing
perversions of truth, was emphatically rejected by the
Allies on December 30th. In their note of reply they said:

"The putting forward by the Imperial Government of a sham proposal lacking all substance and precision would appear to be less an offer of peace than a war manœuvre. It is founded on calculated misinterpretation of the character of the struggle in the past, the present, and the future.

"As for the past, the German note takes no account of the facts, dates, and figures, which establish that the war was desired, provoked, and declared by Germany and Austria-Hungary.

"At The Hague Conference it was a German delegate who refused all proposals for disarmament. In July, 1914, it was Austria-Hungary, who, after having addressed to Serbia an unprecedented ultimatum, declared war upon her in spite of the satisfaction which had at once been accorded.

"The Central Empires then rejected all attempts made by the Entente to bring about a pacific solution of a purely local conflict. Great Britain suggested a conference; France proposed an international commission; the Emperor to go to arbitration, and Russia and Austria Hungary came to an understanding on the eve of the conflict. But to all these efforts Germany gave neither answer nor effect.

"Belgium was invaded by an empire which had guaranteed her neutrality and which had the assurance to proclaim that treaties were 'scraps of paper,' and that 'necessity knows no law.' . . .

PURPOSE OF THE OVERTURES

"In reality these overtures made by the Central Powers are nothing more than a calculated attempt to influence the future course of war and to end it by imposing a German peace. The object of these overtures is to create dissension in public opinion in the allied countries. But that

224

public opinion has, in spite of all the sacrifices endured by the Allies, already given its answer with admirable firmness, and has denounced the empty pretense of the declaration of the enemy powers. . . .

"Finally, these overtures attempt to justify in advance in the eyes of the world a new series of crimes—submarine warfare, deportations, forced labor and forced enlistment of the inhabitants against their own countries, and violations of neutrality.

"Fully conscious of the gravity of this moment, but equally conscious of its requirements, the allied governments, closely united to one another and in perfect sympathy with their peoples, refuse to consider a proposal which is empty and insincere.

"Once again the Allies declare that no peace is possible so long as they have not secured reparation for violated rights and liberties, the recognition of the principle of nationality and of the free existence of small states, so long as they have not brought about a settlement calculated to end once and for all forces which have constituted a perpetual menace to the nations, and to afford the only effective guarantee for the future security of the world. . . ."

PRESIDENT WILSON'S PEACE NOTE

At the very time when that German note was issued, President Wilson, in entire ignorance of it, had in preparation a note addressed to all the belligerent powers, inviting them to make an exchange of declarations of purposes and of terms on which peace would be acceptable. This was issued by him on December 18th, with a brief explanation that it had absolutely no connection whatever with the German note which had been issued a few days before.

This note, signed by the Secretary of State, ran in part as follows:

"The President suggests that an early occasion be sought to call out from all the nations now at war such an avowal of their respective views as to the terms upon which the war might be concluded, and the arrangements which would be deemed satisfactory as a guaranty against its renewal or the kindling of any similar conflict in the future as would make it possible frankly to compare them. He is indifferent as to the means taken to accomplish this. He would be happy himself to serve, or even to take the initiative in its accomplishment, in any way that might prove acceptable, but he has no desire to determine the method or the instrumentality. One way will be as acceptable to him as another, if only the great object he has in mind be attained.

OBJECTS OF THE BELLIGERENTS

"He takes the liberty of calling attention to the fact that the objects, which the statesmen of the belligerents on both sides have in mind in this war, are virtually the same, as stated in general terms to their own people and to the world. Each side desires to make the rights and privileges of weak peoples and small states as secure against aggression or denial in the future as the rights and privileges of the great and powerful states now at war. Each wishes itself to be made secure in the future, along with all other nations and peoples, against the recurrence of wars like this and against aggression or selfish interference of any kind. Each would be jealous of the formation of any more rival leagues to preserve an uncertain balance of power amid multiplying suspicions; but each is ready to consider the formation of a league of nations to insure peace and justice throughout the world.

226

INTERESTS OF THE UNITED STATES

"In the measures to be taken to secure the future peace of the world the people and Government of the United States are as vitally and as directly interested as the governments now at war. Their interest, moreover, in the means to be adopted to relieve the smaller and weaker peoples of the world of the peril of wrong and violence, is as quick and ardent as that of any other people or government. They stand ready, and even eager, to co-operate in the accomplishment of these ends, when the war is over, with every influence and resource at their command. But the war must first be concluded. The terms upon which it is to be concluded they are not at liberty to suggest; but the President does feel that it is his right and his duty to point out their intimate interest in its conclusions, lest it should presently be too late to accomplish the greater things which lie beyond its conclusion, lest the situation of neutral nations, now exceedingly hard to endure, be rendered altogether intolerable, and lest, more than all, an injury be done civilization itself which can never be atoned for or repaired.

"The President therefore feels altogether justified in suggesting an immediate opportunity for a comparison of views as to the terms which must precede those ultimate arrangements for the peace of the world, which all desire and in which the neutral nations as well as those at war are ready to play their full responsible part.

DEFINITE TERMS SOUGHT

"The leaders of the several belligerents have, as has been said, stated those objects in general terms. But, stated in general terms, they seem the same on both sides. Never yet have the authoritative spokesmen of either side avowed the precise objects which would, if attained, satisfy them and their people that the war had been fought out. The world has been left to conjecture what definitive results, what actual exchange of guaranties, what political or territorial changes or readjustments, what stage of military success, even, would bring the war to an end.

PIOUS ASPIRATIONS

"It may be that peace is nearer than we know; that the terms which the belligerents on the one side and on the other would deem it necessary to insist upon are not so irreconcilable as some have feared; that an interchange of views would clear the way at least for conference and make the permanent concord of the nations a hope of the immediate future, a concert of nations immediately practicable.

"The President is not proposing peace; he is not even offering mediation. He is merely proposing that soundings be taken in order that we may learn, the neutral nations with the belligerent, how near the haven of peace may be for which all mankind longs with an intense and increasing longing. He believes that the spirit in which he speaks and the objects which he seeks will be understood by all concerned, and he confidently hopes for a response which will bring a new light into the affairs of the world."

GERMANY'S EQUIVOCAL ACCEPTANCE

Germany and her allies promptly replied to the President's note with an apparent acceptance, so framed as to make it tantamount to a confirmation of the German proposals of December 12th. They made it clear that they would enter into the conference only on the basis which they had themselves already prescribed, and that

228

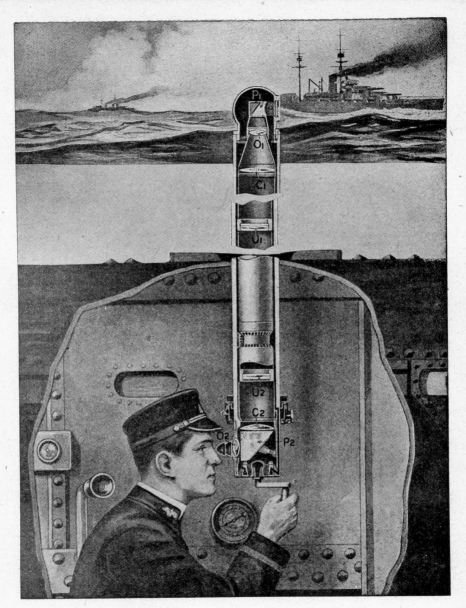

PERISCOPE OF A SUBMARINE

A slender steel column, projecting above the surface of the water, is the eye of the submarine. The image enters at a side of the top, is reflected downward by a prism through lenses and a lower prism to the officer's eye. The periscope may be turned in any direction.

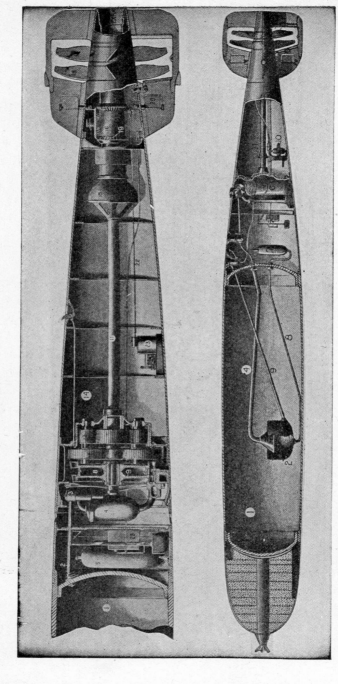

MECHANISM OF THE TORPEDO

At the head of the torpedo is several hundred pounds of gun-cotton, tipped with a cap which fires it on impact. The largest compartment contains compressed air to drive the motor. The rudders are controlled by an automatic device which steers it on a set course.

they would not consider in the peace negotiations any measures for the prevention of further wars of the same kind. The German note ran thus:

"The high-minded suggestion made by the President of the United States of America in order to create a basis for the establishment of a lasting peace has been received and considered by the Imperial Government in the friendly spirit which was expressed in the President's communication.

"The President points out that which he has at heart and leaves open the choice of road. To the Imperial Government an immediate exchange of views seems to be the most appropriate road in order to reach the desired result. It begs, therefore, in the sense of the declaration made on December 12th, which offered a hand for peace negotiations, to propose an immediate meeting of delegates of the belligerent states at a neutral place.

"The Imperial Government is also of the opinion that the great work of preventing future wars can be begun only after the end of the present struggle of the nations. It will, when this moment shall have come, be ready with pleasure to collaborate entirely with the United States in this exalted task."

AN UNEQUIVOCAL REFUSAL

The reply of the Allies was made on January 10th, and was much more elaborate and detailed than that of Germany. It expressed cordial appreciation of and sympathy with the benevolent motives of the American Government, but protested strongly against the assimilation established in the American note between the two groups of belligerents. It referred to the note of the Allies in response to the German peace note as a response also to the President's inquiry concerning the terms of peace which would be satisfactory, and then continued:

"President Wilson desires . . . that the belligerent powers openly affirm the objects which they seek by continuing the war; the Allies experience no difficulty in replying to this request. Their objects in the war are well known; they have been formulated on many occasions by the chiefs of their divers governments. Their objects in the war will not be made known in detail with all the equitable compensations and indemnities for damages suffered until the hour of negotiations. But the civilized world knows that they imply in all necessity and in the first instance the restoration of Belgium, of Serbia, and of Montenegro and the indemnities which are due them; the evacuation of the invaded territories of France, of Russia and of Roumania with just reparation; the reorganization of Europe guaranteed by a stable regime and founded as much upon respect of nationalities and full security and liberty of economic development, which all nations, great or small, possess, as upon territorial conventions and international agreements suitable to guarantee territorial and maritime frontiers against unjustified attacks; the restitution of provinces or territories wrested in the past from the Allies by force or against the will of their populations; the liberation of Italians, of Slavs, of Roumanians and of Tcheco Slovaques from foreign domination; the enfranchisement of populations subject to the bloody tyranny of the Turks; the expulsion from Europe of the Ottoman Empire. The intentions of His Majesty the Emperor of Russia regarding Poland have been clearly indicated in the proclamation which he has just addressed to his armies. It goes without saying that if the Allies wish to liberate Europe from the brutal covetousness of

Prussian militarism, it never has been their design, as has been alleged, to encompass the extermination of the German peoples and their political disappearance. That which they desire above all is to insure a peace upon the principles of liberty and justice, upon the inviolable fidelity to international obligation with which the Government of the United States has never ceased to be inspired.

"United in the pursuits of this supreme object the Allies are determined, individually and collectively, to act with all their power and to consent to all sacrifices to bring to a victorious close a conflict upon which they are convinced not only their own safety and prosperity depends but also the future of civilization itself."

THE PRESIDENT'S PEACE MESSAGE

Following this, on January 22, 1917, President Wilson addressed the United States Senate on the subject, not with a request for action but in explanation of his policy, and thus ended the discussion of peace, which was already obviously futile. In his address he reviewed the notes of the belligerents, insisted that when peace was finally made the United States must have a part in the work, and indicated what must be the general tenor of the peace terms to be satisfactory to this country; saying in conclusion:

"In holding out the expectation that the people and the Government of the United States will join the other civilized nations of the world in guaranteeing the permanence of peace upon such terms as I have named, I speak with the greater boldness and confidence because it is clear to every man who can think that there is in this promise no breach in either our traditions or our policy as a nation, but a fulfillment rather of all that we have professed or striven for.

231

A MONROE DOCTRINE FOR ALL NATIONS

"I am proposing, as it were, that the nations should with one accord adopt the doctrine of President Monroe as the doctrine of the world: That no nation should seek to extend its policy over any other nation or people, but that every people should be left free to determine its own policy, its own way of development, unhindered, unthreatened, unafraid, the little along with the great and powerful.

"I am proposing that all nations henceforth avoid entangling alliances which would draw them into competition of power, catch them in a net of intrigue and selfish rivalry, and disturb their own affairs with influences intruded from without. There is no entangling alliance in a concert of power. When all unite to act in the same sense and with the same purpose, all act in the common interest and are free to live their own lives under a common protection.

"I am proposing government by the consent of the governed; that freedom of the seas which in international conference after conference representatives of the United States have urged with the eloquence of those who are the convinced disciples of liberty; and that moderation of armaments which makes of armies and navies a power for order merely, not an instrument of aggression or of selfish violence.

"These are American principles, American policies. We can stand for no others. And they are also the principles and policies of forward-looking men and women everywhere, of every modern nation, of every enlightened community. They are the principles of mankind and must prevail."

CHAPTER XVIII

AMERICA AS A BELLIGERENT

AMERICA'S entrance into the War of the Nations was tardy and deliberate. We have seen how numerous, persistent and extreme had been her provocations, during more than two and a half years. Yet she waited until nearly every great nation in the Eastern Hemisphere was involved, and indeed until some of her neighbors in this hemisphere were beginning to consider participation in it. Our declaration of war with Germany, made on April 6, 1917, was the thirty-sixth that had been made in this war since Austria's breach with Serbia on July 28, 1914—a period of less than thirty-three months.

It will be interesting, as a matter of reference and record, to recapitulate the various declarations which had been made; bearing in mind that in some cases nations against which war was declared did not respond with counter-declarations. For example, Germany declared war against France on August 3, 1914; but France has never yet made any declaration against Germany. Her

233

only answer to the German declaration was, to fight.
The following is a list of declarations down to our own:

1914

July 28—Austria on Serbia.	Aug. 11—France on Austria-Hungary.
Aug. 1—Germany on Russia.	" 11—Montenegro on Germany.
" 3—Germany on France.	" 12—Great Britain on Austria.
" 3—Germany on Belgium.	" 23—Japan on Germany.
" 4—Great Britain on Germany.	" 25—Austria on Japan
" 5—Austria-Hungary on Russia.	" 29—Austria on Belgium.
" 8—Montenegro on Austria.	Nov. 2—Russia on Turkey.
" 9—Austria on Montenegro.	" 5—Great Britain on Turkey.
" 9—Serbia on Germany.	" 5—France on Turkey.

1915

May 22—Italy on Austria.	Oct. 15—Great Britain on Bulgaria.
" 22—Italy on Turkey.	" 16—France on Bulgaria.
June 3—San Marino on Austria.	" 19—Italy on Bulgaria.
Oct. 14—Serbia on Bulgarial	" 19—Russia on Bulgaria.

1916

Mar. 8—Germany on Portugal.	Aug. 28—Bulgaria on Roumania.
" 10—Portugal on Germany.	" 28—Turkey on Roumania.
" 15—Austria on Portugal.	" 28—Germany on Roumania.
Aug. 27—Roumania on Austria.	" 28—Italy on Germany.

1917

Apr. 6—United States on Germany.

Since the action of the United States on April 6, 1917, the
following additional declarations of war have been made:

1917

Apr. 7—Cuba on Germany.	Aug. 14—China on Austria-Hungary.
" 7—Panama on Germany.	" 14—China on Germany.
July 2—Greece on Bulgaria.	Oct. 26—Brazil on Germany.
" 2—Greece on Germany.	Dec. 7—United States on Austria-Hungary.
" 22—Siam on Austria-Hungary.	" 10—Panama on Austria-Hungary.
" 22—Siam on Germany.	
Aug. 4—Liberia on Germany.	

1918

Apr. 22—Guatemala on Germany.	July 19—Honduras on Germany.
July 16—Hayti on Germany.	

FORMS OF DECLARATIONS OF WAR

In finally making our declaration of war against Germany, we might well have adapted the words of Shakespeare and said, "Stand not upon the order of declaring, but declare." There was much discussion and there were many differences of opinion as to the order, or the form; whether we should "declare war" or should merely declare that "a state of war existed." There was thought to be much and important difference between the two, as though the former would impose far more responsibility upon us than the latter. The former seemed to be looked upon as an announcement that we should begin war against Germany, while the latter was merely a recognition of the fact that Germany had begun to wage war against us.

But the two phrases are practically synonymous. To declare does not mean to wage war or to announce an intention of doing so. It means nothing more than to state, to announce, to publish, to make clear, an already existing fact. Our phrase, as finally adopted by Congress, was that a state of war "is hereby declared." That did not mean at all that we purposed to create a state of war. It meant that we recognize the fact that one already existed, and the preceding context made it abundantly clear that it was Germany that created that state of war and thrust it upon us; which was, of course, precisely correct and the very thing that we ought to have said.

UNREADY FOR WAR

Seldom, if ever, has any nation made a declaration of war in a greater state of unreadiness for war than the United States was in when it finally joined issues with Germany. For more than a century the policy of Wash-

235

ington and Jefferson, the traditional policy of this nation, had been neglected and ignored. For several years there had been much discussion and agitation of the matter, but little had been done. The nation was bewitched by the siren song of pacifism into believing, first, that there was no danger of our ever getting into war with a great power, and second, that if we did we should show ourselves able to "lick all creation."

Our army, unsurpassed in character, was a mere handful in size. Our organized militia, also pitifully small in numbers, was disorganized and demoralized by the fatuous manner in which it had been mismanaged in our campaign against Mexico. Our navy, superb as its units were, was lacking in submarines and battle cruisers, and was so undermanned that half the battleships were laid up for lack of crews. We had scarcely any aviation service, and our supplies of artillery, rifles and ammunition were wofully inadequate.

THE COST OF UNPREPAREDNESS

In all this we were blind to the lessons of history. Washington in the Revolution dwelt frequently and bitterly upon the murderous folly of arraying raw recruits against trained soldiers, and urged thorough training and universal service. In the War of 1812 we had been unprepared and had trusted to green militia, with the result that our land forces were usually beaten and our national capital was abandoned to the foe. In the Civil War it took us two years to get ready to fight. In the Spanish War our unpreparedness and the mismanagement of our camps and commissary formed a national scandal. Yet we ignored these lessons of history, and for more than two years faced a world in flames of war, with a growing assurance that

236

Photo by *Underwood and Underwood, N. Y.*

United States Battleship "Oklahoma"

One of the latest types of super-dreadnaught is here shown, racing along at 20½ knots an hour on a speed test. This great warship is a sister-ship of the "Nevada." Her displacement is 27,500 tons, her engines develop 28,000 horsepower and she is armed with ten 14-inch guns in her four turrets, twenty-one 5-inch and four 3-pounders, together with four 21-inch Torpedo Tubes. She cost over $6,000,000.

AN AMERICAN FIGHTING MACHINE

The U. S. Battleship "Wyoming," making a "smoke curtain," behind which
submarines or destroyers might launch an attack on the enemy.

we ourselves would be involved in it, without making any real preparations to meet the tremendous crisis.

EFFORTS AT PREPARATION

The moment war was declared, however, Congress began with frantic haste to atone so far as possible for the delay. Vast sums were voted for expansion and equipment of the army and navy, and a large increase of forces was authorized. A small band of pacifists opposed these measures, but their opposition was speedily overridden. At first public sentiment on the subject was supposed to vary greatly in different parts of the country, the Middle West being least disposed toward war, and some states, in which German residents were numerous, being reputedly strongly opposed to it. Day by day, however, brought the nation into harmony, until all sections were rallying to the support of the government.

The authorized increase of the army and navy was at first sought through the familiar system of volunteer enlistment. But this dragged, and it became evident that more strenuous methods must be employed. The President finally declared himself in favor of compulsory service, through a system of selective conscription, and a bill to that effect was introduced into Congress. Opposition to it was noisy but otherwise feeble, and at the middle of May the necessary legislation was enacted. The nation was awake and rising to meet the crisis.

Chapter XIX

OUR RESOURCES: ACTUAL AND POTENTIAL

Our Population and Wealth, and Production of Bread and Iron, Compared with the Other Great Powers — Our Financial Resources — Size of the Army and Navy Before the War — The Organized Militia — Submarines and Airships American Inventions — Agricultural Resources and How They Might be Quadrupled — Our Commercial Marine — Deplorable Lack of Ocean-going Tonnage — Comparisons with Other Countries — Urgent Need of an Increase of the Mercantile Marine.

VAST ARE the resources of America. At the time of her entry into the war, thirteen other nations were already involved in it. They included the six so-called Great Powers of Europe. But save for the population of two of them, the United States decisively outranked them all in the chief elements of material greatness. Apart from population the three chief elements of greatness are wealth, wheat and iron. The first means the aggregate wealth of the real and personal property of all the people of the nation. In that particular, the United States surpasses any two other nations in the world, put together. The second, wheat, is the most important article of food in civilized lands, and the production of it is an essential factor in the nation's economic independence. The third, iron, is the most important of all the metals, and the production of it is a gauge of the nation's industrial potency.

The following tables show, in round numbers, the population and wealth, and the wheat and iron production, of the chief belligerents, according to the latest available statistics:

238

Countries.	Population.	Wealth.
United States............	103,287,000	$230,000,000,000
British Empire............	438,000,000	130,000,000,000
Russian Empire...........	175,000,000	60,000,000,000
France (omitting colonies)..	40,000,000	65,000,000,000
Italy (omitting colonies)....	36,000,000	35,000,000,000
Germany................	68,000,000	80,000,000,000
Austria-Hungary	53,000,000	45,000,000,000

Countries.	Wheat, Bushels.	Iron, Tons.
United States...............	1,000,000,000	36,500,000
British Empire..............	813,250,000	18,000,000
Russia.....................	840,000,000	4,150,000
France.....................	258,000,000	3,500,000
Italy......................	170,500,000	380,000
Germany...................	160,000,000	14,160,000
Austria-Hungary............	212,900,000	1,500,000

AMERICAN FINANCIAL RESOURCES

The financial ability of the United States to pay the expenses of the war for itself, and to assist its allies, may be estimated from the following statistics:

Annual national income..................	$50,000,000,000
Total bank resources.....................	35,000,000,000
Individual deposits......................	24,000,000,000
Cash held by the banks..................	2,500,000,000
Total gold stock in the country...........	3,000,000,000
Available additional commercial credits on basis of present cash holdings...........	6,000,000,000

It is estimated that the borrowing power of the American Government is not less than $40,000,000,000, from domestic sources, without seriously disturbing the ordinary financial and economical affairs of the nation.

THE ARMY AND NAVY

The figures already given of population and wealth suggest the collossal potency of the United States in war. But at the outbreak of the present war that potency was undeveloped, and the actual army and navy stength of the nation was small. The following table indicates the actual strength of the army establishment at the end of the last fiscal year before our entry into the war, June 30, 1916:

Organizations.	Officers.	Men.
General Officers	24	....
General Staff Corps	32	....
Adjutant General's Department	23	....
Inspector General's Department	17	....
Judge Advocate General's Department	13	....
Quartermaster Corps	258	5,492
Medical Corps	443	4,670
Medical Reserve Corps	154	....
Dental Surgeons	38	....
Corps of Engineers	228	1,826
Ordnance Department	83	740
Signal Corps	71	1,472
Bureau of Insular Affairs	3	....
Chaplains	64	....
Professors	7	....
Total	1,458	14,200
Cavalry, 15 regiments, etc.	782	15,160
Artillery, 6 regiments, etc.	257	5,627
Infantry, 31 regiments, etc.	1,607	34,313
West Point detachments	....	603
Indian Scouts	....	39
Casuals and recruits at depots and en route	....	8,798
Total	....	9,440
Total, Regular Army	4,843	97,013
Philippine Scouts	182	5,603
Grand total	5,025	102,616

THE NAVY

The actual strength of the navy in October, 1916, was 3,761 officers and 54,214 men, a total of 57,975. In the Marine Corps there were 410 officers and 11,044 men, a total of 11,454.

According to the United States "Navy Year Book" for 1916, there were at its date of publication the following vessels in the navy listed as fit for service:

Type.	No.	Displacement.
Dreadnoughts	12	307,450
Predreadnoughts	25	340,146
Armored cruisers	10	140,080
Cruisers, first class	5	46,465
Cruisers, second class	4	25,065
Cruisers, third class	16	50,820
Monitors	7	24,964
Destroyers	49	43,585
Coast torpedo vessels	16	6,695
Torpedo boats	17	3,146
Submarines	42	15,722
Tenders	8	31,927
Gunboats	28	25,967
Transports	4	22,235
Supply ships	4	25,400
Hospital ship	1	5,700
Fuel ships	21	253,900
Naval yachts	14	8,957
Tugs	47	19,568
Special types	8	45,954
Total	338	1,444,746

ADDITIONS TO BE MADE

The following vessels were listed as under construction:

Type.	No.	Displacement.
Dreadnoughts	5	160,600
Destroyers	9	9,911
Submarines	33	21,093
Gunboat	1	1,575
Transport	1	10,000
Supply ship	1	8,500
Hospital ship	1	9,800
Fuel ships	2	29,000
Tugs	2	1,150
Total	55	251,269

And these were provided for and contracted for:

Type.	No.	Displacement.
Dreadnoughts	4	130,400
Battle cruisers	4	137,200
Second-class cruisers	4	28,400
Destroyers	20	23,700
Submarines	30	22,590
Special type	1	10,600
Total	63	354,800

THE NAVY IN PROSPECT

There was thus in being and in assured prospect for the immediate future the following naval force:

Type.	No.	Displacement.
Dreadnoughts	21	598,450
Predreadnoughts	25	340,146
Battle cruisers	4	139,200
Armored cruisers	10	140,080
Cruisers, first class	5	46,465
Cruisers, second class	8	53,465
Cruisers, third class	16	50,820
Monitors	7	24,964

Type.	No.	Displacement.
Destroyers	78	77,196
Coast destroyers	16	6,695
Torpedo boats	17	3,146
Submarines	105	54,455
Tenders	8	31,927
Gunboats	29	27,512
Transports	5	32,225
Supply ships	5	33,000
Hospital ships	2	15,500
Fuel ships	23	282,230
Naval yachts	14	8,957
Tugs	49	20,718
Special type	9	56,504
Total	456	2,050,265

THE ORGANIZED MILITIA

The organized militia, commonly known as the National Guard, was of the following strength in 1916:

States.	Officers.	Men.
Alabama	166	2,391
Arizona	54	866
Arkansas	81	834
California	245	3,218
Colorado	58	770
Connecticut	227	3,476
Delaware	35	426
District of Columbia	94	1,741
Florida	85	1,181
Georgia	225	2,859
Hawaii	93	2,548
Idaho	63	901
Illinois	500	6,099
Indiana	150	2,411
Iowa	218	3,182

States.	Officers.	Men.
Kansas	127	1,925
Kentucky	170	2,252
Louisiana	63	1,119
Maine	111	1,428
Maryland	168	2,024
Massachusetts	418	6,600
Michigan	220	3,430
Minnesota	210	2,889
Mississippi	71	1,085
Missouri	207	3,746
Montana	50	734
Nebraska	110	1,507
Nevada	0	0
New Hampshire	83	1,175
New Jersey	301	4,021
New Mexico	67	867
New York	1,014	15,309
North Carolina	208	2,846
North Dakota	55	735
Ohio	492	5,916
Oklahoma	70	966
Oregon	96	1,595
Pennsylvania	701	9,450
Rhode Island	90	1,527
South Carolina	102	1,424
South Dakota	65	857
Tennessee	113	1,634
Texas	185	2,720
Utah	32	546
Vermont	76	878
Virginia	197	2,808
Washington	90	1,358
West Virginia	106	1,505
Wisconsin	192	3,247
Wyoming	35	579
Total	8,589	123,605

A MODERN MILITARY TRACTOR AEROPLANE

A machine of the latest model, carrying a pilot and observer and drawn by a 90 horsepower, eight cylinder water-cooled engine. Its wing area is 359 square feet, wing span overall, top 43 feet 7$\frac{3}{16}$ inches, lower, 33 feet 11$\frac{1}{2}$ inches. Overall length of machine 26 feet 10$\frac{1}{2}$ inches. Net weight empty, 1170 pounds, gross weight with load, 1850.

TOKENS OF OUR NATURAL RESOURCES

Above, harvesting in the west; below, steam harvester and thresher.

SUBMARINES AND AIRSHIPS

Our military services were insufficiently supplied with submarine boats and with aeroplanes; which was an irony of fate, seeing that both those devices were chiefly of American origin. The submarine dates back to Robert Fulton, who years before he initiated steam navigation with the Clermont made successful trips under the waters of the British Channel in a hand-propelled submarine. For many years his achievements in that direction were all but forgotten. But the general idea was taken up in our own time by two other Americans, Simon Lake and John P. Holland, and from their inventive genius proceeded the development of the submarine fleets which have so largely transformed the naval warfare of the world. So, too, Langley and the Wright brothers, Americans, were pioneers in the development of aeroplanes, or "heavier than air" flying machines.

AGRICULTURAL RESOURCES

Some mention has already been made of America's production of wheat, the most important of all foodstuffs. This country annually produces more than 3,000,000,000 bushels of corn, 1,000,000,000 bushels of wheat (in 1915, the record year), 1,500,000,000 bushels of oats, 225,000,000 bushels of barley, 35,000,000 bushels of rye, 20,000,000 bushels of buckwheat, 400,000,000 bushels of potatoes, 75,000,000 tons of hay, 28,000,000 bushels of flaxseed, 7,500,000,000 pounds of cotton, 1,000,000,000 pounds of tobacco, 1,900,000 long tons of sugar, and 300,000,000 pounds of wool. It has 65,000,000 swine, 65,000,000 head of cattle, 25,000,000 horses and mules, and 60,000,000 sheep. It produces more than 500,000,000 tons of coal, 1,000,000,000 pounds of copper, and 225,000,000 barrels of petroleum a year. It has 268,000 manufacturing establishments with a yearly output worth $20,000,000,000. Its farm products are worth more than $10,500,000,000 a year.

Vast as are these resources, however, they are small by the side of what they might be. Even in the completely settled and cultivated states, scarcely fifty per cent of the available agricultural land is actually under cultivation, while that which is cultivated is not made to produce more than one-half as much as it should. Thus the average yield of wheat is from 15 to 17 bushels to the acre, while in some European countries it is 33 bushels; and the average yield of potatoes seldom reaches 100 bushels, while in Germany it is considerably more than 200 bushels to the acre. Double the cultivated area, and double the acre yield, and the enormous figures given above would be quadrupled.

OUR COMMERCIAL MARINE

One of the weakest points in our resourcefulness at the beginning of the war was that of the commercial marine. Enormous as was our foreign trade, it was chiefly conducted in foreign vessels under foreign flags. We have at New York the greatest seaport of the world, reckoned in the value of its trade, while in the year before the war the second was German, the third and fourth English, and the fifth Belgian:

New York	$1,966,256,617
Hamburg	1,960,779,855
London	1,866,930,782
Liverpool	1,816,983,279
Antwerp	1,214,725,495

These were the five first-class ports. No other in the world reached the billion-dollar mark. Now let us see what were our imports from and our exports to the principal countries involved in this war:

	Imports.	Exports.
Austria-Hungary	$12,969,000	$70,761,000
Belgium	20,010,000	79,869,000
France	83,346,000	172,221,000
Germany	166,626,000	377,464,000
Italy	50,554,000	99,462,000
Netherlands	54,478,000	145,525,000
Russia	9,274,000	45,026,000
United Kingdom	147,180,000	655,005,000

OUR LACK OF TONNAGE

The total tonnage of American shipping was indeed large; perhaps the second largest in the world. But the major part of it was on the Great Lakes and in purely coastwise traffic. In foreign trade our total steam tonnage was pitifully small in comparison with that of other countries. Thus:

	Tons.
United States	667,896
United Kingdom	19,202,770
Germany	4,380,348
Russia	790,075
Austria-Hungary	777,729
Denmark	671,000
Holland	983,049
France	1,500,000
Italy	987,559
Japan	1,146,977
Norway	1,422,006
Sweden	782,508
Spain	746,748

The natural consequence of these conditions was seen in the small figure which American vessels presented in the commerce of our own ports. In 1913 the total clearances of American steam vessels in foreign trade from our own seaports were 4,520,697 and of foreign vessels 31,221,160. The clearances of shipping from our ports under the flags of the actual and potential belligerents in the present war were as follows:

	Tons.
Austro-Hungarian	427,246
Belgian	356,231
British	19,359,581
French	1,033,931
German	4,587,050
Italian	802,103
Russian	129,635

THE GREAT SHIPPING COMPANIES

A list of the great shipping companies of the world, just before the war, arranged in the order of total tonnage, showed that by far the largest was a German line, while another German line was easily second and the next four were British.

One of the earliest results of the war in 1914 was to stimulate the increase of American merchant shipping, to do the neutral carrying trade of the world, and the implication of this country in the war is certain still further to promote the same movement, for the supplying of our allies across the sea with the necessaries of existence and for replacing the vast amount of their tonnage which the German submarine campaign has destroyed.

CHAPTER XX

OUR MILITARY GEOGRAPHY

Our "Isolated Position" Less Marked than of Old — All the World Now Within Reach — Two Alien Frontiers — One Marked with a Century of Peace — The Troublous Mexican Frontier — Our Extended Frontage on Two Oceans — Fortunate Formation of the Atlantic Littoral for Defense — Possibilities of an Inland Coastal Waterway, Valuable in Peace, Invaluable in War — Utility of the Panama Canal and Need of Its Defense — American Interest in the Gulf and Caribbean.

IN THE early days of the republic we enjoyed, geographically, a "splendid isolation." The oceans formed practically insuperable barriers against serious invasion. When we got rid of France and Spain as neighbors by taking Louisiana and Florida for our own, there were left abutting upon us the territories of only one important power, and in 1815 we established with it a peace which has ever since remained unbroken; a peace in the perpetuity of which we had so much confidence that we agreed to leave the frontier between us and that power entirely unfortified.

Modern inventions, however, have destroyed our isolation, and all the world is now within reach and within striking distance of us. The Atlantic Ocean is now scarcely more of a barrier than was the Hudson or the Delaware River in Washington's time. Our efficiency on the sea and our military preparedness on the land, must now be depended upon to protect us from foreign invasion.

TWO LAND FRONTIERS

There will probably never be occasion for anxiety concerning the longer and more important of our two land frontiers. The peace which has been unbroken for more than a century is now being mightily confirmed by the union of the two nations in war against a common foe. At the southwest, however, the prospect is not so reassuring. Already twice in our history we have crossed the Mexican border with force and arms, and the unhappy condition of that country provokes a fear that other troubles may hereafter occur in that same region. It cannot be said, however, that there is any grave menace there to the integrity of this republic. It is true that during the present war, while still our relations with her were friendly, Germany plotted to use Mexico as a channel for invasion of the United States, for purposes of conquest and the partitioning of our territory. It does not appear, however, that any serious Mexican statesman gave the vicious intrigue encouragement, and we may probably feel assured that none is likely to do so. An attack upon the United States from that direction would be of all most difficult for the invader to prosecute.

OUR GREAT COAST LINE

It is rather to our enormously extended coast line that we are to look as the potential scene of attack, and therefore as the region to which most defensive attention is to be given. Apart from Alaska and our insular possessions, we have a coast line of thousands of miles, on the Atlantic and Gulf, and on the Pacific, and along it or close to it are seated some of our most important cities.

The defense of these cities and of the entire coast line against attack or the landing of an army of invasion must be threefold. The first line of defense is, of course, the navy, which should be sufficiently strong to render it impossible for an enemy to land an army at any point, or to attack one of the coast cities. For efficiency in that respect, the navy needs a good supply of submarine boats, and also a supply of aeroplanes for scouting purposes—to watch for and report the approach of an enemy's fleet. Next there must be an adequate system of coast fortifications around all important coast cities and at the entrances of navigable rivers and bays. Finally, there must be an army of ample force, so mobile that it can speedily be massed at any point, to prevent the landing of a hostile army.

NATURE'S PROVISION FOR DEFENSE

It is an interesting and most gratifying circumstance that the most important and most exposed portion of our coast, the Atlantic frontage, has been provided by nature with exceptional advantages for defense, needing only a little human co-operation to make them available. The reference is, of course, to the actual and potential system of inland coastal waterways extending from New England to the Gulf. It is a system which, if put into full use, would be of inestimable service in time of peace as a high-way of travel and transportation, and which in time of war would be literally invaluable, since it would provide an intracoastal course of navigation well sheltered and secure from alien attack, and at the same time a means of shifting our coast defense and submarine fleet from point to point in both security and secrecy. The Panama Canal is prized because it will enable us to transfer a fleet swiftly from the Atlantic to the Pacific, or *vice versa*. This intra-coastal waterway would enable us to keep our fleets of torpedo boats, destroyers and submarines lying secure in sheltered waters and ready to issue forth for action from any of a multitude of inlets along the coast.

THE INTRACOASTAL HIGHWAY

Boston is generally accepted as the northern and eastern terminal of the highway. Beyond that point the coast does not, save in a few places, readily lend itself to inland navigation. But Boston is the last important port in that direction. It is in value of its commerce the second port of the United States. It is the point where the intracoastal waterway most directly emerges upon the high seas, and where it is nearest to Europe. It is also a point where an exceptional number of great trunk railroad systems converge upon tidewater. For these reasons it will most appropriately constitute the upper terminal and perhaps on the whole the most important center of traffic of the whole coast system.

Boston is now connected with the intracoastal route by way of the Cape Cod Canal. That is beyond doubt a most useful passage, and will always enjoy an extensive patronage. It is not, however, suited to the chief purposes of the intracoastal waterway. Its principal utility is for ocean-going craft. Between it and Boston lies the broad stretch of Cape Cod Bay, almost a part of the high seas and not well adapted to navigation by the barges and other vessels which will throng the intracoastal route. For vessels which have hitherto gone from Boston to New York or southward around Cape Cod, and for those coming down from Portland and other points above Boston, to ports below the latter, it should always be of much value. But for the purposes of canal and other inland navigation there is needed a most sheltered route from Boston Harbor to Long Island Sound. This will be provided by the contemplated canal from Quincy or Weymouth to Fall River, supplemented by another through Rhode Island, from Narragansett Bay through Point Judith Pond and the other lagoons to Watch

COAST DEFENSE GUN

A modern 14-inch coast defense gun at Sandy Hook. The gun is mounted on a disappearing carriage, which lowers it out of sight behind the breastworks after firing. This is one of the powerful guns of the world, firing a projectile which would pierce the armor of a battleship more than five miles away.

A BATTERY OF 12-INCH U. S. COAST DEFENSE MORTARS

These powerful weapons fire a projectile which weighs from 700 to 1,046 pounds, depending on the range desired, and which is capable of piercing the deck armor of any battleship. They have a range of 20,000 yards with the 700-pound projectile. The gun is

Hill and Fisher's Island Sound. From the latter water the route is direct, down Long Island Sound to New York.

AT THE METROPOLIS

There are, however, plans for an alternative route which would possess great advantages for both commercial and military purposes. That is, to cross from Fisher's Island Sound to Gardiner's Bay and Peconic Bay, and thence by a short canal across the sand plains to the great chain of lagoons along the southern edge of Long Island, including the Great South Bay and Jamaica Bay, the last-named water giving a superb frontage in the metropolitan borough of Brooklyn. Thence passing back of Coney Island the waterway would reach New York Bay at Gravesend; from which point it could proceed to the Raritan River and trans-Jersey canal either by way of the Lower Bay or by way of the Kill van Kull, Newark Bay and Staten Island Sound. The latter route would doubtless be followed by all vessels which desired to be in touch with the trunk railroad lines, and very largely by all which came by way of Long Island Sound and the East River. It would take them directly to the doors of Newark and Elizabeth, and past the immense industrial and commercial establishments which will soon cover the Newark and Elizabeth meadows and will make those hitherto neglected regions one of the chief centers of business activity in the United States.

FROM THE DELAWARE SOUTHWARD

The remainder of the route is pretty well determined. A notably easy canal route has been surveyed across New Jersey, from Raritan Bay to the Delaware River and Philadelphia, whence improvement of the Delaware and Chesapeake Canal will carry it to Chesapeake Bay with access to Baltimore and Washington. From the neighborhood of Norfolk a canal will traverse the Dismal Swamp region to the Pasquotank River, or else will go directly from the Chesapeake and the James River to the head of Currituck Sound. In either case the route thence would be by way of Albemarle, Croatan, Pamlico, Core and Back sounds, to Beaufort, N. C. There is already a channel along which small vessels can thus pass from the Chesapeake to Beaufort inland, avoiding the terrors of Hatteras and Cape Lookout. Indeed, they may proceed about thirty miles further, along Bogue Sound to Bogue Inlet, at the mouth of White Oak River, where, however, there are no port facilities.

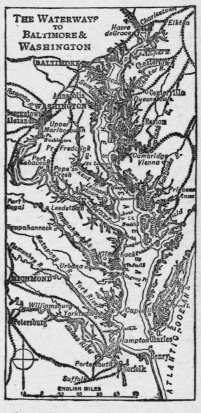

Here, however, the inland thoroughfare now ends, and vessels must take to the open Atlantic to proceed to Wilmington, N. C., to Charleston, S. C., to Savannah, and other Southern ports. Obviously, that fact enormously impairs the value of the whole route. It makes it a waterway from Massachusetts Bay merely to Onslow Bay, on the North Carolina coast, instead of to the Gulf of Mexico, and it leaves Wilmington and the traffic of the Cape Fear River, Georgetown and the Great Pedee River, Charleston,

Savannah and Brunswick all cut off from inland connection with the North. Moreover, while torpedo boats and submarines may now pass inland from Norfolk to Beaufort, they cannot get from the latter port to Charleston, the chief naval station south of the Chesapeake, without navigating the open ocean for nearly two hundred and fifty miles along a dangerous coast.

FROM THE CAROLINAS TO TEXAS

To fill this gap with a suitable waterway would not be a formidable task. From Beaufort to Cape Fear, nearly half the distance, natural thoroughfares exist which need nothing but deepening and connecting with short stretches of canal. From Cape Fear to the confluence of the Waccamaw and Great Pedee rivers, in South Carolina, would be the hardest part of the undertaking, but army engineers have estimated that a canal could be constructed between those points for only $3,000,000. Then from Winyah Bay, at the mouth of the Great Pedee, to Charleston, to Savannah, to Brunswick, to Fernandina, to Jacksonville and so on to Key West, nature has provided passages which need nothing but a little improvement. From the St. John's River across upper Florida a canal may readily be constructed giving access to the Gulf near or at Apalachee Bay, whence St. George's Sound, Choctawatchee Bay and other coastal waters give natural passage to Pensacola, to Mobile Bay, to Mississippi Bay and to New Orleans; while from the latter city nature has provided an inland thoroughfare along almost the entire Louisianian and Texan coast, to Galveston and thence to the Rio Grande.

THE VALUE OF THE SCHEME

The value of such a waterway, from Boston Harbor to the Rio Grande, is to be estimated from two points of view. One is the commercial. In connection with that, a few figures will be pertinent. In the first ten years of the present century, along the very stretch of coast which this inland waterway is to serve, 1,675 vessels with a tonnage of 483,743 were lost and 4,040 with a tonnage of 3,289,200 were more or less seriously damaged. The loss to vessels was more than $30,000,000, and the loss to cargoes was more than $10,000,000. The number of lives lost was 2,223. Now it is not to be contended that all these losses would have been spared if the intracoastal waterway had been in existence and operation. But if we reckon that only half of them would have been spared, which is a most conservative estimate, we shall have a saving of $20,000,000, or $2,000,000 a year, which is as much as it would cost to open the entire route to navigation; not to mention the saving of more than 1,100 human lives. Surely it would be better to spend the money for the canal than to send it to the bottom of the sea.

FOR COAST DEFENSE

So much for the utility of the intracoastal waterway in time of peace. It should not be an objection to the project, not even to the most extreme pacifist, that it would be of still greater, vastly greater, utility in time of war, particularly as its military usefulness would be entirely for defensive and not at all for aggressive purposes. Such a waterway would not be of sufficient capacity to accommodate great battleships, and these indeed would have no occasion to use it. But its utility for the mosquito fleet, the functions of which are exclusively defensive, would be simply inestimable. It would enable submarines, torpedo boats, and small gunboats, transports, and tenders, to move freely from one part of the coast to another without being exposed to the perils of the open and stormy ocean, or to attack or even observation by the enemy. It would enable them to be concentrated swiftly and secretly at any point on the coast where they might be needed; to swarm out of the nearest inlet to repel an approaching enemy. It would make any attempt to blockade any port of our coast futile, since that port would be in inland communication by water with all other ports along the coast. An enemy's fleet approaching any part of our coast would be confronted by a mobile fleet. There has been talk of the possibility of an enemy making a landing in force upon some remote and undefended part of our shores. That might readily be done, in present circumstances, if our battle-fleet were evaded or defeated. It would be impossible if the coast were lined at all points with a navigable inland waterway swarming with submarines and destroyers. And of course the peaceful commerce of this route could be maintained in time of war in a security which would be impossible outside of the coast line.

PANAMA AND THE CARIBBEAN

The great need of the Panama Canal was felt at the beginning of our Spanish War; and its immense potential utility in war as well as its actual utility in peace is now increasingly obvious. It would enable our fighting fleet to be quickly transferred from one coast to the other, as danger threatened. In proportion to its value, however, is the need of protecting it from hostile seizure or destruction. Such protection is not to be afforded by mere fortifications at the terminals, though of course these are essential and the wisdom of our government in securing the treaty right to construct them is manifest.

The security of the Canal depends upon our dominance in

the adjacent waters, and particularly the Gulf of Mexico
and the Caribbean Sea. It was in order to have a foot-
hold from which to attack the Canal that Germany so
persistently intrigued for the possession of territory, if
only a naval station, somewhere about the Caribbean, and
it was to hamper us in our plans for defense of the Canal

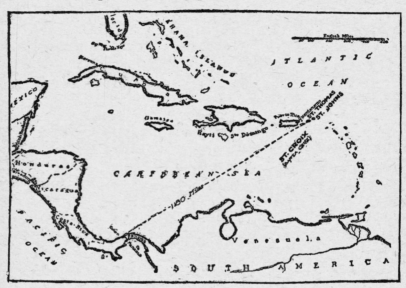

MAP SHOWING THE DANISH WEST INDIES

that she opposed, on one occasion successfully, our acquisition of the Danish West Indies. Her extreme desire a few
years ago to inveigle Holland into becoming a member of
the empire was partly, of course, in order to gain Holland's
frontage on the North Sea, but it was also in no small
measure in order to be able to plant the German flag upon
the Dutch Islands in the Caribbean. There is no more
essential feature of our scheme of national defense than
the maintenance of American dominance in those waters.

CHAPTER XXI

THE MEANING OF THE WAR

War Means War — The Initial Preparations — Increase of the Army and Navy — Appropriating a War Budget — Seizure of German and Austrian Vessels which Had Been Interned — Arrest of German Spies and Conspirators — Warnings and Orders to Alien Enemies — Government Confiscation of Wireless Telegraphy — The Nation Placed upon a War Footing — The Coming of War Commissioners from the Allies — Our Practical Alliance with European Powers — A New Era in the Foreign Relationships of the United States.

WAR MEANS WAR. That fact was not instantly grasped by the American nation upon our declaration of war with Germany. The scene of the conflict was far away. Surely we should not actually be mingled in the fighting. We should lend money to the allies, of course, and use our ships for conveying to them the supplies which they needed. But that would be all. It did not take long, however, for a truer conception of the situation to dawn upon even the easiest-going American mind. More than half a century ago Lowell wrote

"It's war we're in, not politics;
It's systems wrastlin' now, not parties;"

and in the fateful month of April, 1917, the American people began to realize the fact.

Immediately upon the declaration of war, bills were introduced in Congress for the prosecution of the conflict. A war loan of $7,000,000,000, the largest single appropriation ever made by any government in the world, was passed without a dissenting vote in either House. Later an Urgent Deficiency bill, appropriating $2,827,000,000

259

more for war expenses was passed, only a single vote being cast against it in the House of Representatives. Bills for the increase of the army and navy were enacted, one of them providing for "selective conscription" in place of the discredited volunteer system. This last supremely important measure, through scandalous "playing politics" in Congress, was not enacted until May 19th, and then the humiliating announcement was made by the War Department that, owing to the "depletion of supplies," none of the 500,000 conscripts would actually be called to the colors before about the first of September!

GERMAN SHIPS SEIZED

Meantime administrative acts were strenuous. A few hours after the enactment of the war resolution United States officers took possession of the vast and valuable array of German merchant vessels which had been interned for safety at various American ports. There were ninety-one of these vessels, including the largest steamship in the world and several others of the largest and swiftest class. Their total tonnage was in the neighborhood of 400,000, and their value was probably much more than $100,000,000. A catalogue of this gigantic argosy, the largest by far ever seized in the history of the world, is as follows:

At the port of New York, including Brooklyn and Hoboken:

	Gross Tons.	Approximate Value.
Vaterland, passenger	54,282	$7,500,000
George Washington, passenger	27,000	5,000,000
Kaiser Wilhelm II, passenger	19,361	4,000,000
President Lincoln, passenger	18,168	3,600,000
President Grant, passenger	18,072	3,600,000

	Gross Tons.	Approximate Value.
Pennsylvania, passenger	13,333	2,600,000
Grosser Kurfürst, passenger	13,243	2,600,000
Barbarossa, passenger	10,915	2,000,000
Princess Irene, passenger	10,881	2,000,000
Friedrich der Grosse, passenger	10,695	2,000,000
Hamburg, passenger	10,531	2,000,000
König Wilhelm II, passenger	9,410	2,000,000
Prinz Eitel Friedrich, passenger	8,797	1,500,000
Armenia, freighter	5,471	1,000,000
Adamsturm, freighter	5,000	1,000,000
Pisa, freighter	4,967	1,000,000
Prinz Joachim, passenger	4,760	1,000,000
Allemannia, freighter	4,630	1,000,000
Harburg, freighter	4,472	1,000,000
Magdeburg, freighter	4,497	800,000
Bohemia, freighter	4,284	800,000
Nassovia, freighter	3,092	800,000
Portonia, freighter	2,778	600,000
Maia, freighter	2,555	600,000
Indra, ship	1,746	400,000
Clara Mennig, freighter	1,685	500,000
Matador, bark	1,468	300,000

At twenty-three other ports, in the United States and the insular possessions:

	Tons.		Tons.
Boston:		**Baltimore:**	
Amerika	22,622	Bulgaria	11,440
Kronprinzessin Cecilie	19,503	Rhein	10,058
Cincinnati	16,339	Neckar	9,835
Koln	7,409	**Philadelphia:**	
Wittekind	5,640	Rhaetia	6,600
Ockenfels	5,621	Prinz Oskar	6,026
New London:		**Newport News:**	
Willehad	4,761	Arcadia	5,454

261

	Tons.		Tons.
Wilmington, N. C.:		Honolulu—*Continued*	
Kiel	4,494	Staatssekretär Kraetke	2,009
Nicaria	3,974	Governeur Jaeschke	1,738
Savannah:		Hilo:	
Hohenfelde	2,974	C. J. D. Ahlers	7,490
Charleston:		San Juan, P. R.:	
Liebenfels	4,525	Odenwald	3,537
Pensacola:		Pago Pago, Samoa:	
Rudolph Blumberg	1,769	Elsas	6,591
Vogesen	3,916	Manila:	
Jacksonville:		Andalusia	5,433
Frieda Leonhardt	2,822	Buchum	6,161
New Orleans:		Camilla Rickmers	5,130
Breslau	7,524	Carl Diederichsen	1,243
Andromeda	2,554	Clara Jebsen	1,735
San Francisco:		Coblenz	3,130
Serapis	4,756	Elmshorn	4,594
Neptun	197	Esslingen	4,902
Ottawa	3,659	Johanne	1,531
Portland, Ore.:		Lyeemoon	1,925
Dalbeck	2,723	Mark	6,579
Seattle:		Pong Tong	1,631
Saxonia	4,424	Rajah	2,028
Winslow, Wash.:		Sachsen	8,007
Steinbeck	2,164	Sambia	4,765
Astoria:		Suevia	3,789
Arnoldus Vinnen	1,859	Tubingen	5,586
Kurt	3,109	Zamboanga:	
Honolulu:		Borneo	2,168
Pommern	6,557	Marudu	1,514
Prinz Waldemar	3,227	Darvel	1,308
Setos	4,730	Cebu:	
Holsatia	5,649	Prinzess Alice	10,981
Locksun	1,657	Tsintau	1,685
Loong Moon	1,971	Wiegand	499

Many of these vessels had been maliciously damaged by their crews, by the breaking of parts of the engines, etc., before surrender; but none so seriously but that they could soon be repaired and put into service.

AUSTRIAN SHIPS ALSO TAKEN

A few days later, upon severance of diplomatic relations with Germany's ally, Austria-Hungary, the government similarly took possession of fourteen ships of that nationality, as follows:

	Gross Tonnage.	Approximate Value.
New York Bay:		
Martha Washington	8,312	$4,000,000
Dora	7,037	2,000,000
Ida	4,730	1,500,000
Newark Bay:		
Himalaia	4,958	1,500,000
Boston:		
Erny	6,515	3,000,000
New Orleans:		
Clara	3,932	1,000,000
Teresa	3,769	1,000,000
Anna	1,575	200,000
Pensacola:		
Lucia	6,744	3,000,000
Galveston:		
Campania	3,551	1,500,000
Morawitz	4,795	2,000,000
Newport News:		
Budapest	3,651	1,000,000
Philadelphia:		
Franconia	4,637	2,000,000
Tampa:		
Borneo	3,621	1,000,000

The pier and water-front property at Hoboken, which had been occupied by the great German steamship lines as their terminal, was taken by the United States Government as a center for shipment of supplies to the allies.

RADIO STATIONS SEIZED

The government also, immediately upon the declaration of war, took possession of all wireless telegraphic stations, public and private, and caused all that it did not need for its own purposes to be dismantled. This was, of course, to prevent the misuse of such apparatus by German spies, and also to prevent anybody from evading the censorship and transmitting information which the government did not wish sent out. In New York City alone more than two hundred amateur plants were thus seized and dismantled.

MANY SPIES ARRESTED

The day after the declaration of war no fewer than sixty-five German spies, or suspects, were arrested by the military authorities in various places throughout the country, while thousands more were placed under the observation of the Secret Service. This was the first time since the War of 1812 that such measures had been taken against aliens.

The President also issued a proclamation, which was followed by state and municipal orders everywhere, prescribing the conditions on which unnaturalized Germans might continue to live in the United States and enjoy their freedom. They were required to surrender at once all arms and ammunition, and not to live or go within a certain distance of any arsenal, munitions factory, or other establishment named in the proclamation. Subject to these conditions, they were permitted to go about their business as usual.

264

The agencies of German insurance companies, which were doing an enormous business in this country, carrying some $3,500,000,000 in risks, were permitted to continue operations, but all their assets were to be kept here.

BUSINESS ORGANIZING FOR WAR

All over the country, business began to organize for war. More than fifty railroad presidents, representing 250,000 miles of roads, met at Washington to perfect plans for placing their roads at the disposal of the government for purposes of military transportation. The Federal Shipping Board began arrangements for the building of numerous cargo ships to take the place of those destroyed by German submarines, and General George W. Goethals, the builder of the Panama Canal, was placed in charge of this colossal undertaking.

Meantime, for the protection of existing shipping and to minimize the danger of unexpected raids of hostile cruisers or submarines, barred zones of from two to ten miles in radius were established across the approaches to all harbors, which vessels were forbidden to enter at night, or without permission by the harbor patrol.

INDUSTRY AT THE NATION'S SERVICE

Within three days of the declaration of war about 32,000 manufacturing establishments, including the largest in the country, placed themselves at the nation's service and offered to turn their plants and workmen over to the government, if needed.

The American Federation of Labor, comprising nearly all labor organizations in the United States, through the unanimous action of its advisory committee pledged itself not to take advantage of the country's necessities to change existing standards of hours or wages, thus averting strikes.

CO-OPERATION WITH THE ALLIES

One of the most interesting and significant achievements of the period immediately following the declaration of war was the entering of the United States into a co-operative *entente* with the allied powers of Europe. Two important commissions came at once from Great Britain and France to this country and held a series of war conferences with the President and his Cabinet at Washington. That from Great Britain was headed by Arthur James Balfour, Foreign Secretary and formerly Prime Minister, one of the foremost British statesmen of his time, and one who throughout his career had been distinguished for friendliness to America. The French commission was headed by M. Rene Viviani, formerly Prime Minister, and Field Marshal Joffre, the hero of the battle of the Marne. These commissions were cordially received by the President and Congress, and with vast enthusiasm by the general public. One of their earliest acts was to pay a visit of homage to the home and tomb of Washington at Mount Vernon.

They made it quite clear to the American Government that there was urgent need of our aid, in money, in ships and in men; to keep the European allies supplied with food, and to reinforce the armies in France which for so long a time had been enduring the awful strain of holding back the German hordes. As a result of their representations our government was incited to redoubled efforts, and it was decided to send an American army to France at the earliest practicable date.

NO "ENTANGLING ALLIANCES"

It was also made clear, however, that the United States was not asked or expected to renounce the Monroe Doctrine

266

or to depart from its fixed policy of not forming permanent alliances with European powers. On this point Mr. Balfour, speaking for all his collegues, was most explicit.

"I am told," he said, "that there are some doubting critics who seem to think that the object of the mission of Great Britain and France is to inveigle the United States out of its traditional policy and to entangle it in a formal alliance, secret or public, with European powers. I cannot imagine any rumor with less foundation, nor can I imagine any policy so utterly unnecessary. Our confidence in the assistance which we are going to get from this country is not based upon such considerations as those which arise out of formal treaties."

PURPORT OF THE ENTENTE

There was no treaty, then, but there was a "gentlemen's agreement," or an entente, no less specific and binding. It was to the effect that the United States and the European allies would co-operate in the war to the end, and that no power should make a separate peace with Germany. At the end of the war, the United States would take an equal part in the peace conference, and terms would be insisted upon which would be satisfactory to all. But there would be no thought of dragging the United States into any permanent league of European powers, unless it were a league for maintaining peace, or into matters which did not directly concern it.

Thus was begun a new era in the relationships between America and the European powers, which was in fact merely a reversion to and fulfilment of the policy enunciated by the founders of the republic but never before put into execution.

CHAPTER XXII

OUR RELATIONS WITH THE ALLIES

Mutual Misunderstandings at the Beginning of the War — The President's Ideals of Perfect Neutrality — Seeking the Impossible — Reasons for Our Official Attitude — Effect of the German Propaganda — Astonishment of the Allies at Our Course — America Saved by Three European Powers from German Invasion — The Service of the British Fleet — Radical Difference Between the Two Belligerent Leagues — Allied Legality and German Illegality — Dollars or Human Lives — America at Last Realizing the Difference — Mutual Understanding and Co-operation at Last Attained Without Sacrifice of American Principles.

A DRAMA of misunderstanding; that is what we must consider the great war to have been before our entry into it; at least so far as America and the Allies—now our allies—were concerned. Never, perhaps, was there another war in which the essential issues were so little appreciated by the chief neutral power, or in which the chief neutral and one of the belligerent sides so little understood each other; though in the end the most complete mutual understanding came. We speak now of the official attitude of mind. Doubtless there were many individuals on each side of the Atlantic who had the Vision, and who from the beginning rightly appreciated the position and the conduct of both America and the Allies. But diplomacy is directed and history is largely made by the official and not the individual course.

THE PRESIDENT'S CONCEPTION OF NEUTRALITY

The official attitude of the United States was set forth by the President in his proclamation of neutrality, at the very beginning of the war. The proclaiming of neutrality was of course not only proper but necessary, unless we

268

were at once to implicate ourselves in the war. But the President went further than merely to proclaim official neutrality. He sought popular neutrality as well. He was aware of the large numbers of our own citizens of British, French and other allied nations origin and sympathy, and of the large though lesser numbers of those of Teutonic affiliation, and he dreaded the possible dissensions and conflicts which might arise in this country between the respective partisans of the two belligerent leagues. With this in mind, he exhorted all Americans to observe strict neutrality, not merely in acts and words, but even in thought. We must not, he insisted, permit our inner and secret sympathies to turn toward one side or the other.

That was impossible, of course. It was an exhortation against nature. It is doubtful if many ever seriously tried to obey his injunction; and it is practically certain that few ever succeeded in doing so. But that impossible attitude was the official attitude of record, and it was that by which foreign nations were compelled to judge us. Indeed, even to a date only a little while before the American declaration of war, that attitude was nominally still maintained. As related elsewhere in this volume, in his note suggesting overtures for peace, in December, 1916, President Wilson referred to the two belligerent leagues of Europe as having at least professedly the same objects and purposes in the war; a suggestion against which the Allies strongly protested.

REASONS FOR OUR ATTITUDE

Suggestion has already been made of the President's motive, or of one of his motives, in recommending this impossibly neutral attitude. There were other reasons why many of the American people were at first unable to perceive the real issues of the war, and were slow in realizing how immediate and intense was American interest in it.

We had been at peace with the world for many years, and had got out of the habit of thinking in terms of war or of analyzing and comprehending the causes and purposes of war. A stupendous and complex problem was presented to us, and we were unfamiliar with the method of its solution and even with the value of its various factors.

There had grown up in America, too, the strange delusion that we had a traditional policy of complete isolation from European affairs, and that all European wars were necessarily matters of indifference to us, in which we were by no means to become involved.

We must also recognize the facts that there had long been here a persistent and often vigorous anti-British propaganda. It not infrequently happens that dissensions between near relatives are more bitter, up to a certain point, than those between strangers. Thus America, being chiefly of British origin, indulged in a family feud with the Mother Country.

The large and important Irish element in the United States, too, promoted a certain disapproval of and even resentment at Great Britain on account of the undoubted grievances which Ireland had formerly for many years suffered under British rule.

THE GERMAN PROPAGANDA

Another potent factor in misleading American opinion at the beginning was the shrewd, insidious and altogether unscrupulous German propaganda, which was Protean in form and often ingenious in the superlative degree. It took the guise of peace societies, of anti-militarist leagues, of petitions against the sale of military munitions, and of other ostensibly neutral and benevolent movements; all organized and directed, however, by Germans or German sympathizers, largely financed with German money, and all aiming at the same end, to create sympathy with Germany and to exacerbate animosity against England.

A single example—one of many—may be cited. Early in the war certain German intriguers and conspirators started the circulation of petitions to Congress to enact an embargo upon the exportation of munitions. This was signed by more than a million persons, all over the country, under the auspices of a so-called "Organization of American Women for Strict Neutrality." The signatures were solicited on the ground that we ought not to sell munitions to the foes of Germany because "Germany did not permit her citizens to sell arms or munitions of war to Spain during our war with that nation," and that same statement was embodied in the text of the petition itself. The fact is that that statement was a deliberate falsehood, first put forward by a notorious German agent in New York and later used at German instigation in this petition, for the direct purpose of deceiving and misleading the American people. The indisputable official record of our own government is that during that entire war vessels freely carried ammunition from German ports to Spain.

THE ALLIES ASTONISHED

All these things had their effect in America, to the astonishment of the Allies. Those countries saw through the German intrigues and falsehoods far more quickly and more clearly than did we, and they could not understand our blindness. They realized, too, from the very beginning the real character of the war, that it was a war on their side of democracy against autocracy, of the rights

271

of man against the "divine right of kings." They saw in the violation of treaties, the repudiation of international law, and the subversion of independent nationalities a direct menace to every nation in the world. If Germany could override the rights of Belgium, any nation could override the rights of any other.

All this was very clear to the British and French minds, and they could not understand why it was not equally obvious to the American mind. They could not understand why the United States failed to do so much as to file a protest or a remonstrance against the violation of Belgium, when it was one of the signatories of that treaty of The Hague which declared and covenanted, on the faith of all the signatory nations, that the territory of that kingdom—that is, of all neutral states—should be inviolate.

NOT ASTONISHED BUT ASTOUNDED

They were not merely astonished, they were astounded, at some of the further developments. They could not understand why, after the appalling tragedy of the Lusitania, we did not promptly hold Germany to the "strict accountability" which we had threatened. They could not understand how we could continue on terms of friendly diplomatic intercourse with a power after we had found that its Ambassador, attaches and consuls in this country had been systematically conspiring for the commission of felonies against our domestic peace, law and order, and against our status as a neutral power.

They did not, of course, give due weight to the circumstances of this nation—its utter unpreparedness for war, its habitual disinclination toward war, and the essential difference between its point of view and manner of thought and their own. In a lesser emergency there might have been

272

less misunderstanding. But this world cataclysm was so stupendous, so stupefying, so overwhelming, that neither they nor we could appreciate the other's feelings or point of view.

OUR THREE SAVIORS

Meantime three European nations were our saviors. The fact was largely ignored at the time, and was even ignorantly or maliciously denied. But it was and is a fact, which must abide in history. The ultimate purpose of Germany in beginning this war was universal conquest of all nations; and, as John Hay once remarked, "all nations includes America." That fact was made sufficiently clear in the writings of General von Bernhardi and other German militarists. It was unmistakably suggested by the pains with which Germany's army and navy departments secured, long before this war, the most elaborate, accurate and detailed maps and plans of our chief harbors and seaboard cities and the country surrounding them. It was openly boasted at the beginning of the war, by many prominent and authoritative Germans. "In three weeks," they said, "we shall have Paris; in three months, England; in three years, America!" It may be added that since his return home Mr. Gerard, our Ambassador to Germany from before the beginning of the war until our breach of relations with that country, has amply and emphatically confirmed, from knowledge acquired at Berlin, this account of Germany's intentions.

Now there were three things which frustrated this design of the Kaiser's, and which therefore saved the United States from having to fight for its life against a wholesale German invasion. The first was the sublime heroism and self-immolation of Belgium in resisting with her puny might the onset of the German legions. She was quickly crushed, and has ever since been suffering martyrdom for her temerity. But the few days of delay of the German army in battering down the forts of Liege enabled France to get her troops together and England to send a handful of her "contemptible little army" across the Channel, to make a stand at the Marne, near the very ground where, more than fourteen centuries before, Aetius and the Gauls had defeated Attila and his Hunnish hordes fresh from their ravishing of Belgium. It was that victorious stand at the Marne that prevented the modern Attila and his Huns, fresh from their ravishing of Belgium, from fulfilling their boast of "Paris in three weeks."

But even before that, and at that time, and ever since down to the present moment, it was and is the British fleet that saved America and the world from the German menace. Month after month and year after year, the French and British armies, at fearful cost, held in Champagne and Picardy the line that never was broken, and kept the Teutonic armies in check. Month after month and year after year, too, in the stormy northern seas, the British fleet kept the German navy locked within its mine-guarded ports, and thus preserved the freedom of the seas for us and for all peaceful nations, and protected America from fulfilment of the German boast of conquest within three years. It is the British fleet and it alone that enables us to enter this war with Germany on our own terms, and not confronted with German dreadnoughts thundering at the gateways of our ports, and with German legions debarking upon our unguarded coasts.

DIFFERENCE BETWEEN THE BELLIGERENTS

All this is quite clear to America today. It was clear to the Allies beyond the sea from the very beginning of the war. And their understanding of it, and their failure to understand our apparent lack of understanding of it, account for their astonishment at our earlier attitude. These things also account for some of the friction which arose between them and us in the former stages of the war.

There was undoubtedly some French and British interference with our commerce and our mails, and those powers appeared upon the face of the case to be violating our rights and denying the freedom of the seas. They did not proclaim a true blockade of the German coast, under which they would of course have had an undeniable right to stop all commerce. Yet they did stop and forbid our commerce with Germany and even with certain neutral states, and they exercised a certain censorship over our mails. These things were regarded as grievances by us, and led to some more or less animated diplomatic controversy.

Here again there was misunderstanding. The Allies regarded themselves as fighting our battles for us as well as their own, as indeed they were, as we now see and confess. Therefore they thought that we ought not to object to such measures as were necessary for the successful prosecution of their campaign. That was a point of view which was very real to them, but which we did not in the least appreciate.

COMMERCIAL ABUSES

There were other reasons for their course. They did not declare a blockade, because to have done so would have imposed far greater hardships upon us than those which we did suffer. It would have meant the confiscation instead of the mere turning back of vessels which attempted to break through the line.

But they did interfere with our commerce with neutral states, because those states were bordering upon Germany or were in commercial intercourse with her, and the goods which we shipped to them were perfectly well known to be destined for Germany. It would have been folly for the Allies to prohibit our shipping supplies to Germany directly, and yet permitting us to ship them in unlimited quantities to Denmark, to be sent right across that country into Germany. That such was the destination of the goods, there was no doubt; there was not even a pretence at denial of it. It was perfectly obvious from the fact that immediately after the outbreak of the war the importations into those neutral states—Denmark, Norway, and Holland—enormously increased. It would have been absurd to pretend that because of the war or for any other reason those countries suddenly needed for their own use three or four times as great supplies as ever before.

An example of this abuse of commerce may be cited. A concern in Holland began soliciting from Japan shipments of Japanese bronze statuary, as "works of art" which of course could not be considered contraband of war. But it stated explicitly that it did not care what the subjects were, nor whether the pieces were artistically meritorious or not, so long as they were of solid bronze, the heavier the better. They need not even be finished and polished; in the roughest form they would be just as acceptable. Yet, however rough they were, they should be packed in thick sheets of india rubber, to protect them from being scratched or dented! Of course it was nothing in the world but a scheme for getting supplies of bronze and rubber for military purposes.

MISUSING THE MAILS

There were similar abuses of the mails. Germans in America and elsewhere made use of them to ship into Germany goods which if sent as freight would instantly have been seized as contraband. Tons of copper and india rubber and other goods were offered for transmission through the parcels post, and indeed large quantities were sent at great expense by first-class letter post. Of course military and naval information, secured by German spies, was also sent through the mails, especially after the United States Government established supervision over the wireless telegraphic stations and forbade the transmission of non-neutral messages by that means.

In brief, the Allies were not interfering with legitimate mails or commerce, but were merely putting a stop to their illegitimate use under cover of specious pretences.

DIFFERENCES BETWEEN BELLIGERENTS

From the beginning of the war, moreover, there was a radical difference between the belligerents in their attitude toward this country, and in the character of those acts of theirs which gave or were supposed to give us cause for offense. The acts of the Allies in interfering with our commerce and mails were at worst of disputable legality. There was not one of them for which some justifying argument based on international law and precedent could not be adduced; some of the precedents having been set by this country itself in its treatment of neutral commerce during the Civil War. Thus we had intercepted and confiscated a cargo bound in a British ship from one British port to another—to wit, from Liverpool to Nassau, New Providence—on the ground that it was contraband and was meant to be transshipped from the second port to a belligerent destination; and that act was sustained by our Supreme Court and was acquiesced in by the British Government. That certainly gave some ground for the interception of cargoes bound from an American to a Dutch or Danish port when there was reasonable cause for belief that they were to be transshipped thence to a German destination.

On the other hand, the acts of Germany were indisputably and confessedly illegal; gross violations of international law and treaty rights, for which not even the most vehement partisan of Germany could offer a pretence of legal justification. Thus there was nothing more clear in law than that merchant vessels must not be destroyed until visit and search had demonstrated the contraband character of their cargo; that even then they were not to be destroyed unless the conveyance of them to port was physically impossible; and that in case of destruction satisfactory provision was to be made for the safety of their passengers and crew. All these principles were flagrantly and defiantly violated by Germany, simply on the ground that she had adopted a new method of warfare—submarine—which made it impossible, or unsafe, or inconvenient, for her to obey the law.

DOLLARS AND HUMAN LIVES

There was another difference, of a still more striking and impressive character. That was, that at most the Allies destroyed our property, while the Germans destroyed human lives. The Allies interfered with our commerce, seized our property, lessened our financial profits, and delayed the transmission of our mails; but nothing more. They did not destroy nor imperil a single American life.

Germany, on the other hand, not only did all these

things which the Allies did, but also she imperiled and destroyed the lives of many American citizens. There was a contrast which smote upon the sensibilities of humanity itself with convincing force. On the one hand dollars, on the other human lives. Between the two it was impossible for us to hesitate.

REALIZING THE DIFFERENCE

These radical and essential differences, differences of kind and not merely of degree, were not at first fully appreciated by the American Government and people. But as the war proceeded the realization became more and more complete. President Wilson emphasized it when he denounced the German submarine campaign as necessarily contrary to law and to humanity; something which could not be mended but must be ended.

The result was that by the beginning of the present year the American Government and people, with exceptions so few as to be negligible, had by the inexorable logic of events been brought to take almost precisely the view of the war which the Allies had taken from the beginning, and when after our declaration of war against Germany the commissioners of the chief allied powers came hither to confer with our government, complete accord was found to prevail.

MUTUAL UNDERSTANDING

The mutual understanding was as complete as the misunderstanding had been at the beginning of the war. On the one hand, the United States appreciated the necessity of co-operation with the Allies and of persistence in the campaign until Prussian militarism should be thoroughly defeated and it would be possible to restore peace on a

279

basis of justice and of assurance against the recurrence of the war. The idea, once expressed, of "peace without victory," was seen to be erroneous, and peace with victory —victory for justice and international law and the principles of humanity—to be a necessity of mankind.

On the other hand, the Allies understood the reason and the righteousness of the American resolution to maintain the long-established policy of this country not to meddle with affairs beyond its own concern and not to enter into permanent alliances with European powers. It was perceived that co-operation did not require complication, and that it would be possible for the United States to fight this war through and participate in the establishment of terms of peace in the most loyal and complete co-operation with the Allies, and yet not to bind itself to anything beyond those limits.

In such an understanding America and the Allies came together in April and May, 1917, and together engaged in the transcendent task of bringing order out of chaos and of restoring law and justice, humanity and the rights of man, in the midst of an all but universal cataclysm. After that the understanding became still stronger and more close, through the placing of all troops in the war under a single Generalissimo, and the creation of an Allied War Council, under the deliberations of which all the Allies act in harmonious concert.

CHAPTER XXIII

PAN-AMERICA AND OTHERS

Our Relations with Latin America — German Influences Hostile to Us in Several States — Suspicion of Our Motives — German Schemes of Invasion — The Awakening of Latin America — Approval of Our Breach of Relations with Germany — Similar Course of the European Neutrals, and of China — Universal Condemnation of the German Submarine Campaign — Our Declaration of War Similarly Approved — Brazil's Breach of Relations with Germany — Course of Other States — Latin America Practically United in Support of This Country.

WHAT OF Latin America? That was one of the first and most interesting questions asked in and concerning the war, and one the answer to which has been supremely significant and gratifying. It must be borne in mind that for some little time before the outbreak of the war our relations with the countries to the south of us had not been as cordial and confidential as might have been desired. With some of them, indeed, our relations were strained and unsympathetic. We had been practically if not technically at war with Mexico. Colombia still cherished resentment for her loss of Panama, with which, though not equitably, she charged the United States. Chili had not altogether forgotten our unwarranted meddling in her domestic affairs away back in 1891. And in all three of these countries German financial as well as diplomatic influence was particularly strong, and of course was exerted to the fullest extent against the United States. In fact, as suggested in another chapter, the unpleasantness between this country and Colombia was almost entirely of German incitement and fomentation, while if the troubles in Mexico

281

were not of German origin it was largely because of German intrigues and conspiracies that they were turned against this country.

In two of the southern states of Brazil, moreover, there were considerable colonies of German immigrants and their descendants, who had purposely been kept purely German and quite unassimilated with the Brazilians, in hope some day of forming the nucleus of a German colonial empire in that region, and the extent of their influence upon the course of Brazil was an unknown quantity.

SUSPICION OF THE UNITED STATES

Beside these specific circumstances, it is undeniable that a certain degree of suspicion concerning the intentions of the United States toward them prevailed at that time among nearly if not quite all the states of Latin America. Our mischievous meddling in Chili, our acquisition of the Panama Canal, our coercion of Venezuela, our establishment of virtual protectorates over Haiti and Santo Domingo, our action toward some of the Central American states, and above all our extraordinary policy toward Mexico, had given anti-American intriguers and agitators apparently plausible ground for insinuating that we had a purpose to override the independence of all those countries and to make them tributary to us.

Not for many years had our relations with Latin America been in so delicate if not so critical a condition, and it was in full understanding of that fact that early in the war the German Government began plotting to form an alliance with Mexico and to strike at the United States through that country, backed with the moral if not the military aid of all the countries at the south.

282

PAN-AMERICAN AWAKENING

But in that expectation Germany was grievously disappointed. Probably no countries in the world are more versed in international law and jurisprudence, or have a more scrupulous regard for the sanctity of the same, than those between the Rio Grande and Cape Horn. They were quick, therefore, to perceive the iniquity of the German course, and to perceive in it a menace against themselves and all other nations. Even in Mexico, amid the domestic chaos of that unhappy country, the real animus of the German intrigues was understood, and little or no encouragement was given to the anti-American temptations. "*Timeo Teutones,*" said the land of the Aztecs, "*et dona ferentes.*"

There began, then, an awakening of Latin America such as that continent had not known before, and a turning toward the United States similar to that which had followed the promulgation of the Monroe Doctrine and which had not been known since. It was universally felt that Germany was renewing that menace of the Holy Alliance which the Monroe Doctrine had been designed to combat and which it had in fact defeated. In such circumstances there was just one thing to do. That was, to align themselves with the United States.

PAN-AMERICA AGAINST GERMANY

So long as we remained neutral and on friendly terms with Germany, the South and Central American countries did the same. When we severed diplomatic relations with Germany, at the beginning of February, 1917, they did not indeed follow our example but they showed unmistakably their sympathy with it. Brazil took the lead. On February 6th Lauro Mueller, the Brazilian Foreign

Minister, himself of German origin, informed the German Government that Brazil could not recognize the validity of the submarine blockade and campaign against merchant shipping, but protested against it, and would hold Germany responsible for any acts involving Brazilian citizens or property which were contrary to international law or treaty rights.

Chili, in which German commercial and financial influences were particularly strong, assumed a similar attitude, even more tersely and emphatically expressed; reserving liberty of action for the protection of her citizens and their property. Argentina did the same, declaring that she would act at sea according to her fundamental rights and the principles of international law. Bolivia, Uruguay, Panama and Cuba issued similar notes. Peru specifically demanded reparation and indemnity for the sinking of one of her vessels by Germany; adding that she could not admit the resolution of which Germany had given notice, regarding it as opposed to international law and the legal rights of neutral nations.

COURSE OF OTHER NEUTRALS

Other neutral nations also strongly protested against Germany's announcement of unrestricted submarine warfare. Spain declared that Germany's note "caused a very painful impression," and denounced it as "contrary to the principles observed by all nations even in moments of the greatest violence."

Holland declared that her government was "obliged to object with extreme energy," and that she could see in the German policy "violation of the rights of nations, to say nothing of an attack upon the laws of humanity."

Switzerland, the incarnation of neutrality and peace,

had no shipping to be menaced by submarines; but she was dependent for her imports upon the shipping of other nations, and she was also much interested in international law and in humanity. Therefore she promptly condemned Germany's policy as "an attack upon the right of peaceful commerce," and protested energetically against it.

The three Scandinavian governments, of Sweden, Norway and Denmark, conferred together for a week, and then united in an identical note, protesting in the strongest manner against the policy which Germany had announced, and holding Germany responsible for any injury which their people might suffer through it.

China, also, aligned herself with America and the other neutral powers in protesting energetically against Germany's course. She added that if Germany persisted in it, she would have to sever diplomatic relations with her, and would take such other action as might be necessary for the maintenance of the principles of international law.

Thus practically the entire neutral world was arrayed on the side of America in her resistance to the arrogant, unlawful and immoral pretensions and menaces of the German Government.

APPROVING OUR WAR DECLARATION

Our declaration of war against Germany caused a wide spread confirmation and intensification of that attitude. Brazil took the lead on April 11th in severing diplomatic relations with Germany, and on June 28th, the decree of neutrality was formally revoked, 46 German vessels were seized, and Brazil entered upon a defensive war against Germany. On April 13th, Bolivia also severed relations with Germany.

Argentina issued a note recognizing the justice of our

course in declaring war against Germany because of the latter's violation of the principles of neutrality established by the rules of international law. Later, in September, 1917, it was discovered that the German Chargé d'Affaires had grossly abused Argentine neutrality and had recommended to his government that when Argentine vessels were destroyed they should be sunk "without a trace being left." He was at once dismissed from the country and the Argentine Congress voted to sever all relations with Germany. The President, however, a pro-German, declined to approve such action.

Uruguay approved the American declaration of war and described Germany's submarine warfare as "an insult to humanity." On June 18th it announced that the neutrality laws would not be enforced against the United States, and on October 7th it gave the German minister his passports. Paraguay expressed sympathy with the United States in its action, recognizing that this country had been "forced into war to rehabilitate the rights of neutrals," and on September 11th proclaimed through its minister at Washington its "sincere adhesion to the cause which the States and the other Entente Powers defend."

Panama, a protectorate of the United States, announced her readiness to assist this country in any way for the protection of the Isthmian Canal, while Cuba, another protectorate, squarely declared war against Germany, and seized and gave to the United States four German ships.

Chili, of all South American States perhaps the least cordial toward the United States, because of our ill treatment of her years ago, has remained neutral, though many of her leading statesmen have openly expressed sympathy with this country. Peru severed diplomatic relations with Germany on October 7th, having long before approved our declaration of war against Germany. Ecuador on October 8, 1917, announced that she would not receive a German minister should he come thither, and on December 8th formally severed diplomatic relations with Germany. Colombia and Venezuela have taken no specific action.

Guatemala took the lead in Central America in severing relations with Germany on April 28, 1917, because of "plots against the safety and independence not only of Guatemala but the whole of Central America." Costa Rica early waived her neutrality laws in our favor, and on September 21st severed relations with Germany at the discovery of German plots against the government. Honduras, and the insular republic of Hayti, declared war against Germany in July, 1918.

Mexico, busied with domestic rehabilitation, maintained neutrality, and unfortunately remained a scene of German intrigue.

"This support of Latin-America," said the eminent Chilian statesman, Dr. Alejandro Alvarez, formerly Counsellor of the Foreign Office, "can be explained as being an expression of gratitude for the aid given by the United States one hundred years ago, when the other American countries were winning their independence, as well as being the result of the solidarity of interests and of sentiment between the American States, which has shown itself especially during the course of the nineteenth century. In view of this solidarity, there could be no doubt that the United States would have the support and sympathy of all the countries of Latin-America."

AFTER MANY YEARS

It has been a full century since the Holy Alliance had begun its menace against American democracy. It had been a hundred years less six since the culmination of that menace in the preparation for overt acts had roused this country to acceptance of the challenge and to the offering of resolute and militant defiance. That heroic assertion of American democracy had for a year evoked a glad and sympathetic response from all our southern neighbors. Then, in an hour of crassest folly, and for the sake of maintaining a national crime, we had repulsed that sympathy and alienated those whom we assumed to protect.

In the fulness of time, and with the fitness of fate, the work of a century before was resumed, confirmed and perfected. Before the insolent menace of a league of autocracy, more reactionary and more hostile to the rights of nations and of men than was the unholy Holy Alliance at its unholiest estate, the democracy of America, North, Central, South and Insular, arose in resolute and harmonious union.

GIANT GUNS—THEIR MUZZLE-ENERGY, PROJECTILES, AND PENETRATING POWERS

The British 13.5, which was known as the 12-inch-A until the "Lion" was launched, has a length of 45 calibers, and a muzzle-energy ten per cent greater than that of the 50-caliber 12-inch of 1909 and 1910. It may be noted that the caliber is the diameter of the bore of a gun. The statement that a gun has a length of 45 calibers, for example, implies that the gun's length is forty-five times the bore's diameter. Thus a 12-inch gun of 45 calibers is 45 feet long.

MINING. TRENCH AND SAP - A PERSPECTIVE VIEW - AFTER

A

B

SECTION FROM A TO B.

B C

PESTLE

LIP OF CRATER

MINE

PLAN OF GALLERY

ENEMY
TRENCHES

APPROXIMATE DIAME
OF CRATER

Sapping and Mining the Enemy's Trenches.

When the hostile trenches are near together an open zig-zag trench is dug to a point very close to the enemy's line, then a covered gallery is excavated to a point almost under the hostile trench.

ORGANISATION OF DEFENCES BY JOINING CRATER WITH SHELL-HOLES

SECTION FROM C TO D.

LIP OF CRATER

SECTION OF GALLERY.

GAINING A FOOT OF GROUND PER HOUR.

Here a charge of explosive is placed and fired from a distance by an electric wire. At the same instant the men charge over the ground and occupy the ruined trench of the enemy. (*Ill. L. News copr.*)

MACHINE-GUN AND ITS CREW

American boys operating one of several varieties of machine-guns which have done fearful execution in France.

Chapter XXIV

HOW MODERN WARS ARE WAGED

All the Resources of Science Drafted into War — The Scope of Warfare Doubled — Directing a Modern Battle — Mathematics and Mechanics — Torpedoes and Submarines — Many Lethal Inventions — High Power Firearms — The Hospital Service — A Notable Change in the Garb of All Armies but One — Cryptic Coloration Learned from Animals — The Origin of "Khaki" — Purpose of Such Coloration — American "Army Blue" Abandoned — The French Alone Stick to the Old Uniform.

TIMES CHANGE, and wars change with them. In no respect, probably, is human progress more strikingly shown than in the ways and means of war. The contrast between the cave or the hut and the modern mansion or great office building, between the stage coach and the express train, between the candle and the electric light, between the stylus and the printing press—these contrasts are not more marked than that between the methods of warfare of early ages and those of today.

That is, of course, because many of the most advanced achievements of science, in chemistry, mechanics, engineering and what not have been applied to the arts of war; if indeed they have not, as many certainly have, been effected expressly for military purposes. Thus gunpowder was invented for use in war. It became of vast utility also in the arts of peace, but the improvements which have been made in it, and the development of other far more powerful explosives, have had their stimulus largely in the desire to increase the efficiency of military firearms. Steam navigation was of course applied to warships as well as to merchant vessels. Submarine navigation, which

Fulton undertook before he invented his steamboat, was meant almost exclusively for warlike purposes. The telegraph, the telephone, wireless telegraphy, and the electric light, have been made adjuncts to the army. The most striking developments of the balloon and the aeroplane have been for military purposes. The automobile has been made a vehicle of war.

DOUBLING THE FIELD OF WAR

The present generation has seen the field of military operations doubled in extent, and more. Formerly war was waged on the surface of the earth and on the surface of the sea. Now it is waged with equal fury in the heavens above the earth and in the waters beneath the surface of the sea; to which we may add that it is also waged under ground to an extent never dreamed of in earlier wars.

The ride of Paul Revere, and the beacon fires of the days of the Armada, are now supplanted by the telegraph and telephone as means of arousing the people and of summoning troops to the scene of conflict. Armies no longer march great distances to meet the foe, but are conveyed by trains, perhaps on railroads specially built for the purpose. Supplies of food and ammunition instead of being brought by mule wagon are conveyed by trains of automobile trucks.

BATTLEFIELD COMMUNICATIONS

A hundred or even fifty years ago, the commanding general of an army sought some coign of vantage from which he could survey the entire field of battle; or if that was impossible, he stationed himself as close to the firing line as might be prudent and kept himself informed of the progress of the battle and sent his orders to his lieutenants by relays of mounted messengers.

290

Now he may be miles from the scene of battle, seated in his tent or in a house, following the movements of the troops on a topographical map and transmitting orders and receiving reports by telephone to and from all parts of the field. Thus an army of hundreds of thousands, operating on a battle front of twenty or thirty miles, is as directly under control of the distant commander-in-chief as was a single regiment in olden times.

NAVAL MECHANICS AND MATHEMATICS

Equally striking has been the transformation of naval warfare. In Nelson's day, and even in Farragut's, the captain or the admiral stood on the quarter-deck, directing the navigation of the ship and the fighting of the crew, while the ammunition was brought to and placed in the guns by hand. Now the commander stands in his armored conning tower, giving commands by telephone, and the ammunition is handled and the guns are loaded by mechanical or electrical devices. The whole battleship is an intricate, elaborate engine or congeries of engines, operated by steam or electricity.

One great cause of the American naval victories in the War of 1812 was their use of sights on cannon. But now a warship's guns are aimed by machinery, according to elaborate mathematical calculations. Instead of laying hostile ships side by side, gun-muzzles touching, as Paul Jones loved to do, the fighting is conducted at a distance of miles. The huge guns, loaded with smokeless explosives, hurl shells of half a ton weight each a distance of a dozen miles, with force sufficient to pierce the vitals of a ship at seven or eight miles, and with fuse gauged to explode the projectile within a second or two of the appointed time; while the mathematical and mechanical accuracy of the aiming is so great that at a distance of several miles a shot can be landed within a few feet of any designated point, and that when both vessels are moving at full speed.

TORPEDOES AND SUBMARINES

A hundred years ago the torpedo was a cask filled with powder, which drifted or was thrust against a vessel and

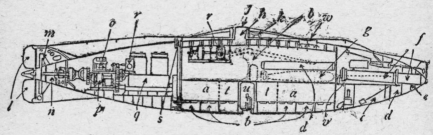

SUBMARINE TORPEDO-BOAT OF THE HOLLAND TYPE

a, a, storage-batteries; *b, b*, main ballast-tank; *c*, gasolene tank; *d*, torpedo compensating-tank; *e*, forward trimming-tank; *f*, torpedo-tube; *g, g*, torpedoes; *h*, conning-tower; *j*, water-tight hatch on top of conning-tower; *k*, steering-compass; *l*, ordinary steering-rudder, the horizontal diving-rudder not shown; *m*, screw-propeller; *n*, after trimming-tank; *o*, air-compressor; *p*, combined dynamo and motor; *q*, gasolene engine; *r, r*, periscope motors; *s*, ventilating-tube; *t*, auxiliary ballast-tank; *u*, adjusting ballast-tank; *v*, air-storage tanks; *w*, forward water-tight hatch.

was exploded by percussion caps on contact. Today the torpedo is an elaborate mechanism capable of being dispatched with unerring aim for a great distance. It can penetrate the hull of an enemy's ship at the range of a mile, and it may explode on contact or be exploded by a time mechanism at the designated second.

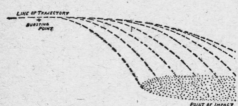

THE GROUND COVERED BY SHRAPNEL IS ELLIPTICAL, ABOUT 200 x 25 YARDS

Such projectiles are now discharged from submarine vessels. These vessels range in size up to 5,000 tons, and are capable of cruising

FRENCH SUBMARINES ATTACKING

A photograph of the French submarine fleet taken during a series of naval maneuvers, in which it was demonstrated that the submarines could have annihilated the entire force of battleships.

ESCAPING A TORPEDO BY RAPID MANEUVERING

This destroyer escaped a torpedo from a hunted submarine by quick turning. Generally the torpedo travels at about fifteen feet under water.

across the Atlantic and back, or around the world. Some of them now carry in addition to torpedo tubes cannon of as much as six inches caliber, for use when they are not fully submerged

MANY INVENTIONS

War in the air comprises the use of vast dirigible balloons, and of swift and agile aeroplanes driven at almost incon-

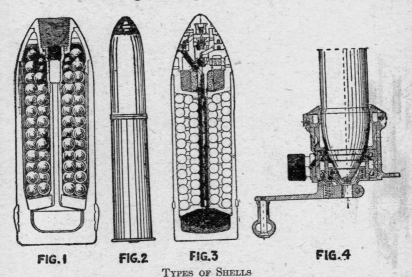

FIG. 1   **FIG. 2**   **FIG. 3**   **FIG. 4**

TYPES OF SHELLS

Fig. 1.—Shrapnel shell, packed with bullets that spread. Fig. 2.—A French quick-firer shell, like an enlarged rifle cartridge. Fig. 3.—The "Universal" shell, combining the action of shrapnel and high explosives. Fig. 4.—A fuse-setting machine.

ceivable speed. Bombs and rockets are used for signaling and for illuminating purposes on a scale never before known. Poisonous gases are employed, blown against the enemy through pipes from vast retorts. These gases are sometimes asphyxiating and life-destroying, sometimes they are calculated to destroy the sight of the enemy, and some-

Section of Intrenchment in Firm Soil and Military Names of Parts

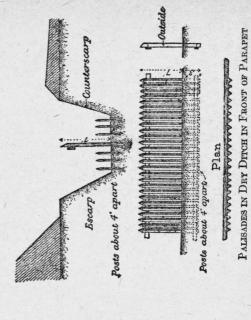

Palisades in Dry Ditch in Front of Parapet

Field Casements and Bomb-proofs

Loopholes Made of Sandbags

times they merely cause a stifling or a weeping sufficient to prevent the men from fighting but without fatal results.

Armored and artillery-armed automobile cars have been much used in battle, capable of driving over ditches and through walls and fences, and impervious to all but the heaviest artillery fire.

Trench warfare has been developed as never before. Instead of a mere ditch and embankment running along the front of the army, there is now an elaborate network of ditches covering a vast extent of country, with tunnels and dormitories, dining rooms and kitchens many feet below the surface of the ground. Many of these excavations are lined with concrete walls and are floored

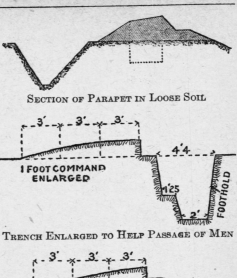

SECTION OF PARAPET IN LOOSE SOIL

TRENCH ENLARGED TO HELP PASSAGE OF MEN

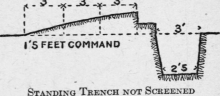

STANDING TRENCH NOT SCREENED

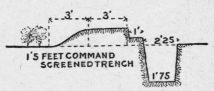

SCREENED STANDING TRENCH

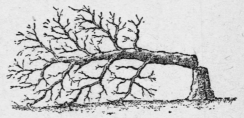

FELLED TREE OBSTACLE, BRANCHES POINTING OUTWARD

with planking, and supplied with water, heating and lighting systems.

HIGH POWER RIFLES

The old-fashioned musket went to the scrap heap long ago. The modern soldier is armed with a repeating rifle capable of killing a man at a distance of three miles. Indeed, the pistol of today has a longer effective range than the musket of a century ago.

Machine guns of various types, some of them capable of discharging scores of bullets in a minute, are largely

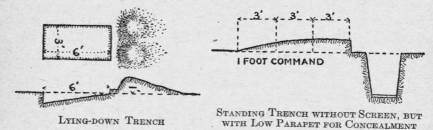

LYING-DOWN TRENCH

STANDING TRENCH WITHOUT SCREEN, BUT WITH LOW PARAPET FOR CONCEALMENT

used; some of them so compact as to be used by a single man after the manner of an ordinary rifle.

THE HOSPITAL SERVICE

Happily, the ways and means of saving life have not lagged behind those of destroying it. The Japanese set an example to the world of sanitary and hospital efficiency in their war with Russia, which other nations have been prompt to emulate. The Red Cross and other organizations have developed a service for the wounded that is comparable with the fighting efficiency of the army. In our Civil War more men died in hospitals from wounds than on the field of battle. Today the deaths in hospitals are insignificant in number.

296

THE CHANGE OF UNIFORM

The present war emphasizes more strongly than ever one of the ways in which we have learned the art of war from the lower orders of the animal creation. That is not in simple destructiveness, in what we call brute force. We have had no need to emulate the fury of the tiger or the shark. Human nature supplied it without effort or study. But in the most subtle adjuncts to actual slaughter, and in those which most implicate some of the most delicate and complex scientific processes, we have learned much from quadrupeds, birds, reptiles, fishes and insects.

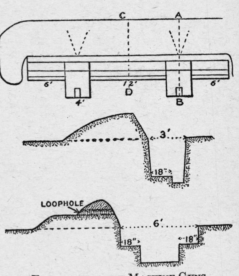

EMPLACEMENT FOR MACHINE GUNS

The German army in the field is wearing what is described as the most effective uniform ever devised in the world. Its effectiveness is both offensive and defensive, and is due entirely to its color, which is a greenish-yellowish gray, which blends so perfectly with the prevailing color-tone of the landscape as to render the troops invisible, or at least indistinguishable, even at so short a distance as half a mile or less. The same end was aimed at by the American, British and other armies some years ago in the adoption of "khaki" colored cloths, but it was not attained as perfectly as by the Germans, because that color was selected empirically, or perhaps

SIMPLE GUN PIT

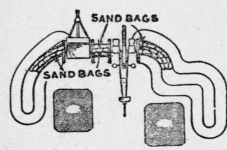

HASTY INTRENCHMENTS FOR FIELD ARTILLERY

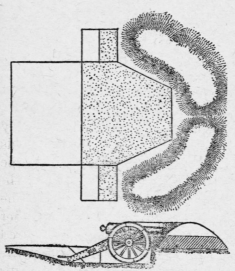

HASTY GUN PIT PROTECTED AT FRONT SIDES

298

we should say traditionally, seeing what its unpleasant origin was, while that of the German uniforms is the result of painstaking scientific study and experiment.

LEARNING FROM ANIMALS

In this, man is, of course, merely imitating the natural gifts of the humbler members of creation. Naturalists have long been familiar with the varied and important uses of color in the scheme of animate creation, and have realized that of those uses the cryptic is by far the most common and probably the most important in the struggle for existence. Cryptic coloration is employed both in attack and in defense, and is commonly associated with other qualities, such as speed, agility and strength. Those animals which are most perfectly concealed by their coloring generally show, when discovered, great speed in flight, as the rabbit; or great strength and fury in defense or attack, as the tiger. Pro-cryptic coloring, for concealment for purposes of safety and defense, widely prevails among small animals and insects, and is far

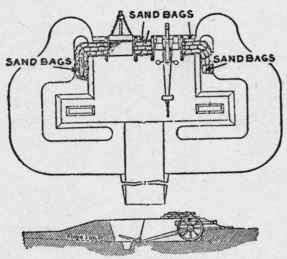

DELIBERATE INTRENCHMENTS FOR FIELD ARTILLERY
WHEN DEPRESSION IS NECESSARY FOR CONCEALMENT

more common than the anti-cryptic coloring which facilitates aggression and attack; since creatures which are preyed upon are more numerous than those which prey upon them.

THE PURPOSE OF DISGUISE

In the vast majority of cases all these colorings have for their object precisely the same object as the assumption of "khaki" by our soldiers has: The dual object, of concealing the wearer from the enemy and of enabling the wearer to get close to the prey before being perceived.

299

This object has become more and more important with the changes in armament which have enabled fighting to be done efficiently at long range. When the combat was hand to hand, with sword or battle-axe, the color of armor or dress mattered little. When the rifleman can kill his foe at a distance of two miles or more, it does matter much. So it has come to pass that cryptic coloring of uniforms is one of the very latest developments of military science.

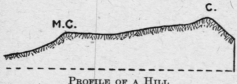

PROFILE OF A HILL

m, *c* is the "military crest," though *c* is higher.

GUN PIT ON CREST OF A HILL

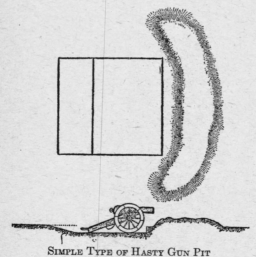

SIMPLE TYPE OF HASTY GUN PIT

NO MORE "ARMY BLUE"

At the present time the American army wears as a service uniform cloth of an olive-drab hue, which is commonly called "khaki" though it is really not of that peculiar color, but is much lighter than it. Khaki, which was adopted as the service color of the British army in and after the Boer War, had a peculiar origin. The word is the name of a Hindoo sect of Vishnuites, founded by Kil, a disciple of Krishna Das, has reference to the practice

Photo by Paul Thompson.

One of the coast batteries of British artillery.

THE BRITISH GUNS

At the left of the picture is seen a range finder and in the center a group of officers watching the effect of the fire.

RUSHING A GUN TO THE FIRING LINE.

With the Royal Horse Artillery in Flanders. Always the guns follow closely in the wake of an infantry advance to break up counter attacks and speed the fleeing Germans on their way.

of those religionists of sprinkling their clothing and their faces with the ashes of dried and burned cowdung. The color of those unsavory ashes is "khaki." It is interesting to observe that while it is of Indian origin, uniforms of that color are not worn by the native Indian army, unless in some regiments of the British contingent; but the strong and showy colors of the old style dress are adhered to. This is doubtless in large part because of an unwillingness of the other sects and creeds thus to identify or associate themselves with the Khaki sect..

GERMAN AND FRENCH CONTRAST

In Germany, as we have seen, the spectroscope and all manner of scientific devices have been brought into use to ascertain precisely what combination of tints conforms most perfectly to the general hue of the average landscape. Never was so much attention paid to the analysis of the spectrum of comet or star as to this problem in military cryptic coloring. Most other armies have approximated to the same system. Russia has an inconspicuous green-gray service uniform, and Italy one of a neutral bluish gray. France alone ignores the scheme and sticks defiantly to the blue tunic and red trousers of her former wars. Whether in so doing she has placed herself at a disadvantage in this war remains to be declared. Nothing to that effect has yet been heard. And of course it will not escape remembrance that in the animal world there are, both in aggression and in defense, some noteworthy exceptions to the rule of cryptic coloring.

Chapter XXV

WOMEN AND WAR WORK

Historical Examples of Women in War — Unexampled Interest of Women
in the Present Struggle — Women's Work for Relief of Suffering and for National
Preparedness — Employment in Various Industries — The Scarcity of Food —
Enormous Increase of Exports and Diminution of Supplies — Proposals for Relief —
Conservation and Increased Production the Natural Methods — The Work of
Housewives for the Saving of Food — A Notable Example — The President's
Proclamation to the People — Garden Work and Kitchen Economy Urged —
Notable Response by the Women of America to the Call of Duty.

"THE FEMALE of the species," wrote Kipling, "is
more deadly than the male." In poetic fashion he proved
his point, and with him both nature and history measurably
agree. We are not without striking examples of the efficient heroism of women in warfare, even in actual conflict
on the field of battle. The fancies of Spenser and Ariosto
have justification in the facts of Boadicea and Zenobia
and Jeanne d'Arc. Even in our own age we have the
plain but inspiring record of "Sergeant Molly" Pitcher,
and we know that in the Balkan War of 1912 hundreds of
Macedonian women marched and fought in the ranks by
the side of their brothers and husbands.

It would have been by no means surprising if the present
war had at an early date summoned to service a whole
army of vengeful Amazons, for surely never was there
one which so unspeakably outraged womanhood in all its
capacities. The truthful tale of German ravishings, tor-
tures, mutilations and murders of women in Belgium and
302

northern France, told from German soldiers' own statements and confessions, and of the wholesale deportation
of young women and girls from those countries into Germany, to be enslaved for the vilest uses, and all this done
not in the hot passion of battle but by the deliberate,
cold, calculated order of the most exalted dignitaries of
the Imperial Government—this forms a chapter in history
beside which Cawnpore seems clean and Sioux and Apache
massacres seem merciful.

Promptly at the outbreak of the war in Europe the
women of America organized themselves in vast numbers
for two major purposes. One was for the relief of the war
sufferers in European lands. The appeal to them to do
this was especially strong for the reason already suggested
—the unprecedented extent to which women and children
were made to be direct sufferers from and victims of the
war. The greater part of the relief work which was done
by this country on so large a scale was due to the energy
and devotion of women; in the Red Cross and in many
special organizations.

WOMEN AND PREPAREDNESS

The other great purpose which animated the women
of America, even before this country became involved
in the war, was that of promoting our national preparedness.
The nauseous doggerel of a one-time "popular" song,
"I Didn't Raise My Boy to Be a Soldier," was righteously
resented by the women of America, who had no thought
of suckling cowards, and in innumerable multitudes they
thronged forward into patriotic organizations intended to
urge universal military training and service and to provide
the essential adjuncts thereto which women can best
supply.

WOMEN IN INDUSTRY

Great Britain and other European countries had set the example of women's engaging in agricultural and other industries, to take the places of men who had gone to fight. In the cities women were successfully employed as elevator operators, street car conductors, and in many other occupations, beside places in munition works and other factories in which men had formerly been employed. In the country women successfully practiced gardening and agriculture.

In the United States women have begun to prepare themselves for such tasks, if it should be necessary for them to undertake them. Particularly have they undertaken farm and garden work, for of that there is actual, imperative and widespread need. At the time of the declaration of war it was realized that the country was on the verge of something almost approximating famine. Scanty crops here, and unprecedented demands for food supplies abroad, caused us to be confronted with a condition which demanded that in 1917 every available acre and square rod of ground should be made to produce the largest possible crop.

THE INCREASE IN FOOD EXPORTS

The enormous increase in exports of foodstuffs of various kinds, and the consequent depletion of our domestic reserve, may be realized from a review of data given by the Department of Commerce at Washington:

	1914 Exports.	1916 Exports.	Increase.
Bacon (lbs.)	193,964,252	579,808,786	385,844,534
Barley (bu.)	6,644,747	27,473,160	20,828,413
Beans and dried peas (bu.)	314,655	1,760,383	1,445,728
Beef, canned (lbs.)	3,464,733	50,416,690	46,951,957
Beef, fresh (lbs.)	6,394,404	231,215,075	224,820,671
Buckwheat (bu.)	580	515,304	514,724
Butter (lbs.)	3,693,597	13,503,279	9,809,682

	1914 Exports.	1916 Exports.	Increase.
Cheese (lbs.)...............	2,427,577	44,394,251	41,966,674
Corn (bu.).................	9,380,855	38,217,012	28,836,157
Cornmeal (bbl.)...........	336,241	419,979	83,738
Cottonseed meal (lbs.)......	799,974,252	1,057,921,569	257,947,317
Cottonseed oil (lbs.)........	192,963,079	266,529,960	73,566,881
Eggs (doz.)...............	16,148,849	26,396,206	10,247,357
Hams and shoulders (lbs.)...	165,881,791	282,208,611	116,326,820
Milk, condensed (lbs.)......	16,209,082	155,734,322	139,525,240
Mutton (lbs.).............	4,685,496	5,552,918	867,422
Oatmeal (lbs.).............	15,998,286	54,748,747	38,750,461
Oats (bu.).................	1,859,949	95,921,620	94,061,671
Peaches, dried (lbs.)........	6,712,296	13,739,342	7,020,046
Pork, canned (lbs.)........	3,074,303	9,610,732	6,536,429
Pork, fresh (lbs.)...........	2,668,020	63,005,524	60,337,504
Potatoes, extra sweet (bu.)..	1,794,073	4,017,760	2,223,687
Raisins (lbs.)...............	14,766,416	75,014,753	60,248,337
Rice (lbs.).................	18,223,264	120,695,213	102,471,949
Rye (bu.).................	2,222,934	14,532,437	12,309,503
Salmon, canned (lbs.).......	87,750,920	152,951,962	65,201,042
Sugar, refined (lbs.).........	50,895,726	1,630,150,863	1,579,255,137
Wheat (bu.)...............	92,303,775	173,374,015	80,880,240
Wheat flour (bbl.)..........	11,821,461	15,520,669	3,699,208

SHORTAGE IN 1916

Now the fact that we were able to increase our exports so enormously did not mean that we had correspondingly increased our production. It meant that there were exceptionally large harvests in 1914 which left a great surplus on our hands, which we were able to send abroad in 1916. The fact is that in 1916, because of bad weather and other causes, our production was much decreased from the average of the preceding years, so that our surplus stocks were depleted, and the nation was confronted with potential scarcity of the severest kind. Here are the official figures showing the decrease in 1916:

	Average Production 1910-1914.	Production 1916.	Shortage.	Excess.
Wheat.........	728,225,000	639,886,000	88,339,000	....
Corn..........	2,732,457,000	2,583,241,000	149,216,000	....
Oats..........	1,157,961,000	1,251,992,000	....	94,031,000
Barley........	186,208,000	180,927,000	5,281,000	....
Rye...........	37,568,000	47,383,000	....	9,815,000
Buckwheat.....	17,022,000	11,840,000	5,182,000	....
Rice.., ...	24,378,000	41,982,000	....	17,604,000
Potatoes.......	360,772,000	285,437,000	75,335,000	....

There was also a marked decrease in the quantity of food supplies in cold storage warehouses throughout the United States, as these figures show:

	March 1, 1917.	March 1, 1916.	Per Cent Decrease.
Cheese, American (lbs.)........	9,499,466	13,373,424	29.3
Eggs, cases (30 doz.)...........	4,759	34,761	86.3
Lard (lbs.)....................	76,389,599	111,897,182	31.7
Lamb and mutton (lbs.)	4,007,465	5,812,144	31.1
Frozen pork (lbs.).............	55,926,367	88,603,621	36.9

PROPOSALS FOR RELIEF

This undoubtedly serious state of affairs called for prompt action for relief, and various plans were proposed. Some urged an embargo on foodstuffs, but they were chiefly German sympathizers or Germans themselves in disguise. It was obvious that such a procedure would mean ruin to the Allies and the triumph of Germany; and that was not to be thought of, at any rate after we had ourselves entered the war as the opponent of Germany and as an ally of the Allies.

Others suggested government seizure, control and distribution of all supplies of food; but that was obviously an extreme measure which should be resorted to only in case of the most dire necessity.

The two measures which were most obvious, most natural, and most desirable, and which, indeed, gave greatest promise of being effective, were these: that we should economically conserve our existing supplies and that we should seek to increase our products to the greatest possible degree; and these were measures in which the active co-operation of women was indispensable.

THE CONSERVATION OF FOOD

The Secretary of Agriculture was recently quoted as saying that American families had been wasting $700,000,-000 worth of food in their kitchens every year. Thoughtful observers and investigators were inclined to think that he underestimated rather than overestimated the amount. The complaint was not that Americans ate too much, or too good, food, but that they wasted too much. They had wasteful methods of purchasing, of cooking, and of serving, and they threw too much of the perfectly good surplus from their meals into the garbage cans instead of utilizing it for subsequent meals. It was a phase of our characteristic and proverbial American profligacy—the same profligacy in resources which caused more first-class lumber to be destroyed in the cutting and by forest fires than was sent to market.

This was obviously an evil to be corrected chiefly by the women, who were the housekeepers and cooks, and who could therefore check such waste. How readily a reform in that respect could be effected was strikingly shown in New York City, where in the week following an appeal by the Mayor for greater carefulness in the use of food, there was a very large percentage of reduction of the number of tons of garbage collected. That simply meant that so many tons of perfectly good food had been saved for subsequent meals instead of being thrown away, and also that housekeepers had gauged their requirements more accurately and had thus had smaller surpluses to dispose of.

WORK ON THE FARMS

The need of increasing the productiveness of our farms was so pressing that President Wilson on April 14th issued a special address to the people of the nation on the subject, in which he said:

"I take the liberty of addressing this word to the farmers of the country and to all who work on the farms: The supreme need of our own nation and of the nations with which we are co-operating is an abundance of supplies, and especially of foodstuffs. The importance of an adequate food supply, especially for the present year, is superlative. Without abundant food, alike for the armies and the peoples now at war, the whole great enterprise upon which we have embarked will break down and fail. The world's food reserves are low. Not only during the present emergency, but for some time after peace shall have come, both our own people and a large proportion of the people of Europe must rely upon the harvests in America.

"Upon the farmers of this country, therefore, in large measure rests the fate of the war and the fate of the nations. May the nation not count upon them to omit no step that will increase the production of their land or that will bring about the most effectual co-operation in the sale and distribution of their products? The time is short. It is of the most imperative importance that everything possible be done, and done immediately, to make sure of large harvests. I call upon young men and old alike and upon

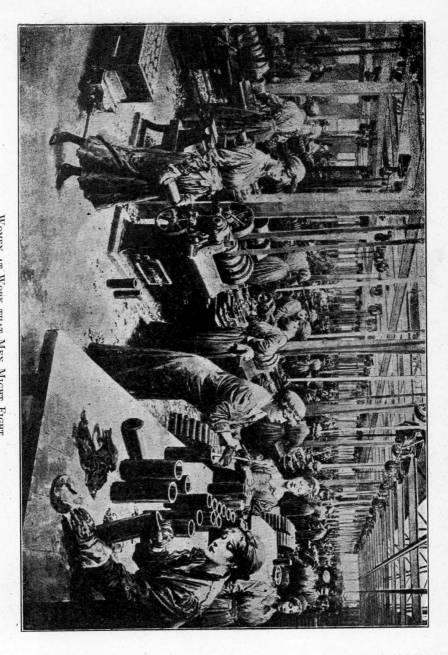

WOMEN AT WORK THAT MEN MIGHT FIGHT

A busy scene in one of the munition workshops. The women in the foreground are testing shells for accuracy of size and those in the background are turning the shells on engine lathes.

MAKING ARMOR PLATE

View of the armor plate machine shop at the Bethlehem Steel Company. The varied and complex machining required on armor plate demands tools of enormous size and strength as well as varied purpose. In this shop the different groups of armor are assembled in the position they will occupy on the vessel for which they are intended, and inspected before shipment.

the able-bodied boys of the land to accept and act upon this duty—to turn in hosts to the farms and make certain that no pains and no labor is lacking in this great matter.

THE GARDEN AND THE KITCHEN

"Let me suggest, also, that every one who creates or cultivates a garden helps, and helps greatly, to solve the problem of the feeding of the nations; and that every housewife who practices strict economy puts herself in the ranks of those who serve the nation. This is the time for America to correct her unpardonable fault of wastefulness and extravagance. Let every man and every woman assume the duty of careful, provident use and expenditure as a public duty, as a dictate of patriotism which no one can now expect ever to be excused or forgiven for ignoring."

SPECIAL APPEAL TO WOMEN

To this the Secretary of Agriculture added this appeal:

"Every woman can render important service to the nation in its present emergency. She need not leave her home nor abandon her home duties to help the armed forces. She can help to feed and clothe our armies, and help to supply food to those beyond the seas, by practicing effective thrift in her own household.

"Every ounce of food the housewife saves—all food which she or her children produce and preserve—every garment which repair makes it unnecessary to replace—all lessen the draft on the insufficient world supplies.

MUST NOT WASTE FOOD

"To save food the housewife must learn to plan economical and properly balanced meals, which, while nourishing each member of the family properly, do not encourage overeating or offer excessive and wasteful variety. It is her duty to protect food from spoilage by heat, dirt, mice or insects; she must acquire the culinary ability to utilize every bit of edible food that comes into her home; she must learn to use such foods as vegetables, beans, peas and milk products as partial substitutes for meat, and she must see that nothing nutritious is wasted.

"Waste in any household may seem to be insignificant, but if only a single ounce of edible food, on the average, is allowed to spoil or to be thrown away in each of our 20,000,000 homes, over 1,300,000 pounds of material would be wasted each day. It takes the fruit of many acres and the work of many people, to raise, prepare and distribute 464,000,000 pounds of food a year. Every ounce of food thrown away, therefore, tends also to waste the labor of an army of busy citizens.

URGED TO DROP FASHION

"Clothing is largely an agricultural product, and represents the results of labor on the sheep ranges, in cotton fields and in mills and factories. Whenever a useful garment is needlessly discarded material needed to keep some one warm or dry may be consumed merely to gratify a passing fancy. Women would do well to look upon clothing at this time more particularly from the utilitarian point of view.

ENCOURAGE THRIFT!

"While all honor is due the women who leave their homes to nurse and care for those wounded in battle, no woman should feel that because she does not wear a nurse's uniform she is absolved from patriotic service. The home women of the country, if they will give their minds fully to this vital subject of food conservation and train themselves in household thrift, can make of the housewife's apron a uniform of national significance.

"Demonstrate thrift in your homes and encourage thrift among your neighbors.

"Make saving rather than spending your social standard.

"Make economy fashionable lest it become obligatory."

The response of the American people, and particularly of American women, to this appeal was prompt and gratifying. Women not merely practiced economy in the kitchens, but thousands of them undertook the cultivation of gardens, while the men, released from that task, gave themselves to the heavier farm work. It was estimated that in Great Britain 2,000,000 women were doing work formerly done by men. It seems not unlikely that in the United States almost as large a proportion of women are at least engaging in special and unaccustomed labor of some kind in order to "do their bit" toward sustaining the nation and assuring its victory in the great war.

Chapter XXVI

ARMY AND NAVY ORGANIZATION

Origin and Development of Our Military Arm — The Present Chief Officers — The Secretary of War and General Staff — Various Departments of the Army — The Infantry Organization — How the Cavalry is Organized — The Artillery Service — The Militia, Organized and Unorganized — Military Schools and Training Camps — The American Navy — Composition of a Standard Fleet — Organization of the Navy Department — Its Various Bureaus — The Naval Militia — The Marines, the "Soldiers of the Sea."

"ARMS AND THE MAN!" The army and navy are, after all, the center of interest in time of war. It is they that do the actual fighting. Let us see how they are composed, organized, commanded, and employed.

The army of the United States was created by the Continental Congress, and at the close of the Revolution its strength was fixed at one regiment of infantry of twelve companies, and one regiment of artillery of four companies, a grand total of 1,216 officers and men. The next year, 1791, an additional infantry regiment of 900 men was authorized. In 1798 a provisional force of 10,000 was raised in view of the danger of war with France, but it was disbanded two years later. Another such force was raised for the War of 1812 and was disbanded at its close. A regiment of dragoons was authorized in 1833, and two more in 1836, and ten years later, at the outbreak of the Mexican war, the army contained 7,244 men. During that war it was increased to 20,000, but at the end of the war it was reduced to its former size, with the addition of one regiment of mounted rifles. Two regiments of infantry and two of cavalry were added in

1855, and at the outbreak of the Civil War the army had a line strength of 12,931 officers and men, and a total in all departments of 16,367.

The greatest increase of the regular army in the Civil War was on January 1, 1863, when the total number was 25,463. There was a gradual decline until at the end of the war the number was 21,669. In August, 1876, Congress fixed its maximum strength at 25,000 enlisted men. On January 1, 1893, it contained 28,502 officers and men. At the beginning of the European war, in the summer of 1914, it consisted of 4,701 officers and 87,781 men. Deducting the quartermaster and hospital corps, the coast artillery, practically stationary in coast defense works, and some others, there remained a mobile army, for field work, of 2,935 officers and 51,446 men. In the navy there were 52,667 enlisted men. The authorized strength of the army was considerably greater than the actual strength, many of the organizations being below their full strength.

ARMY DEPARTMENTS AND OFFICERS

For many years before our war with Germany the Continental United States had been divided into four military departments, the Eastern, Central, Southern and Western, with headquarters respectively at New York, Chicago, Fort Sam Houston (Texas), and San Francisco. But in March, 1917, just on the verge of our entry into war, the President ordered the division of the Eastern Department into three, known as the Eastern, Northeastern and Southeastern, with headquarters at New York, Boston and Charleston.

THE THREEFOLD ARMY ORGANIZATION

Soon after the declaration of war, additional legislation provided for the increase of the army to a size never before dreamed of, approximating 3,000,000 men. It was to consist of three parts, unified for the purposes of this war. The first was—and now is—the Regular Army, the increase of which by voluntary enlistment was authorized from less than 100,000 to 300,000 men. By the middle of August it was completed with a total of 305,700 men. The second part consists of the National Guard, or State militia regiments, which have lost their identity and their numerical designations as State organizations and have become "Nationalized." They numbered at the date mentioned 311,000 men. They were sent in the early fall to the following training camps:

Camp	Location
Camp Bowie	Fort Worth, Tex.
Camp McArthur	Waco, Tex.
Camp Logan	Houston, Tex.
Camp Doniphan	Fort Sill, Okla.
Camp Cody	Deming, N. M.
Camp Kearny	Linda Vista, Cal.
Camp Sevier	Greenville, S. C.
Camp Wadsworth	Spartanburg, S. C.
Camp Hancock	Augusta, Ga.
Camp Wheeler	Macon, Ga.
Camp Sheridan	Montgomery, Ala.
Camp McClellan	Anniston, Ala.
Camp Greene	Charlotte, N. C.
Camp Shelby	Hattiesburg, Miss.
Camp Beauregard	Alexandria, La.
Camp Fremont	Palo Alto, Cal.
Camp Mills	Mineola, N. Y.

The third part of the military establishment is the so-called National Army, composed of conscripts, or men chosen by a "selective draft." On June 5th all men in the country between the ages of twenty-one and thirty were registered, for conscription, to the number of 9,659,382. On July 20,

687,000 of these were drafted by lot. Later they were summoned, in instalments, to sixteen training camps, situated in various parts of the country, each containing more than 40,000 men, and each under the command of a major-general, as follows:

Camp Devens...	Ayer, Mass............	Maj.-Gen. H. F. Hodges
Camp Dix......	Wrightstown, N. J......	Maj.-Gen. C. W. Kennedy
Camp Upton...	Yaphank, N. Y........	Maj.-Gen. J. F. Bell
Camp Meade...	Annapolis Junction, Md.	Maj.-Gen. Joseph E. Kuhn
Camp Jackson..	Columbia, S. C.........	Maj.-Gen. F. H. French
Camp Lee......	Petersburg, Va.........	Maj.-Gen. Adelbert Cronkhite
Camp Gordon..	Atlanta, Ga............	Maj.-Gen. Eben Swift
Camp Sherman.	Chillicothe, Ohio......	Maj.-Gen. E. F. Glenn
Camp Pike.....	Little Rock, Ark.......	Maj.-Gen. S. D. Sturgis
Camp Custer...	Battle Creek, Mich.....	Maj.-Gen. J. T. Dickman
Camp Taylor...	Louisville, Ky.........	Maj.-Gen. Harry C. Hale
Camp Grant....	Rockford, Ill..........	Maj.-Gen. Thomas H. Barry
Camp Dodge...	Des Moines, Iowa......	Maj.-Gen. E. H. Plummer
Camp Funston..	Fort Riley, Kan........	Maj.-Gen. Leonard Wood
Camp Lewis....	American Lake, Wash...	Maj.-Gen. Henry A. Greene
Camp Travis...	Fort Sam Houston, Tex.	Maj.-Gen. Henry T. Allen

Additional drafts were made from time to time, as troops were sent abroad and room was thus made in the training camps for fresh levies. By the Fourth of July, 1918, over one million men had been sent, and the camps were still filled. As many young men who were under twenty-one on June 5, 1917, had now come of age, a new registration was held in June, 1918, for their enrollment, with the result that nearly 800,000 names were added to the conscription lists. On June 27th another lottery was held to determine the order in which they should be drafted when needed.

OUR MILITARY ESTABLISHMENT

The General Staff was created by Act of Congress in February, 1903, on the recommendation of Elihu Root then secretary of war. It is the expert military advisory board to the President and the Secretary of War. Its members are employed in the study of military problems, the preparation of plans for the national defense, the utilization of the various army organizations in time of war, etc. It is ultimately, by July 1, 1920, to consist of fifty-five officers.

VARIOUS ARMY DEPARTMENTS

The Adjutant-General's Department is the medium through which all orders of the War Department are issued, and all regulations for the control of the army; in which all records are kept; and through which all correspondence is conducted.

The Inspector-General's Department is charged with the careful inspection of all parts of the army, the Military Academy, hospitals, transports, cemeteries, and in fact every detail of the entire military establishment, and of reporting upon their condition and making recommendations for their maintenance and improvement.

The Judge Advocate-General's Department is the law bureau of the military establishment, and has custody and supervision of the records of all general courts-martial, courts of inquiry and military commissions, and also of the titles of land held by the War Department.

The Quartermaster-General's Department has charge of all barracks, storehouses and other buildings; ships, railroads and transportation generally; horses, mules, wagons, etc.; clothing and camp and garrison equipment; food and forage; and the distribution of funds for payment of the army.

The Surgeon-General's Department is the medical corps of the army, having charge of sanitation, hospitals, transportation and care of the sick and wounded, etc. Its members

HERBERT C. HOOVER

Appointed Food Administrator to conserve the food resources of the nation and control their distribution.

MAJOR-GENERAL JOHN J. PERSHING

Who was selected to lead the first American expeditionary force to France.

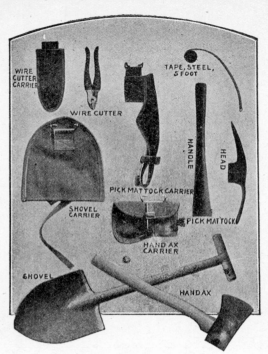

UNITED STATES INFANTRY TOOLS

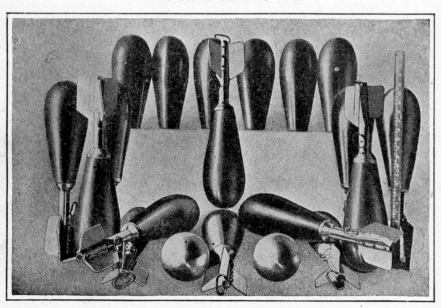

BOMBS TO BE DROPPED FROM AIRCRAFT

are unarmed, and are protected from harm by international agreement.

The Engineering Corps is charged with surveying sites for camps and fortifications and the construction of defensive works, the laying out and making of roads, the erection of buildings, bridges, piers, etc., and river and harbor improvements.

The Ordnance Department has the task of providing all the munitions of war, from pistols and rifles to the largest cannon, tools, machinery, harness and other equipments. It also provides the small arms for the Navy Department. It has, of course, charge of the arsenals.

The Signal Corps, under the chief signal officer, constructs, maintains and operates all telegraph and cable lines, telephones, radiographic plants, heliographs, and all other means of communication.

The Bureau of Insular Affairs has jurisdiction over Porto Rico and the Philippines.

INFANTRY ORGANIZATION

The great body of an army consists of infantry. In the United States army an infantry regiment is composed as follows, when its ranks are full:

One colonel, 1 lieutenant-colonel, 4 medical officers, and 1 chaplain; a headquarters company, including the band, color sergeants, etc., numbering 59; a machine gun company, of 57; a supply company, comprising wagoners, numbering 39; and three battalions of four companies each. The battalions are numbered first, second and third. The companies are designated by the letters of the alphabet, A, B, C and D companies being in the first, E, F, G and H in the second, and I, K, L and M in the third battalion. Each company has a captain, first lieutenant, second lieutenant, first sergeant, mess sergeant, supply sergeant, 6 sergeants, 11 corporals, 2 cooks, 2 buglers, 1 mechanic, 19 first-class privates, and 56 privates, making 103 in all. The entire regiment thus contains 1,404 officers and men. That is the peace footing. In time of war there are added 21 to the machine gun company, and 50 to each of the twelve companies in the battalions, or 221, raising the war strength of a regiment to 1,625.

Each infantryman carries a pack, rifle, ammunition and rations, weighing in all about forty-five pounds.

The various units of an army are as follows, with their composition and commander: Squad, composed of 8 men, commanded by a corporal; platoon, 40 to 50 men, lieutenant or sergeant; company, 2 to 4 platoons, captain.

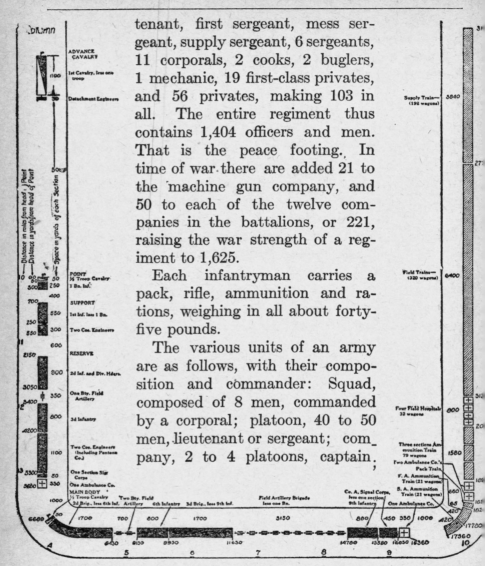

THIS DIAGRAM, DRAWN TO SCALE, SHOWS THE LENGTH OF ROAD OCCUPIED BY THE VARIOUS UNITS OF A DIVISION OF 20,000 MEN ON THE MARCH IN THE PRESENCE OF THE ENEMY

battalion, 4 companies, major; regiment, 3 battalions, colonel; brigade, 3 regiments, brigadier-general; division, 3 brigades, major-general; army corps, 2 or more divisions, lieutenant-general; army, 2 or more army corps, general.

CAVALRY ORGANIZATION

A cavalry regiment has a colonel, lieutenant-colonel, chaplain, 4 medical officers and 2 veterinarians; a headquarters troop of 55, raised to 86 in war; a machine gun troop of 74, raised to 95 in war; a supply troop of 50, raised to 54 in war; and three squadrons of four troops each, the squadrons and troops being designated by numbers and letters corresponding with those of battalions and companies of infantry. Each squadron is commanded by a major and each troop by a captain. Each troop comprises 73 officers and men, increased to 108 in war.

Thus the peace strength of a cavalry regiment when its ranks are full is 1,070 and its war strength 1,546 officers and men.

THE ARTILLERY SERVICE

The field artillery includes mountain, light, horse and heavy artillery. Each regiment consists of six batteries, with guns or howitzers all of the same or of different calibers. The standard heavy field artillery of our army consists of 4.7-inch guns and 6-inch howitzers. We have no monster siege howitzers such as Germany has been so effectively using. The light artillery uses 3-inch guns and 3.8-inch howitzers. Larger pieces have been designed and are in course of manufacture.

The coast artillery has both fixed and movable batteries, using guns of from 3 to 12 inches and mortars of 12 inches caliber. Guns of 14 and 16 inches have been designed, and a few made. The permanent fortifications at the principal ports comprise direct-fire rifles, largely mounted on disappearing carriages; mortars for high angle fire; and submarine mines for under-water attack upon hostile vessels.

OUR MILITARY SCHOOLS

The military establishment of the United States comprises an elaborate educational system. There is the Military Academy, at West Point, which, as a school of engineering and science, ranks among the best colleges in the world. There are at all military posts schools for the general instruction of enlisted men, and schools for the instruction of the officers in matters appertaining to their duties. Then there are nearly a score of service schools of different kinds, including the Army War College, the Army Staff College, the Coast Artillery School, the Engineer School, the Mounted Service School, the Army Medical School, the Army Signal School, the Army School of the Line, the School for Bakers and Cooks, the Army Field Engineer School, the School of Fire for Field Artillery, the School of Musketry, and the Signal Corps Aviation School.

In addition to these, there are numerous colleges and preparatory schools throughout the country to which army officers are detailed as military instructors.

CAMPS OF INSTRUCTION

A system of camps for training and instruction was established in 1913, through the efforts of General Leonard Wood, for the benefit of college students and other civilians who wished to become practically familiar with military affairs. A little later that year a number of college presidents and camp students formed the Society of the National Reserve Corps, to promote the system of universal military training. As a result several camps of instruction were established, the most notable being that for business men at Plattsburg, N. Y.

Since the declaration of war against Germany, numerous instruction camps for officers have been created, in three series, as follows:

Series I.—Plattsburg Barracks, N. Y.; Madison Barracks, N. Y.; Fort Niagara, N. Y.; Fort Myer, Va.; Fort Oglethorpe, Ga.; Fort McPherson, Ga.; Fort Benjamin Harrison, Ind.; Fort Sheridan, Ill.; Fort Logan H. Roots, Ark.; Fort Snelling, Minn.; Fort Riley, Kan.; Leon Springs, Tex.; Presidio of San Francisco, Cal.

Series II.—Plattsburg Barracks, N. Y.; Fort Niagara, N. Y.; Fort Myer, Va.; Fort Oglethorpe, Ga.; Fort Benjamin Harrison, Ind.; Fort Sheridan, Ill.; Leon Springs. Tex.; Fort Snelling, Minn.; Presidio of San Francisco, Cal,

Series III.—One in each division of the Regular Army, of the National Guard Army, and of the National Army; also one each at Fort Bliss, Tex.; Fort Sam Houston, Tex., and Chickamauga, Tenn.; and in the Philippines, Hawaii, and the Panama Canal Zone.

There are Reserve Engineers' training camps at Belvoir, Va.; American University, D. C.; Fort Leavenworth, Kan., and Vancouver Barracks, Wash.

There are also numerous aviation training camps and schools of military aeronautics, further mention of which will be found elsewhere in this volume.

The Embarcation Camps are Camp Merritt, Dumont, N. J., and Camp Stuart, Newport News, Va.

United States arsenals are at Augusta, Ga.; Benicia, Cal.; Frankford, Pa.; New York, N. Y.; Picatinny, N. J.; Rock Island, Ill.; San Antonio, Tex.; Sandy Hook. N. J.;

Springfield, Mass.; Watertown, Mass., and Watervliet, N. Y.

There are hospitals at Hot Springs, Ark.; Presidio of San Francisco, Cal., and Washington, D. C.; and Disciplinary Barracks at Fort Alcatraz, Cal.; Fort Jay, N. Y., and Fort Leavenworth, Kan.

THE AMERICAN NAVY

The navy of the United States was established by the Continental Congress in 1775, as a means of protecting the coasts of the insurgent colonies from the ravages of British cruisers. Its first commander-in-chief was Esek Hopkins, but its chief founder was John Paul Jones. Its history down to recent years presents a record of discouragement and neglect, illuminated with many splendid deeds achieved not because of, but in spite of, the naval policy of the government.

Elsewhere in this volume is given an account of the present strength of the navy. The bulk of it is divided into three active fleets, each under a commander-in-chief with the nominal rank of admiral but the real rank of rear-admiral. One is the Atlantic Fleet, whose field of operations comprises the Atlantic Ocean, the Gulf of Mexico, the Caribbean Sea, the Mediterranean Sea, and other tributary waters. Another is the Pacific Fleet, which guards the western coasts of North, Central and South America, Alaska, Hawaii and Samoa. The third is the Asiatic Fleet, which serves in the western part of the Pacific Ocean, the China Seas, the Indian Ocean and the East Indies.

FLEET ORGANIZATION

Ships of the navy which are in commission are divided among three classes or conditions. Those in full commission are completely manned and officered, and are in all respects ready for immediate service. Those in reserve are laid up at a navy yard or elsewhere, practically ready for service excepting that their crews are of reduced strength and must be increased before service. Those in ordinary are thus laid up with only enough officers and men aboard to serve as caretakers.

In time of peace a fleet consists of one battleship used as the flagship of the commander-in-chief; four divisions containing four battleships each; several divisions of armored cruisers; and various auxiliary and supply ships, and when practicable flotillas of torpedo boats, destroyers, and submarines.

The entire naval establishment is under the President, as commander-in-chief, and, after him, under the Secretary of the Navy. The officers who serve on the ships are of two kinds, line and staff. The officers of the line are, in order of rank: The admiral of the navy, an office not always filled; vice-admirals, offices also not always filled; rear-admirals, captains, commanders, lieutenant-commanders, lieutenants, lieutenants of junior grade, and ensigns. The staff officers are medical, dental and pay officers, chaplains, professors of mathematics, naval constructors and civil engineers. Midshipmen, graduated from the Naval Academy, are ranked as officers of the line.

THE NAVY DEPARTMENT

The Secretary of the Navy is the head of the Navy Department. He has an assistant secretary and a chief clerk. In the absence of both the secretary and the assistant secretary, the chief of naval operations is acting head of the department.

The chief of naval operations is a rear-admiral, ranking as

admiral, and he is charged with the operations of the fleet and with the preparation of it for use in war.

The General Board corresponds with the General Staff of the army, and is composed of the admiral of the navy, the chief of naval operations, the commandant of the Marine Corps, the director of naval intelligence, the president of the Naval War College, and such other officers as the Secretary of the Navy may choose.

The judge advocate-general corresponds with the officer of the same title in the army.

The Bureau of Yards and Docks has jurisdiction over all navy yards and naval stations, buildings and other public works of the department.

The Bureau of Navigation has charge of the training and education of officers and men and their enlistment and assignment to duty; of the Naval Academy and other schools; and of all records of service.

The Bureau of Ordnance has to do with all arms and ammunition, including torpedoes, and with those portions of ships directly concerned with arms and munitions.

The Bureau of Construction and Repair has to do with the designing of all ships, and the construction of all that are built in the government's own navy yards; with the supervision and inspection of all that are built by private contract; and with alterations and repairs.

The Bureau of Steam Engineering has under its care all the engines for the propulsion of vessels, electrical equipment, fuel, etc.

The Bureau of Supplies and Accounts is the fiscal or business agency of the department.

The Bureau of Medicine and Surgery corresponds with the Medical Corps of the army.

THE NAVAL MILITIA

The Naval Militia was first organized n Massachusetts, in 1890, as a part of the national guard of that state. There are now more than a score of such organizations, in as many states, with nearly 600 officers and more than 8,000 enlisted men. The Navy Department lends ships for the practice of the militia, and Congress appropriates money for arms and equipment. There is a National Naval Militia Board, consisting of five officers of the Naval Militia, representing the various lake and seacoast regions of the United States, which meets at Washington for general advice and direction of the Naval Militia.

In the summer of 1916 more than 2,000 members of the Naval Militia went on a two weeks' practice cruise, on nine battleships of the reserve fleet. The militia has also organized aeronautic sections.

THE MARINES

The Marine Corps has been described as the soldiers of the sea. It dates from November 10, 1775, and has a record of efficient service not surpassed if equaled by that of any other part of the navy or army. Its members have the training of infantry soldiers, but their service is rendered in connection with the navy. They form the landing parties which are occasionally sent ashore in foreign lands for the protection of American lives and property, and they do a vast variety of work, both on ship and ashore.

The Revenue Cutter Service and the Life Saving Service are normally under the jurisdiction of the Treasury Department, but by an act of Congress in 1915 they were consolidated into the United States Coast Guard, and were placed in time of emergency at the command of the Secretary of the Navy.

Such, in brief, is the organization of the two great services upon which the nation depends for protection and for victory in war.

UNITED STATES ARMY TABLE

RANK	DUTIES
General	In supreme command of all.
Lieutenant-General	Second in command.
Major-General	Commands a Field Army or a Division.
Brigadier-General	Commands Brigade (4,000 rifles).
Colonel	Commands Regiment (1,500 rifles).
Lieutenant-Colonel	Assistant to Colonel, commands Regiment in his absence.
Major	Commands Battalion (400 rifles).
Captain	Commands Company (100 rifles).
First Lieutenant	Commands Platoon (24 to 32 rifles) and assists Captain.
Second Lieutenant	Commands Platoon (24 to 32 rifles) and assists Captain.
First Sergeant	Commands Platoon (24 to 32 rifles), acts as file closer and commands Company in absence of Officers.
Sergeant	Assists Officers and First Sergeant.
Corporal	Commands Squad (8 rifles).
Private	Performs duties assigned by Officers.

UNITED STATES NAVY TABLE

RANK	DUTIES
Admiral	Chief of Operations, or Commander of Atlantic, Pacific or Asiatic Fleet.
Vice-Admiral	Second in command of Atlantic, Pacific or Asiatic Fleet.
Rear-Admiral	Command of a Division of a Fleet or Department Duty.
Captain	Commander of Battleship or Cruiser.
Commander	In command of second or third-class ships or special duty on board first-class ship.
Lieutenant-Commander	Commands fourth-class ship or special duty.
Lieutenant	Assigned to command of a department of first-class ship or subordinate duty on smaller ship.
Lieutenant (Junior Grade)	Junior Officer assigned to special duty.
Ensign	Junior Officer assigned to special duty.
Midshipman	Naval Academy Student.
Chief Warrant Officer	In charge of department of ship.
Warrant Officer	In charge of department of ship.
Mate	In charge of special department of ship.
Chief Petty Officer	In charge of small department.
Petty Officer, first class	In charge of group of seamen or special duty.
Petty Officer, second class	Same as first class.
Petty Officer, third class	Same as first class.
Seaman, first class	Performs duties assigned by Officers.
Seaman, second class	Performs duties assigned by Officers.
Seaman, third class	Performs duties assigned by Officers.

CHANGES IN COMMAND

The offices of General and Lieutenant-General, and of Admiral and Vice-Admiral, have usually been left vacant; and indeed have not always existed. Before the present war only Washington, Grant, Sherman and Sheridan had held the rank of General, and Farragut, Porter and Dewey that of Admiral. But the magnitude of the forces which were mustered for the Great War, as well as the extreme desirability of having American commanders of equal rank with those of the other Allied armies, caused the revival of those offices.

Accordingly, John J. Pershing, a Major-General, who was chosen to command our expeditionary forces in France and Belgium, was promoted to the full rank of General, and Rear-Admiral Henry T. Mayo was made Admiral, and Commander-in-Chief of the Fleet in the Atlantic Ocean. There were also numerous promotions to the ranks of Major-General and Brigadier-General, as well, of course, as to the lower offices of the military establishment; and to the various ranks in the navy.

CHAPTER XXVII

FINANCING A NATION AT WAR AND ITS ALLIES

America Learning to Think in Terms of Billions — Appropriations of Unprecedented Magnitude — The First Liberty Loan — Response of the Nation to the Call for "Sinews of War" — The Second Liberty Loan — Thrift Certificates and War Savings Stamps — Millions of Eager Contributors to the Nation's War Chest — An Enormous Revenue Secured by Extraordinary Taxation — Loans to Our Allies — Security of the Nation's Credit.

THE GREAT WAR has set America to thinking financially in terms of billions. In a single appropriation bill Congress has voted more, and in a single issue of bonds the nation has raised more, than the entire cost of our four years' Civil War. Yet these stupendous expenditures are probably not as great, in proportion to our resources and our ability, as were those of 1861–65.

From the beginning it was obvious that we should have to raise enormous sums, both to meet the expenses of our own unprecedented military preparations and operations, and to supply the needs of our allies. Mention has already been made of the first huge appropriation bill which was passed by Congress soon after our entry into the war. On May 9th the Secretary of the Treasury announced the details of the first "Liberty Loan" which the government proposed to ask the nation to subscribe. It was to be a loan of $2,000,000,000, bearing interest at 3½ per cent, and payable in 1947, though redeemable by the government at will any time after 1932 at par and interest. It was dated June 15, 1917, on which date subscriptions closed. It was

328

BUILDING A BRIDGE OF BOATS TO EUROPE

A typical scene in one of our many shipyards where huge freighters like the one in this picture are being rushed to completion for the United States government to carry supplies abroad to our troops and our Allies. This vessel is nearly completed and almost ready for launching.

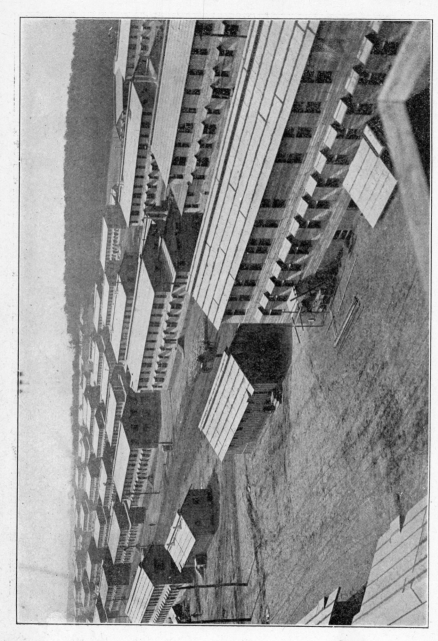

WHERE UNCLE SAM IS TRAINING SOLDIERS FOR THE NATIONAL ARMY

A general view of a cantonment where men selected for service in our National Army under the Selective Draft Law are being trained into fighters. A cantonment like the one in this picture includes barracks, store-houses, administration buildings, etc., for 40,000 men.

then found that it had been enormously over-subscribed. More than four million people had offered the government no less than $3,035,226,850. Of this sum only the two billions asked for was accepted, all the small subscriptions being taken, and the large ones being scaled down.

THE SECOND LOAN

This was a splendid beginning, but it was only a beginning. On September 5th a second credit was voted, of $11,538,000,000; of which four billions were to be loans to our allies, three billions were to be raised in a second "Liberty Loan," two billions were to be sought in Thrift and War Saving certificates, and two billions in Treasury certificates of indebtedness. The second "Liberty Loan" was at 4 per cent interest. On October 27th it was closed, and it was found that to provide the three billions asked for, some nine and a half million persons had subscribed $4,617,532,300. The government decided to accept the sum for which it had asked and 50 per cent of the surplus, making $3,808,766,150 in all. Subscribers to the first loan had the privilege of exchanging their 3½ per cent bonds for the 4 per cent bonds of the second loan, and many of them did so.

WAR SAVINGS

Following this, in the late fall of 1917, the system of War Savings Certificates and Stamps, and Thrift Cards and Stamps was put forward, for the raising of $2,000,000,000 during the year 1918. Their object was to promote thrift among people of small means, and to enable them as well as wealthier people to loan money to the government at profitable rates.

These certificates and cards have been placed on sale

at postoffices, banks and elsewhere, and have been widely purchased.

The third "Liberty Loan" was issued at 4¼ per cent, at the latter part of April, 1918. The sum of $3,000,000,000 was asked for, but it was stated that if it was over-subscribed the government would take all that was offered. The result was that when the subscriptions closed on May 4th, bonds to the amount of $4,170,019,650 had been purchased by the people. That was a magnificent over-subscription. But still more gratifying and significant was the number of subscribers. The number of subscribers to the first loan had been more than four millions, or one in every twenty-five of the population. The second loan had nine and a half million subscribers, or about one in every ten and a half. But the subscribers to the third numbered about 17,000,000 or one in every six of the population. In that respect the third loan was probably the most successful, and the most truly popular, ever floated.

THE INCOME TAX

In addition to these loans the government planned also to raise during the year about $3,400,000,000 by taxation, of which approximately one-third was to come from taxes on personal and corporate incomes, one-third from taxes on business profits in excess of a prescribed maximum, and one-third from miscellaneous taxes, including stamp taxes on business and legal documents, and increase of postage rates. The income tax, of course, most directly affects the masses of the people, since the lowering of the exemption limit to $1,000 for unmarried persons and $2,000 for heads of families enormously increased the number from whom the tax would be collected. The income tax law provides

330

for a tax to be paid by unmarried persons of 2 per cent on income above $1,000 but less than $3,000, 4 per cent on the income between $3,000 and $5,000, and so on. Heads of families are taxed 2 per cent on income above $2,000 but less than $4,000, 4 per cent on income between $4,000 and $5,000, and so on. But above $5,000 incomes are subjects to an extra levy, or surtax, so that the amount of income between $5,000 and $7,500 is subject to a total income tax, including both normal and extra, of 5 per cent; and between $7,500 and $10,000, 6 per cent. The surtax further increases with higher incomes, so that amounts of $1,000,000 are taxable at 65 per cent, with 1 per cent additional for each half million up to $2,000,000. All incomes over the latter amount are taxable at 67 per cent.

Typical income tax levies on heads of families are as follows: Income of $2,500, tax is $10; income of $3,000, tax is $20; income of $3,500, tax is $30; income of $4,000, tax is $40; income of $4,500, tax is $60; income of $5,000, tax is $80. Unmarried persons would pay in this way: Income of $1,500, tax is $10; income of $2,000, tax is $20; income of $2,500, tax is $30; income of $3,000, tax is $40; income of $3,500, tax is $60; income of $4,000, tax is $80; income of $4,500, tax is $100; income of $5,000, tax is $120.

SEVEN MILLIONS TAXED

This income tax was first levied on incomes received during 1917, and was to be paid on or before June 15, 1918, the amount of income being reported to the government by March 1st. Because of the lowering of the exemption limit, it was estimated that no fewer than seven million persons would be subject to this tax, against fewer than half a million under the old law which applied to the incomes of 1916. The numbers of persons taxed on incomes of various sizes in 1916 were as follows:

Size of Incomes.	Number of Taxpayers.
$3,000–$4,000	85,122
4,000–5,000	72,027
5,000–10,000	150,551
10,000–15,000	45,305
15,000–20,000	22,621
20,000–25,000	12,956
25,000–30,000	8,055
30,000–40,000	10,068
40,000–50,000	5,611
50,000–100,000	10,452
100,000–150,000	2,900
150,000–200,000	1,284
200,000–250,000	726
250,000–300,000	427
300,000–400,000	469
400,000–500,000	245
500,000–1,000,000	376
1,000,000 and over	206
Total taxpayers	429,401

It was announced at the beginning of July, 1918, that the total receipts from taxes on incomes and on excess profits for the fiscal year ending June 30th had been $2,821,340,801. At that time the government had in mind a further extension of taxation, perhaps with a lowering of the minimum limit of taxable incomes.

CORPORATION TAXES

Corporations pay income taxes, also, but on a different basis. Their net income is subject to a tax of 6 per cent under the new war revenue act, and certain technical deductions are allowed. Corporation returns are due between January 1st and March 1st for the preceding calendar year, and companies operating on a fiscal year basis must report within sixty days after the end of the fiscal year.

Another kind of tax is laid on excess profits of businesses having invested capital. On this basis, taxes on net incomes or profits in excess of certain deductions are at the rate of 20 per cent of the amount of net income in excess of the deduction and not in excess of 15 per cent on the invested capital; 25 per cent on the amount in excess of 15 per cent and not in excess of 20 per cent; 35 per cent on the amount in excess of 20 per cent and not in excess of 25 per cent; 40 per cent on the amount in excess of 25 per cent and not in excess of 33 per cent, and 60 per cent on the amount in excess of 33 per cent.

Before a tax is levied on excess profits, a business is permitted to make the same percentage of profit on its invested capital that it made on its invested capital during 1911, 1912 and 1913, the so-called "pre-war" period, providing that is not more than 9 per cent, and $3,000 additional for a corporation or $6,000 for a partnership or individual. These are the deductions which are not taxable.

LOANS TO OUR ALLIES

Down to the end of December, 1917, the following loans had been made to the allied nations, largely, of course, in the form of credits for supplies purchased in the United States:

Great Britain	$2,045,000,000
France	1,285,000,000
Russia	325,000,000
Italy	500,000,000
Belgium	77,400,000
Serbia	4,000,000
Total	$4,236,400,000

Of this enormous amount, $3,528,629,750 had actually been paid or credited to them; the remainder awaiting their needs and demands.

By the middle of 1918 the total loans to Allies amounted to $4,765,000,000; the increase being chiefly to France and Great Britain.

MONEY IN AMERICA

In spite of, or perhaps rather because of, these stupendous operations, the stock of money in the United States has greatly increased, as has, also, the per capita circulation The amount of gold coin in the United States at the outbreak of the war in August, 1914, was $1,887,271,000, and by July 1, 1918, it had grown to nearly twice as much, or $3,042,703,219. At the beginning of the war this country had less than one-fourth of the world's gold money, and at the end of 1917 it had more than one-third of it.

The amount of money in circulation in the United States also has increased. In December, 1913, it was $35.03 for every member of the population, and in December, 1917, it was $48.50.

A YEAR OF WAR FINANCE

In the fiscal year ending June 30, 1918, more than twelve billion dollars was expended by the United States government on account of the great war; whereas the entire expenditures of the government before the war were less than one billion.

With not quite all the figures in, expenses for the entire fiscal year were reported as follows:

Ordinary expenses for various government departments, $7,567,000,000; payments to Allies, $4,708,000,000; interest on Liberty bonds and other public debt items, $175,000,000;

federal farm loans (to be repaid), $65,000,000; Panama Canal, $19,000,000. In addition, $6,747,000,000 certificates, issued earlier in the year, were redeemed, $27,362,000 one-year Treasury notes were paid, and $21,536,000 national bank and Federal Reserve Bank notes were retired.

RECEIPTS FOR YEAR

Receipts for the year, without records of the last two days, were reported as follows: Liberty loans, $7,563,000,-000; income and excess profits taxes, $2,115,000,000 (with probably $500,000,000 or more yet to come in); miscellaneous revenue sources, $863,000,000; war savings and thrift stamps, $296,000,000; customs (tariff revenue), $178,000,000; miscellaneous revenue, $287,000,000; Panama Canal tolls, $5,846,000. The government also took in $8,468,000 from sale of certificates of indebtedness, redeemed later in the year; $1,020,000 from postal savings bonds; $19,150,000 deposited for purchase of one-year Treasury notes under the federal reserve act, and $10,240,-000 deposited for retirement of national bank and Federal Reserve Bank notes.

The big proportions of government financing in this year are shown sharply by comparison with records of the preceding year, itself a record. Then, ordinary expenses were $1,147,000,000; loans to Allies, $875,000,000, or a total of less than $2,000,000,000. Ordinary revenue receipts were $1,118,000,000 and payments on the first Liberty Loan amounted to $1,485,000,000.

CHAPTER XXVIII

ORGANIZING FOR NATIONAL DEFENSE

Creation of the Council of National Defense — An Advisory Commission of the Nation's Leading Business and Professional Men — A Multitude of Committees and Sub-Committees to Look after All Departments of Activity in the Prosecution of the War — Government Control of the Railroads — Food Administration — The Shipping Board — Building Ten Times Our Former Ocean Tonnage.

IN PURSUANCE of the purpose of marshalling the whole nation for service of some kind in the war, Congress authorized the formation of a Council of National Defense, and also an Advisory Commission to co-operate with it. The Council was charged with the "co-ordination of industries and resources for the national security and welfare," and with the "creation of relations which will render possible in time of need the immediate concentration and utilization of the resources of the nation." In pursuance of those aims the Council was charged with a number of specific duties, to wit:

DUTIES OF THE COUNCIL

1. To supervise and direct investigation, and make recommendations to the President and the heads of executive departments as to—

(a) The location of railroads with reference to the frontier of the United States, so as to render possible expeditious concentration of troops and supplies to points of defense.

(b) The co-ordination of military, industrial, and commercial purposes in the location of extensive highways and branch lines of railroads.

336

(*c*) The utilization of waterways.

(*d*) The mobilization of military and naval resources for defense.

(*e*) The increase of domestic production of articles and materials essential to the support of armies and of the people during the interruption of foreign commerce.

(*f*) The development of seagoing transportation.

(*g*) Data as to amounts, location, method, and means of production and availability of military supplies.

(*h*) The giving of information to producers and manufacturers as to the class of supplies needed by the military and other services of the government, the requirements relating thereto, and the creation of relations which will render possible in time of need the immediate concentration and utilization of the resources of the Nation.

2. To report to the President or to the heads of executive departments upon special inquiries or subjects appropriate thereto.

3. To submit an annual report to Congress, through the President, giving as full a statement of the activities of the Council and the agencies subordinate to it as is consistent with the public interest, including an itemized account of the expenditures made by the Council, or authorized by it in as full detail as the public interest will permit, providing, however, that when deemed proper the President may authorize in amounts stipulated by him, unvouchered expenditures and report the gross so authorized not itemized.

Six members of the President's Cabinet were appointed to this Council, namely: Newton D. Baker, Secretary of War; Josephus Daniels, Secretary of the Navy; Franklin K. Lane, Secretary of the Interior; David F. Houston, Secretary of Agriculture; William C. Redfield, Secretary of Commerce; and William B. Wilson, Secretary of Labor.

THE ADVISORY COMMISSION

The members of the Advisory Council and the departments of work assigned to them were as follows:

Daniel Willard, Chairman, President of the Baltimore and Ohio Railroad—Transportation and communication.

Howard E. Coffin, Vice-President of the Hudson Motor Company—Munitions, manufacturing, including standardization and industrial relations.

Julius Rosenwald, President of Sears, Roebuck & Co.—Supplies, including clothing.

Bernard M. Baruch, financier—Raw materials, minerals, and metals.

Dr. Hollis Godfrey, President of the Drexel Institute—Engineering and education.

Samuel Gompers, President of the American Federation of Labor—Labor, including conservation of health and welfare of workers.

Dr. Franklin Martin, Secretary-General of the American College of Surgeons—Medicine, surgery, and sanitation.

Walter S. Gifford was made director, and Grosvenor B. Clarkson was made secretary of both the Council and the Commission.

Subordinate to the Council there were constituted the following named boards and sections:

The General Munitions Board, Munitions Standard Board, Aircraft Production Board, Medical Section, Commercial Economy Board, Inter-Departmental Advisory Board, Co-operative Committees on the Purchase of Army Supplies (United States Chamber of Commerce), National Research Council, Committee on Shipping, Committee on Women's Defense Work, Committee on Coal Production, Section on Co-operation with States.

The General Munitions Board was presently superseded

338

by a War Industries Board, composed of the following seven members: Daniel Willard, chairman; Bernard M. Baruch, Robert S. Lovett, Robert S. Brookings, Hugh Frayne, Rear-Admiral Frank F. Fletcher, and Lieutenant-Colonel P. E. Pierce. This last-named board acts as a general clearing house for the war industry needs and activities of the government.

MANY OTHER ORGANIZATIONS

There were also constituted, all tributary to the Council of National Defense, the following:

A Director of Steel Supply.

A Commercial Economy Board.

A Committee on Shipping.

A Committee on Inland Water Transportation.

A Committee on Women's Defense Work.

A Section on Co-operation with the States.

A Committee on Coal Production.

A Committee on Engineering and Education, with sub-committees on Universities and Colleges, and on Secondary and Normal Schools.

A Committee on Highways Transportation.

A Committee on Labor, with sub-committees on Mediation and Conciliation, on Wages and Hours, on Women in Industry, on Welfare Work (with nine sectional committees); on Information and Statistics; on the Press; on Publicity; on Cost of Living and Domestic Economy; and an Executive Committee.

A General Medical Board, with more than a score of sub-committees, some of which were again subdivided; and

A Committee on the Standardization of Medical and Surgical Supplies and Equipments.

State Councils of Defense were also organized in the

various states, and the Women's Committee of the Council of National Defense also formed state organizations

RAILROADS TAKEN BY THE GOVERNMENT

Five days after the declaration of war, in April, practically all American railroad companies voluntarily organized themselves for war service. They agreed to waive all competition, and to operate the entire 260,000 miles of road as a single system. To facilitate such operation they formed an Executive Committee, commonly known as the Railroad War Board, to have supreme direction of the entire railroad service of the country. This board consisted of Fairfax Harrison, of the Southern Railway; Howard Elliott, of the New York, New Haven and Hartford; Hale Holden, of the Chicago, Burlington and Quincy; Samuel Rea, of the Pennsylvania; and Julius Krutschnitt, of the Southern Pacific.

The board went promptly to work to increase the efficiency of the roads, particularly for the transportation of soldiers, of war supplies, and of important freight such as food and fuel. The roads were, however, handicapped by the existing laws prohibiting pooling and combinations among competing lines, and they suffered from the fact that while their costs of operation had greatly increased, through the rise in wages and in prices of materials, the government would not permit them to make a corresponding increase in freight rates. The result was that despite their best efforts the roads were unequal to the task which was given to them, and serious congestion of freight occurred, causing scarcity of food, fuel and other supplies.

Partly to remedy, if possible, these conditions, and partly to forefend a threatened general strike of railroad employees, on December 27th the President, acting under the law of August 29, 1916, issued a proclamation taking over for government control and operation every railroad in the United States, together with all appurtenant steamship lines, telegraphs, etc. This act became operative at noon of December 28th. William G. McAdoo, Secretary of the Treasury, while retaining the latter office, was made Director-General of Railroads. The Railroads War Board thereupon resigned, and was replaced by Mr. McAdoo with an Advisory Committee, consisting of John S. Williams, Controller of the Currency; Hale Holden, of the Chicago, Burlington and Quincy Railroad, who had been a member of the Railroads War Board; Henry Walters of the Atlantic Coast Line; Walker D. Hines, of the Atchison, Topeka and Santa Fé Railroad, and Edward Chambers, also of the last-named railroad and Transportation Director of the Food Administration. Under this management the roads were freed from legal restrictions as to pooling and combinations, and were all operated as a single system.

The President, in an address to Congress on January 4, 1918, suggested further legislation dealing with this great undertaking, which was promptly forthcoming. The roads are guaranteed by the government an income equal to their average net operating income for the three years preceding the government's taking of them, and also that their property, fixed and movable, will be maintained and returned to them in as good condition as when it was taken by the government. This action by the government was regarded with general satisfaction by the roads and by the public, a satisfaction which was manifested in a marked rising of the prices of railroad securities.

THE FOOD ADMINISTRATION

Another supremely important war measure was the establishment of government control over the general food supplies of the nation. Following an act of Congress of August 10, 1917, the President appointed Herbert Hoover—who had been at the head of the relief commission in Belgium—Food Administrator, with a Fair Price Committee and a Wheat Purchasing Committee to assist him. A great Federal corporation was formed, with $50,000,000 capital, to handle the entire wheat crop of the country, abolish speculation and equalize and stabilize prices both to the producer and the consumer. A minimum price of $2 a bushel was guaranteed to farmers for 1918 wheat; all elevators and mills of more than 100 barrels a day capacity were required to be licensed; and steps were taken to regulate and standardize the price of bread. The operations of the Food Administrator were also extended to the control of prices of sugar and other commodities, and to the prevention of hoarding. An elaborate system of popular registration and enrolment in a Food Conservation League was conducted throughout the country, the object being to influence people to avoid waste, and to make such substitutions of foods as would enable this country to ship abroad to its army and to the allies the largest possible quantity of wheat, meat, fats, and other articles specially needed there.

The work of the Federal Food Administrator was seconded by State Food Administrators, and by special laws passed in many states. There was also a nation-wide movement to increase production by the cultivation of waste lands and the planting of gardens on vacant lots in city and country.

NATIONAL SHIPBUILDING

Still another gigantic undertaking by the government was the building of a vast fleet of merchant vessels, to take the place, and more, of the vessels destroyed by the German submarine boats. This was necessary in order to provide transportation not only for our own troops and their supplies when they were sent to Europe, but also for the supplies of food and munitions which were absolutely essential to our allies. A United States Shipping Board was created, and under it an Emergency Fleet Corporation, and the latter undertook the construction, both in the government's own yards and by contract with other builders, the construction of the needed vessels. Many of these were to be built of wood, while others were of "fabricated" steel construction, meaning that they were all to be made exactly alike, like so many automobiles, of railroad cars, this uniform construction of course greatly expediting and simplifying the work.

Despite some regrettable delay, due to divided and conflicting counsels, the Emergency Fleet Corporation during 1917 began the construction of 8,246,308 tons of shipping, and by December 1st was able to report that this was 18.2 per cent completed, with an assured prospect of fully completing more than 5,000,000 in 1918. This progress was divided as follows: Wood and composite vessels, 437, of 1,551,900 tons, 10 per cent completed; requisitioned steel ships, 431, of 3,056,008 tons, 39 per cent completed; contract steel ships, 527, of 3,638,400 tons, 4 per cent completed.

A STILL BIGGER PROGRAMME

At the beginning of January, 1918, the Shipping Board contemplated a greatly enlarged programme. It asked Congress for authority to place at once additional contracts for $701,000,000 worth of ships, and $82,000,000 for enlarging shipyards and housing for workmen, which, added to the original authorization of $1,234,000,000, would make more than two billion dollars for shipbuilding and would promise the addition of at least 15,000,000 tons to the American merchant marine on the high seas. How vast an increase this will be may be seen from the facts that in 1916 our entire steam shipping in the foreign trade was only 1,573,705 tons, and that the greatest building of steel and iron steamships in any one year in this century was 442,625 in 1908, while in other years it was less than half as much. The entire steam shipping of the world at the outbreak of the war, including that in coasting trades and on the Great Lakes, was less than 45,500,000 tons, or only three times what the United States is now engaged in building.

The Shipping Board was able to announce on July 2, 1918, the completion of the first million tons of shipping constructed under its direction in American shipyards, and two days later Independence Day was celebrated by the launching at the various shipyards of 93 vessels aggregating 460,200 deadweight tons. The following table shows the deadweight tonnage of vessels completed and put into commission in the first six months of 1918:

January	88,507
February	123,625
March	172,611
April	160,286
May	259,241
June	280,400
Total	1,084,670

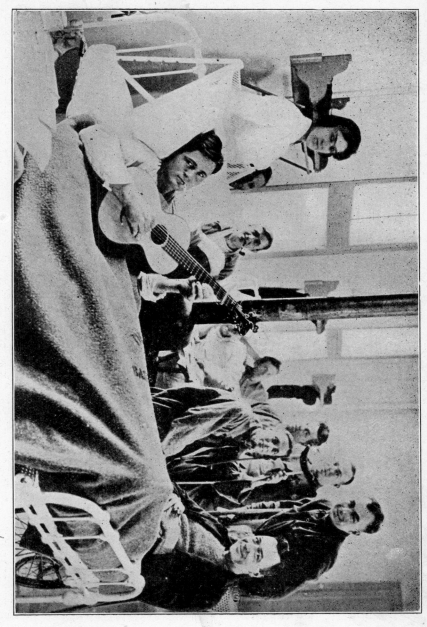

Sickness Cannot Dim Our Fighters' Cheerfulness

A batch of convalescents in a Base Hospital somewhere in France, whiling away the time until they can get back to the firing line. The Red Cross has worked wonders in caring for the health, comfort and happiness of our boys at the front.

UNITED STATES MARINES IN FRANCE PRACTICE GRENADE THROWING

Throwing the deadly hand grenade from the trenches is an accomplishment easily acquired by our marines. The men in this picture are in a practice trench with their French instructors.

Copyright by Committee on Public Information. From Underwood & Underwood, N. Y.

Chapter XXIX

CARING FOR THE SOLDIERS

Construction and Equipment of the Training Camps — Guarding Against Disease — Provision for the Physical, Mental and Social Welfare of Soldiers — Work of the Y. M. C. A., the Young Men's Hebrew Association and the Knights of Columbus, at Home and Abroad — The American Red Cross and Its Gigantic Work — A War Fund of a Hundred Million Dollars and a Membership of Twenty-Two Millions.

MORE THAN thirty new cities were created offhand, in the summer of 1917, for the occupation of our army. Half of them were, it is true, cities of canvas, for the hundreds of thousands of National Guard men of the various states were housed in tents, tens of thousands of them in each of the sixteen camps. But for the more numerous National Army, of men conscribed in the select draft, sixteen permanent cantonments were built, of large two and three-story buildings of wood and steel. The magnitude of these may be estimated from the fact that each of the sixteen cantonments provided quarters for more than 40,000 men.

The sites for these cantonments were chosen with much care, regard being had to their elevation, drainage, dryness of air, water supply, accessibility, and proximity to trunk-line railroads. Selection being made, and possession of the land acquired, tremendous physical tasks presented themselves, all requiring to be done with the utmost possible expedition. The land had to be cleared of timber, buildings, fences and other incumbrances. Ditches and ponds had to be filled up or drained and permanent water-courses regulated. Much grading had to be done. Many miles of macadam road had to be constructed at each cantonment, within its area and also to connect it with railroads and other bases of supply. Miles of sewers had to be built, and other miles of water mains laid. Vast steam and electric systems, for power, heating and lighting, had to be constructed. In some places elaborate processes for the elimination of malaria by the extermination of mosquitoes were necessary. Each cantonment and a one-mile zone surrounding it was thus freed from the pestilence-bearing insects.

BUILDING THE CANTONMENTS

Then came the task of erecting substantial buildings for the housing of more than 40,000 men at each of the sixteen cantonments, for storehouses, and a multitude of other purposes. The speed with which this work was done was little less than marvelous, reminding us of the magic of Aladdin's lamp. The standard barracks buildings were all of uniform size and plan, 43 by 140 feet and two stories high. Lumber and other materials were turned out at mills and factories of the exact sizes needed, so that no cutting and fitting on the ground would be needed. The result was that at Camp Travis, in Texas, such a building was put up, complete and ready for occupancy, in less than two hours! The same speed was achieved at Fort Taylor, in Kentucky, with this added feature of interest, that the lumber used had exactly a week before been in the form of living trees in a forest a hundred miles or more away!

Each cantonment occupies from 3,000 to 7,000 acres of land, or from four or five to eleven or twelve square miles, generally in the form of a circle or ellipse. Around the rim are built the barracks for the men. Inside are the officers' quarters and administration buildings, hospitals, etc. In each a large field is reserved for drilling purposes. The standard barracks building is of wood, the frame covered with matched sheathing and then with a prepared roofing of tarred canvas. On the ground floor are the kitchen, dining rooms, shower baths, lavatories, etc. On the second floor are sleeping quarters for 200 men. Seeing that each such building accommodates only 200 men and that there are more than 40,000 men in each cantonment, the number of buildings required may be reckoned.

At Camp Devens, in Massachusetts, there are more than 1,600 buildings of all kinds, twenty-five miles of sewers, thirteen miles of water mains, and twenty of macadam roads.

The provisioning of the cantonments is another gigantic job. The weekly rations for a cantonment of 40,000 men comprise 150,000 pounds of fresh beef, 75,000 pounds of fresh pork, 75,000 pounds of mutton, 4,000 bushels of potatoes, and 25,000 pounds of butter, besides milk, bread, miscellaneous vegetables, and what not else. Multiply these figures by 32, and we have the weekly market bill of the army in training camps.

WELFARE WORK FOR SOLDIERS

But soldiers do not live by bread alone. Their moral, mental and social welfare must also be regarded. The government provides at each cantonment a hospital with from 1,000 to 1,500 beds, and a theater with about 3,000 seats, and other agencies supply other equipments, of club rooms, libraries, and other establishments to continue to the soldiers in camp a measure of the comforts, pleasures and privileges of home. In such work the lead is taken by the Young Men's Christian Association, the Young Men's Hebrew Association, the Knights of Columbus, the Women's

347

Christian Temperance Union, and the Library Association of America. The Library Association has conducted a nation-wide campaign for supplying the army with books at the rate of at least one volume for every man, which means more than a million volumes collected during 1917. The books selected have a large range, of fiction, history, travel and adventure, and educational works. The Women's Christian Temperance Union provides club houses in which refreshments may be had, with reading rooms, game rooms, etc., so as to lessen the temptation to frequent liquor saloons.

The other three organizations named work harmoniously on parallel lines, serving respectively the Protestant, the Jewish and the Roman Catholic elements of the army. Of the three the Y. M. C. A. is the largest and the most widely known. It has at every cantonment at least one Association Building, which is a center of social welfare as well as of purely religious work. Religious meetings are held, and there are also lectures, moving picture shows, games, reading rooms, and indeed everything possible to serve the social interests of the soldiers.

THE Y. M. C. A. AT THE FRONT

These forms of service are not, however, confined to the training camps and cantonments. They are extended to the battle front, and indeed it is there that they are most active and useful. How varied and practical the work of the Y. M. C. A. is at the seat of war in France has been told by Mr. Francis B. Sayre, writing in "Association Men," a publication of the Y. M. C. A., on his personal observations in the camps and trenches of northern France. He found that the local secretaries were organizing educational classes, study groups, Bible classes, etc., and were

348

·holding personal conferences with many men who needed special advice or encouragement. At one point he found the following programme of social activities for a week:

Monday Evening.—Scotch stories and lecture.

Tuesday Evening.—Regimental Band concert.

Wednesday Afternoon (half-holiday).—Inter-company athletics.

Wednesday Evening.—Minstrel show arranged by a sergeant.

Thursday Evening.—Musical evening—local talent, violin, harmonica, banjo and quartet discovered in the regiment.

Friday Evening.—Men busy with military night maneuvers.

Saturday Night.—Moving pictures. Wild West and Charlie Chaplin received with a whoop of delight. They were the first movies the men had seen in France.

Sunday Morning.—Chaplain's Bible class.

Sunday Evening.—Evening service, good singing and a strong practical message.

SOUND MIND AND SOUND BODY

Mr. Sayre paid special attention to the provision of healthful out-of-door sports for the men, as counter-attractions to less desirable diversion. "Few men," he says, "desire to do evil, least of all the American soldier, who is, in the main, a splendid specimen of manhood; and our constant object, where we see a particular temptation staring a man in the face, is to provide counter-attractions, trusting the soldier to make the right choice. With that thought in mind we have undertaken to develop a resort in the French Alps for soldiers on leave, where snow-shoeing, ski-jumping, and winter sports can be developed, and which should prove far more attractive to the red-blooded man than the danger-ridden streets of Paris. With General Pershing's enthusiastic approval we plan to develop and maintain a great healthy playground for the American Army, where soldiers on leave can forget all about the horrors and nightmare of war, can get refreshed in mind as well as in body, and then go back to their work with new energy and spirit, far more effective fighters."

RELIGION ON THE FIRING LINE

The work of the Association is carried to the very firing line, and it is there that it is most earnest and practical. "The closer one gets to the front," says Mr. Sayre, "the more religion must take on the form of service—the giving of a cup of cold water, which in this case means hot coffee. I think of a typical dugout on the crest of a hard-fought hill, which we came to one evening about sunset. It was a battlefield but freshly taken from the enemy; the stench of the dead was still in the air, and the ground was torn and churned. . . . Further and further we made our way up towards the front-line trenches; finally, at a point under almost constant shellfire, we found a little Y. M. C. A. dugout. It was very filthy and small, with almost no accommodations; and yet here we found a secretary unflinchingly sticking by his post, in spite of the fact that in this dugout twice during the preceding week an orderly was killed by his side—living under shellfire so that he could serve hot coffee to soldiers returning out of the front-line trench and minister to their most immediate needs. No one but a half-frozen soldier coming out of the horrors of a front-line trench could suspect how much religion was contained in that simple giving of a cup of hot coffee. But to many a one it must have preached of Christ's love on

350

earth and the meaning of true religion as they had never understood such things. Men do not soon forget such sermons.

"When the Canadians stormed over the top of a certain famous ridge, and the battlefield was full of needy, suffering men, a Y. M. C. A. secretary appeared serving out hot coffee on the ridge within half an hour after it was stormed, before the line was yet consolidated. 'Everybody else was lying flat in that rain of bullets,' one of the officers said, 'everybody except just that secretary; and the sight of him standing alone, forgetting everything except the men he was risking his life to help is what gave religion to me.'"

THE AMERICAN RED CROSS

Greatest of all the agencies of blessing to the soldier at the front, when he is suffering the wounds of battle, is the American Red Cross. This famous organization has for many years been conspicuous in works of relief and mercy in peace and in war, but in the present emergency it has immeasurably outdone all its former records. Before our participation in this war, the Red Cross organization in America was much smaller, numerically, than in any other important country. But soon after the declaration of war there was a notable rally which increased its membership from a few hundred thousand to about five millions. At the same time a war relief fund of $100,000,000 was raised, and hundreds of thousands of women all over the country entered systematically into the work of making bandages and other supplies for use in the hospitals at the front. Even this, however, was not enough. In December, 1917, culminating on Christmas eve, there was a nation-wide "drive" for the Red Cross, which resulted in the enrolment of nearly 17,000,000 new members, bringing the total up to about 22,000,000, or fully one-fifth the entire population of the United States.

The aims of the Red Cross were officially declared to be:

First, to be ready to care for our soldiers and sailors whenever and wherever that care may be needed.

Second, to aid the shortening of the war by relieving suffering and bolstering up the courage and morale of the civilian populations as well as the armies of our Allies.

Third, the carrying of a message of relief and mercy, as an expression of the sacrifice and sympathy of the American people, to let our Allies know that this is not a *mere* money-making nation, but a great money-making nation—and thus, through promoting a better understanding between ourselves and all the allied nations, lay foundation for an enduring peace after the war.

HOW RED CROSS WORKS

But these aims, thus expressed, give only a slight idea of the variety and magnitude of Red Cross labors. There is an elaborate system of stretcher bearers and nurses and ambulances, beginning in the foremost line of trenches, and extending back to the field-dressing stations, thence by bearers or ambulance to the field hospitals, thence by motor ambulance to the evacuation hospital, thence by Red Cross train to the big base hospital, and finally by Red Cross trains to the convalescent and general hospital zone.

But this is only a part of the work. Far back of the firing line there are millions of non-combatants suffering from the horrors of war. There is famine; there are the plagues which are attendant upon famine; there are myriads lacking clothing; there are ruined homes to be restored. And so the Red Cross works through factories and shops, railroads and motor trucks, steamships and warehouses,

352

lunch-rooms, hospitals, asylums, physicians, traveling dispensaries, shower baths on wheels, carpenters and cooks, chaplains and chauffeurs; undertaking everything that needs to be done to succor and relieve the stricken and to rehabilitate nations prostrated and ravaged by the iron hand of war

SAVING THE CHILDREN

Not the least important work of the Red Cross is that of caring for the children of France, so that they shall not perish of famine and disease in the stress of wartime, but shall live, well and strong, to grow up and take the places of their fathers who are dying that the nation may live. A graphic view of this work—only a single example among thousands—is given in a Red Cross report:

"We have established a temporary children's shelter at Toul, a city in the section of the war zone recently bombarded by the enemy.

Gas bombs are being used by the Germans, and the inhabitants of the nearby villages were obliged to wear face masks to escape asphyxiation. This mode of protection, however, is not feasible for children, and it was found necessary to send the children away at once.

The prefect of the department telegraphed to a worker in Paris that 750 children had been suddenly thrust upon his hands and that he needed immediate assistance.

The next day eight workers left the Red Cross headquarters—a doctor, an experienced nurse, two auxiliary nurses, a bacteriologist and an administrative director and two women to take charge of the bedding, clothing, food, etc.

They found that twenty-one of the children were infants under one year, and the remainder were under eight years.

They were herded together in an old barracks, dirty, practically unfurnished and with no sanitary appliances. Sick children were crowded in with the well, and skin diseases and vermin abounded.

Within two days the children had been thoroughly cleaned and transferred to a new and clean barracks. Medical care had been given and nurses secured for the babies, suitable food provided and a classification of all the refugees made to prevent the separation of members of the same family. The organization of an institution for the care of these children has been worked out."

OTHER RELIEF ORGANIZATIONS

The National Special Aid Society is a nation-wide organization engaged in preparing clothing and other comforts for American soldiers and sailors. A partial list of other war relief organizations is as follows:

American Aid for Homeless Belgian Children. Gifts to be sent to National City Bank, New York City.

American Ambulance Hospital in France. J. P. Morgan & Co., 23 Wall St., New York City.

American Authors' Fund for the Relief of the Wounded Soldiers of the Allied Nations. State Street Trust Co., 33 State St., Boston.

American Artists' Committee of One Hundred Relief Fund for the Familes of French Soldier Artists. William Bailey Faxon, Treasurer, 215 West 57th St., New York City.

American Branch of the Fatherless Children of France Fund. Walter W. Price, Treasurer, 111 Broadway, New York City.

American Comfort Packet Committee, Mrs. Mary Hatch Willard, Chairman, 66 West 39th St., New York City.

American Committee for Armenian and Syrian Relief. Charles R. Crane, Treasurer, 70 Fifth Ave., New York City.

American Committee for Training in Suitable Trades the Maimed Soldiers of France. Mrs. Edmund L. Baylies, Biltmore Hotel, New York City.

American Fund for French Wounded. Mrs. Ethelbert Nevin, Chairman, 122 Madison Ave., New York City.

American Girls' Aid (French). Miss Gladys Hollingsworth, Chairman, 293 Fifth Ave., New York City.

American Hostels for Refugees in Paris and Children of Flanders Rescue Committee. Henry W. Munroe, Jr., Treasurer, 21 East 11th St., New York City.

American Huguenot Committee. Edmond E. Robert, Treasurer, 105 East 22d St., New York City.

American Jewish Relief Committee for Sufferers from the War. Felix M. Warburg, Treasurer, 174 Second Ave., New York City.

American Jewish Relief Committee. Herbert H. Lehman, Treasurer, 20 Exchange Place, New York City.

American Society for Relief of French War Orphans. Thomas Cochran, 120 Broadway, New York City.

American Students' Committee of the Ecole des Beaux Arts. Henry R. Sedgwick, Treasurer, 107 East 37th St., New York City.

American Women's Committee for the Charities of the Queen of Belgium. John Moffat, Honorary Secretary, 200 Fifth Ave., New York City.

American Women's War Relief Fund. John Moffat, Fifth Avenue Building, New York City.

Australian War Relief Fund. A. J. Howard, Treasurer, 435 Fifth Ave., New York City.

Belgian Refugee Workshop Fund. Prof. Albert G. van Flecke, American Security and Trust Co., Washington. D. C.

Belgian Relief Fund. J. P. Morgan & Co., depository, 10 Bridge St., New York City.

Blue Cross Fund for Wounded Horses. Mrs. Elphinston Maitland, Secretary, 55 East 93d St., New York City.

British-American War Relief Fund. Henry J. Whitehouse, Treasurer, 681 Fifth Ave., New York City.

British Red Cross Committee. Edwin S. Marston, President, 12 Bridge St., New York City.

British War Relief Association. Henry Clews, Treasurer, 542 Fifth Ave., New York City.

Bulgarian Relief Committee. Dr. Hugo Schweitzer, Treasurer, 30 Church St., New York City.

Cardinal Mercier Fund, Maryland Committee. James Augustus Whiteley, Chairman, 223 West Lanvale St., Baltimore.

Cardinal Mercier Fund, New York Committee. J. P. Morgan & Co., 23 Wall St., New York City.

Central Committee for the Relief of Lithuanian War Sufferers, M. Salcius, Secretary, 200 Fifth Ave., New York City.

Children of America's Army of Relief. The Federal Trust Co., 85 Devonshire St., Boston.

Commission for Relief in Belgium. Alexander J. Hemphill, Treasurer, 120 Broadway, New York City.

Commission for the Relief of Belgian Prisoners in Germany. James A. Blair, Jr., Treasurer, 200 Fifth Ave., New York City.

Committee for Men Blinded in Battle. William Forbes Morgan, Jr., Treasurer, 17 East 38th St., New York City.

Committee of Mercy. August Belmont, Treasurer, 200 Fifth Ave., New York City.

Dollar Christmas Fund for Destitute Belgians. Henry Clews, Treasurer, 66 Broadway, New York City.

Duryea War Relief. Mrs. Charles H. Ditson, 259 Fifth Ave., New York City.

Emergency Aid Committee (Philadelphia). Mrs. J. Norman Jackson, Treasurer, 1428 Walnut St., Philadelphia.

Fatherless Children of France (Orphelinat des Armées). J. P. Morgan & Co., depository, Fifth Avenue Building, New York City.

Flotilla Committee. Miss Emily Chauncey, Executive, 38 West 39th St., New York City.

Franco-American Committee for the Protection of the Children of the Frontier of France. Frederic R. Coudert, Treasurer, 2 Rector St., New York City.

Franco-Serbian Field Hospital of America. Henry B. Britton, Treasurer, 17 West 30th St., New York City.

General Italian Relief Committee, Longacre Building, West 42d St., New York City.

International Reconstruction League. John Moffat, Executive Chairman, 200 Fifth Ave., New York City.

Irish Relief Fund Committee. Thomas Hughes Kelley, Treasurer, 5 Beekman St., New York City.

Lafayette Fund. Francis Roche, Treasurer, Vanderbilt Hotel, New York City.

Montenegrin Relief Association of America. Jane Stewart Cushman, Treasurer, 105 West 59th St., New York City.

National Allied Relief Committee. Karl Davis Robinson, Secretary, 200 Fifth Ave., New York City.

New York Surgical Dressings Committee. Mrs. Edward Ringwood Hewitt, 19 East 59th St., New York City.

People's Relief Committee for the Jewish War Sufferers. Isaac Goldberg, Treasurer, 171 East Broadway, New York City.

Permanent Blind Relief War Fund. F. A. Vanderlip, Honorary Treasurer, 590 Fifth Ave., New York City.

Persian War Relief Fund. Edward M. Bulkeley, Treasurer, 25 Broad St., New York City.

Polish Hospital Supply and Clothing Committee (auxiliary of the Polish Relief Fund), 681 Fifth Ave., New York City. Miss Eleann Blodgett, Chairman.

Polish University Grants Committee of the Polish Victims' Relief Fund. Mme. Jane Arctowska, 33 West 42d St., New York City.

Polish Victims' Relief Fund, W. O. Gorski, Executive Secretary, 33 West 42d St., New York City.

Prince of Wales National Relief Fund. R. M. Stuart Wortley, Treasurer, 25 Broad St., New York City.

Refugees in Russia. John Moffat, 200 Fifth Ave., New York City.

Relief Fund for the Families of French Soldier Artists. Wm. A. Coffin, Chairman, 58 West 57th St., New York City.

Roumanian Relief Committee of America. 43 Cedar St., New York City. Henry Clews, Treasurer.

Russian American Relief Association. Care National City Bank, 55 Wall St., New York City.

Russian War Relief Committee. John Moffat, Secretary, 200 Fifth Ave., New York City.

Secours National Fund for the Relief of Civilian War Sufferers in France. Mrs. Whitney Warren, 16 East 47th St., New York City.

Serbian Distress Fund (Boston). John F. Moors, Treasurer, 111 Devonshire St., Boston.

Serbian Hospital Fund. Otto T. Bannard, Treasurer, 1 Madison Ave., New York City.

Serbian Relief Committee. Miss F. Hastings, Secretary, 70 Fifth Ave.. New York City.

Shamrock Fund. Miss Mary Dougherty, Secretary, 165 Madison Ave., New York City.

Siberian Regiments American Ambulance Society. Samuel McRoberts, Honorary Treasurer, Flatiron Building, New York City.

Ukrainian War Relief Fund. Simon Yadlowsky, Treasurer, 83 Grand St., Jersey City, N. J.

Union Nationale des Eglises Réformées Evangéliques de France Emergency Relief Fund, 105 East 22d St., New York City.

Vacation War Relief Committee. Miss Emily Chauncey, Executive Secretary, 38 West 39th St., New York City.

War Babies' Cradle. Mrs. Jules S. Bache, Treasurer, 42 Broadway, New York City.

War Relief Clearing House for France and Her Allies. 40 Wall St., New York City. Thomas W. Lamont, Treasurer.

Zionist Medical Unit. Miss Henrietta Szold, Chairman, 44 East 23d St., New York City.

HEALTH OF THE ARMY

With the growth of the army and its active participation in the war, sanitary conditions improved, as the following table of the number of deaths to each thousand will show:

In 1898	20.14
In 1900	7.78
In 1901	6.90
In 1916	5.13
May, 1918	4.89
June, 1918	4.14

These are figures, of course, for only the troops in camps and cantonments in this country. The bed capacity of department hospitals in the United States on June 5, 1918, was 72,667, with a promise of increase soon to 87,344. The number of base and general hospitals in this country had been increased from seven to seventy-two; and the number of officers in the Medical Corps from 900 to 24,000 and of men from 8,000 to 148,000.

MORALS OF THE ARMY

Of the moral condition of the army, the Secretary of War said at the beginning of July, 1918:

"Consensus of opinion is that drunkenness in the army is completely under control, both in the United States and France. General Pershing states: 'As there is little beer sold in France, men who drink are thus limited to the light native wine used by all French people. Even this is discouraged among our troops in every possible way.'

"You may travel for weeks in France without seeing an intoxicated American soldier. In the *Congressional Record* on or about March 31st there is a reprinted statement of a journalist in France, beginning:

"'Every one is on the water wagon at the American front. During the last month I have been at the front daily and often twice a day, seeing thousands of American soldiers. In that time I saw exactly one man drunk, and one other who was under the influence of liquor.'

"The Third Assistant Secretary of War in ten days at a National Army camp adjacent to Chicago saw two men intoxicated

"There is no permanent military camp in the United States with a red-light district in its vicinity."

Chapter XXX

OUR SOLDIERS "OVER THERE"

Departure of the First American Troops for France — Their Enthusiastic Reception in London and Paris — Transportation of the "Rainbow Division" — Learning the Art of War as It is Practiced by the Huns — The First Engagements and the First Casualties — Americans and Aviation — Another Big Detachment Forwarded.

AS EARLY as June 26, 1917, the first detachment of the American Expeditionary Forces set out for France, under the command of Major-General William L. Sibert, to be followed as expeditiously as possible by many more, under the command of General Pershing. For the sake of security and especially of avoiding interception by German submarines, no announcement was made of the departure of troops from America, and the fact was not generally known until some weeks afterward. Thus it was at the middle of October that the so-called "Rainbow Division," composed of troops from every state in the Union, was sent, and it was not until December that the fact was published in the press. The Americans were received with unbounded enthusiasm in London and Paris, as an earnest of America's actual entry into the war.

As related in the press just six weeks later, long after their safe arrival in France, it was in the week of October 15th that the men of the Rainbow Division left Camp Mills, just outside of Mineola, Long Island.

The morning before the men in the Louisiana troop pulled down the canvas which marked the site where General W. A. Mann, commander of the 42d Division, and his staff, had made their headquarters. It was monotonously like the glorious autumn mornings the men of the Rainbow Division had wearied of. The skies were clear and brilliant and there was the faintest touch of cold in the air.

But it was vastly different, for with division headquarters down they knew that the trip to France, for weeks the predominating motif of their dreams by night, loomed dead ahead.

Theirs had been all the uncertainty of the man poised on the edge of a deep abyss. Now all that was gone. They were joyful in the consciousness that the "one big day" in France for which they were living, that day when they would be called on to "go over the top" and give, perhaps, all they had to give, was a vast step nearer.

OFF FOR THE WAR

It was the biggest day these soldier boys had known. Sunset did not bring the usual exodus to Hempstead and the nearby villages. Night came and found every man in camp waiting.

At 11 o'clock the buglers sounded "officers' call." One hour later the great body of the troops knew they were leaving Hempstead Plains the following morning. There was no heavy equipment to take. All that had gone two weeks before. The horses had gone a week before. All each man had to do was to pack his heavy marching equipment and sit tight until the order came.

Nineteen thousand men took part in that first movement. It began early in the morning. Contingents from twenty-four states left in the first batch. Eight thousand men, including units from Alabama, Ohio and the 165th Infantry, New York's "Old 69th," did not go that morning.

The movement began at 3 A. M. A yellow moon hung

like a skull in the skies as they tramped out of camp. They marched quietly. Down Clinton Road they swung, the ranks solid. The sides of the road were lined with the men who were not going yet, their faces white in the dark. There were no cheers. It was solemn departure.

The trains began hauling them away, but the morning sun found others still marching from camp.

Eight o'clock came and with it a rush of people from Mineola, Hempstead and nearby towns. Now there were cheers and shouts. By eleven o'clock the last of the first 19,000 men had left. The trains carried them to Long Island City, from where they proceeded to the transports waiting for them under steam and ready to put out to sea.

A week later the "Old 69th" and the other remaining units left. Their departure was staged in the early afternoon. This time there were crowds, mothers, and sweethearts and brothers. But those who saw the New York unit go were surprisingly few. No one had known the exact date. There had been delays, and so most of the men had already said their last farewells.

FINAL TRAINING FOR BATTLE

After our men had arrived in France, it was necessary for them to undergo a period of training, in order to familiarize them with the conditions of warfare "over there," which were quite different from anything which they had ever known before. They proved, however, apt pupils, surprising and gratifying their French teachers by the rapidity with which they learned and the efficiency which they showed. Before they were actually put upon the firing line many of them were engaged in important engineering work, and in that capacity some of them had their first taste of fighting. Indeed, the first casualties reported were the cases of two American engineers, who were wounded in the Somme region, in early November.

In that same month Americans contributed greatly to the success of General Byng's great stroke near Cambrai, one of the most sensational achievements of the war. They had a large part in pushing forward the railroads which were a vital adjunct to his advance. "The speed with which the lines have been laid through the broken Hindenburg defenses," said a correspondent, "has called forth the highest praise from the British authorities. The Americans have been working in shifts twenty-four hours a day, and no such amount of track has been laid in this region in so short a time before. The manner in which they stood up under the strain has led to their being dubbed the 'force of American athletes.' For these untiring soldiers are today as fit and as willing as they were before the battle began.

COOL WHILE SHELLS BURST

"Naturally, the Americans have for a long time been working under the range of enemy artillery, and more than once they have come under heavy shellfire. One of the most striking sights along the front has been that of the engineers laboring coolly at their tracks while great shells were bursting one hundred yards away.

"At one time the Germans cut loose with their guns on a section of the tracks and tore up three miles of rails which had been laid with much labor, but scarcely had they finished this bombardment when the twin lines of steel began to creep forward once more. After the engineers had reached a point where they were exposed on the skyline it was necessary to work at night or on foggy days in order to avoid enemy observation."

On one occasion a party of Americans engaged in railroad construction were so close to the front as to be involved in a raid by the Germans. Without an instant's hesitation they dropped their shovels and other tools and snatched up rifles and engaged vigorously and effectively in the fray.

THE FIRST DEATHS IN THE TRENCHES

By the first of November American troops were entrusted with the manning of a certain section of trenches at the battle front, and there, on November 3d, the first Americans fighting under the American flag on European soil were killed. It was early in the morning, an hour before daybreak. The Germans, having learned that Americans occupied that part of the trenches, made a surprise attack, expecting to find them easy victims. The attack was made in overwhelming numbers, more than twenty to one, and the Americans were cut off by a heavy barrage fire from relief from the rear. But they stood their ground like veteran heroes, and took several lives for every life they gave.

The German raid on the American trench was carried out against members of the second contingent entering the trenches for training. These men had only been in a few days. Before dawn Saturday the Germans began shelling vigorously the barbed wire front of the trenches, dropping many high explosives of large caliber. A heavy artillery fire was then directed so as to cover all the adjacent territory, including the passage leading up to the trenches, thereby forming a most effective barrage in the rear, as well as in the front.

The young lieutenant in charge of the detachment of Americans started back to the communicating trenches to his immediate superior for orders. The barrage knocked him down, but he picked himself up and started off again. He was knocked down a second time, but, determined to reach his objective, got up again. A third time he was knocked down and badly shell-shocked, and was put out of action.

FIGHT GERMANS BRAVELY

Soon after the Germans rushed through the breaches and wire entanglements on each side of the salient, their general object barrage in the forefield having lifted for a moment. The Germans went into the trenches at several points. They met with stout resistance. Pistols, grenades, knives and bayonets were freely used.

For many minutes there was considerable confusion in the trenches, the Germans stalking the Americans and the Americans stalking the Germans. In one section of the trench an American private engaged two Germans with the bayonet. That was the last seen of him until after the raid, when a dead American was found on the spot. Another was killed by a blow on the head with a rifle butt from above.

The Germans soon retired from the trenches which they had stormed but which they were unable to hold, carrying with them their dead and wounded. The bodies of the American dead, and the wounded, were rescued by their own countrymen. The three killed were the following:

Private Thomas F. Enright; sister, Mrs. Mary Irwin, 6641 Premo Street, Pittsburgh.

Private James B. Gresham; mother, Mrs. Alice Dood, 1001 West Ohio Street, Evansville, Ind.

Private Merle D. Hay; father, Harvey D. Hay, Glidden, Iowa.

THE FINAL HONORS

The bodies of these three brave men were buried near the spot where they fell, with all the honors of war, on November 6th. With a guard of French infantrymen, in their picturesque uniforms of red and horizon blue, standing on one side and a detachment of American soldiers on the other, the flag-wrapped caskets were lowered into the grave as a bugler blew taps and the batteries at the front fired minute guns. As the minute guns went off the French officer commanding the division in this section paid a tribute to the fallen Americans. His words, which were punctuated by the roar of the guns and the whistle of shells, touched both the French and the Americans.

TRIBUTE TO THE FALLEN

In conclusion the French officer said:

"In the name of the —th Division, in the name of the French army and in the name of France, I bid farewell to Private Enright, Private Gresham and Private Hay of the American army.

"Of their own free will they had left a prosperous and happy country to come over here. They knew war was continuing in Europe; they knew that the forces fighting for honor, love of justice and civilization were still checked by the long-prepared forces serving the powers of brutal domination, oppression and barbarity. They knew that efforts were still necessary. They wished to give us their generous hearts, and they have not forgotten old historical memories while others forget more recent ones.

"They ignored nothing of the circumstances and nothing had been concealed from them—neither the length and hardships of war, nor the violence of battle, nor the dreadfulness of new weapons, nor the perfidy of the foe.

367

DIED FACING THE FOE

"Nothing stopped them. They accepted the hard and strenuous life; they crossed the ocean at great peril; they took their places on the front by our side, and they have fallen facing the foe in a hard and desperate hand-to-hand fight. Honor to them. Their families, friends and fellow-citizens will be proud when they learn of their deaths.

"Men! These graves, the first to be dug in our national soil and but a short distance from the enemy, are as a mark of the mighty land we and our Allies firmly cling to in the common task, confirming the will of the people and the army of the United States to fight with us to a finish, ready to sacrifice as long as is necessary until final victory for the most noble of causes, that of the liberty of nations, the weak as well as the mighty. Thus the deaths of these humble soldiers appear to us with extraordinary grandeur.

"We will, therefore, ask that the mortal remains of these young men be left here, left with us forever. We inscribe on the tombs 'Here lie the first soldiers of the Republic of the United States to fall on the soil of France for liberty and justice.' The passerby will stop and uncover his head. Travelers and men of heart will go out of their way to come here to pay their respective tributes.

"Private Enright! Private Gresham! Private Hay! In the name of France I thank you. God receive your souls. Farewell!"

GALLANTRY AT CAMBRAI

A semi-official British report gives an account of the gallant and effective action of the American railroad engineers near Cambrai, already mentioned. "Two and one-half companies of railway engineers," the statement says,

368

"with a strength of eight officers and 365 men, were encamped at Fins on November 30th, having completed their work in the neighborhood. At 6.30 four officers and 280 men went to Gouzeaucourt, arriving at seven and starting to work with Canadian engineers. The entire contingent was under a Canadian major and an American captain. The area was three miles in the rear of the line and none of the troops were armed.

"At 7.15 German barrage fire moved on Gouzeaucourt after heavy shelling to the east. At 7.30 a general retirement was ordered and it was effected with some difficulty due to the artillery, machine gun and airplane fire. A number of losses were sustained at this time and also among men who, cut off by the German advance, had taken refuge in dugouts. Some of these men who had been cut off succeeded in joining British combatant units and fought with them during the day. Meantime there was active shelling against Fins and the men there were ordered to scatter in the fields.

"As the men returned to camp they were assembled under arms and instructions were asked from British headquarters. At three o'clock they were instructed to dig and hold the trenches and the men moved up and started work shortly afterward. At six the trenches were finished sufficiently for the entire command, and division headquarters directed a withdrawal to camp and that the men be held in readiness to man the trenches. Two small details were sent out to repair a distant break in the new track and to assist in transferring ammunition to another point.

"It is stated by British officers that the conduct of the regiment was most satisfactory. They praise its coolness under fire, and the ability of the men to work without interruption is regarded as most commendable."

AMERICAN AVIATORS

A large force of Americans promptly engaged in the aviation service, as forerunners of the vast aerial army which it was designed to put into action, and by the early part of January, 1918, were making raids upon German military posts far within the German lines.

CHAPTER XXXI

OUR SOLDIERS IN THE WAR

Early Engagements—The Allied Call for Aid to Meet the Great German Drive — The Quick and Effective Response — Americans at First "Brigaded" with British and French Troops — Brilliant Achievements at Many Points — Americans Take Over a Large Sector of the Western Front — Operations at Cantigny, Château Thierry, Belleau Wood, and Elsewhere — "Bois des Americains" — American Troops in Italy and on the Shores of the Arctic Ocean — Great Efficiency of American Aviators — A Million Men Sent Abroad by July 4, 1918.

MENTION HAS already been made of various early engagements in which American engineers and others took part as emergency troops. These were in the latter part of 1917. In March, 1918, more serious work began. On March 20th the Germans began one of the greatest drives of the whole war, against the British lines in the region of Arras. Greatly outnumbered, the British slowly retired, in perfect order, inflicting as they did so probably the greatest losses upon the enemy that had been suffered by either side in the war. Despite the slaughter the Germans pressed on, until the British had been forced back to a point beyond which it would be perilous to retire. Then, "with their backs to the wall," as they expressed it, the hard-pressed and long-enduring British called upon their Allies for aid. A French army hastened to their relief, and the drive was stayed.

Then, on March 29th, came a great change in the conduct of the war. General Foch, of the French army, was made Generalissimo, with supreme command over all the allied forces, and on the same day General Pershing placed himself and all the American troops at General Foch's dis-

371

posal. At first, because of their small numbers, the Americans were "brigaded" with the British and French troops, single regiments being placed here and there where needed. But a little later, as their numbers increased, they were entrusted with the defence of a small sector of the battle-front, and this was extended in length week by week, until by early summer of 1918 the Americans were holding many miles of the Western Front.

As early as March 20th American gunners effectively bombarded the German lines at Lahayville, and two days later destroyed their first and second line trenches at Luneville. On March 25th they shelled St. Bausant, and the next day drove the Germans out of Richecourt. On April 8th they routed a German patrol near Toul. They reached the front in force on April 10th, and on April 12th helped to repulse a German attack in Apremont Forest. Their first all-day battle was on April 13th, at Toul, where they successfully met two German attacks; and the next day they were similarly engaged near St. Mihiel. At Seicheprey on April 20th and 21st the Americans and French first lost and then regained ground; on April 29th the Americans took over a sector of the French lines at the tip of the Somme salient; on May 4th in the Lorraine sector they raided the German lines as far as the third trenches; and thereafter they were daily engaged at various points along the lines.

CANTIGNY

Tuesday, May 28, 1918, saw the first really important entry of the American troops into the war. That morning, under cover of a tremendous artillery fire, they stormed the village of Cantigny, near Montdidier, and made a net advance of a mile on a two-mile front. This was strategically important, since it checked the center of the German advance toward Amiens. The engagement was carefully planned in advance, and was carried out strictly according to schedule. In it all the latest methods and devices were employed, including barrage fire, "tanks," grenades, gas masks, and what not, and the Americans showed themselves familiar with them all.

In itself a comparatively small affair, the significance of Cantigny was very great, and it must worthily be recorded as the first American "drive" and victory of the war.

CHÂTEAU THIERRY

Cantigny was quickly followed by Château Thierry. At the end of May the Germans were making another furious drive toward Paris, and were seeking to establish themselves securely on the south bank of the Marne. What happened was well described by a Reuter correspondent who witnessed it, as follows:

On May 31st, when the Germans were already in the outskirts of Château Thierry, an American machine-gun unit was hurried thither in motor lorries. Château Thierry lies on both banks of the Marne, which is spanned by a big bridge. A little to the northward a canal runs parallel to the river and is crossed by a smaller bridge.

The Americans had scarcely reached their quarters when news was received that the Germans had broken into the northern part of Château Thierry, having made their way through the gap they had driven in our lines to the left of the town and then pouring along the streets to the bridge, intending to establish themselves firmly on the south bank and capture the town.

The American machine gunners and French colonials

were thrown into Château Thierry together. The Americans immediately took over the defense of the river bank, especially the approaches to the bridge. Fighting with their habitual courage and using their guns with an accuracy which won the highest encomiums from the French, they brought the enemy to a standstill.

Already wavering under the American fire, the Germans were counter-attacked by the French colonials and driven from the town. They returned to the attack the next night and under cover of darkness crept into the town along the river bank and began to work their way through the streets toward the main bridge. At the same moment a tremendous artillery bombardment was opened upon the southern half of the town.

BLOWING UP THE BRIDGE

When within range of the machine guns the Germans advanced under the cover of clouds of thick white smoke from smoke bombs, in order to baffle the aim of the American gunners. A surprise, however, was in store for them. They were already crossing the bridge, evidently believing themselves masters of both banks, when a thunderous explosion blew the center of the bridge and a number of Germans with it into the river. Those who reached the southern bank were immediately captured.

In this battle in the streets, and again at night, the young American soldiers showed a courage and determination which aroused the admiration of their French colonial comrades. With their machine guns they covered the withdrawal of troops across the bridge before its destruction, and although under severe fire themselves, kept all the approaches to the bank under a rain of bullets which nullified all the subsequent efforts of the enemy to cross the river. Every attempt of the Germans to elude the vigilance of the Americans resulted in disaster.

"BOIS DES AMERICAINS"

The American troops who thus distinguished themselves at Château Thierry were members of the Marine Corps, and the same gallant fighters were very soon engaged again in beating back German attacks on the Marne. The Germans undertook a mass attack at Veuilly Wood, but were mown down by the Marines with machine guns with fearful slaughter. Then, on June 6th, the Americans assumed the offensive, and pushed forward for two miles on a two and a half mile front, occupying important strategic positions northwest of Château Thierry. That night the advance was resumed, through Les Mares Farm to the town of Triangle and the southern edge of the now historic Belleau Wood. For half the night the fighting raged with great fury, and as a result of it the Americans captured the villages of Bouresches and Torcy, securing next day a total advance of two and a half miles on a front of six miles. The losses of the Americans were heavy, but the field was covered with German dead in many places piled three deep.

There followed several days of almost incessant fighting for the possession of Belleau Wood. This was a forest covered hill, held by German infantry and machine gun companies. The Americans began with an artillery attack, throwing more than 5,000 shells, both high explosives and gas shells, into the German works. Then, on the morning of June 10th, the Marines went "over the top" with the bayonet and drove the Germans out of all save a small portion of the wood, and the next day even that portion was cleared and all of Belleau Wood was won. Afterward, on reviewing the victorious American Marines, the French

General commanding that sector of the battle line announced that thereafter Belleau Wood would be forever known as the Bois des Americains.

FIFTY MILES OF AMERICAN LINES

By the middle of June, 1918, the Americans were holding fifty miles of lines, including a small sector in Alsace on what had been German soil since 1871. They had adapted themselves to methods of warfare such as they had never known before, and were winning golden opinions from their allies for their valor and efficiency. They were in daily conflict with the enemy, sometimes entirely on their own account and sometimes in co-operation with the French or British.

Nor were our troops confined to the Western Front. In June, 1918, a great drive at Venice and northern Italy was attempted by the Austrians, and was most successfully repulsed by the Italians and their allies. This gave occasion for recognition of the desirability of sending American troops to that country; not so much for the sake of reenforcing the Italian army as for that of encouraging it and sustaining its morale by giving ocular and tangible proof that America was in the war as a loyal ally of Italy. Some American aviators, indeed, were already there and had done valuable work in helping to repel the Austrian drive, but it was felt that there should be at least a regiment or two of troops. Accordingly, at the end of June a detachment of American engineers was sent thither from France by General Pershing, and it was presently followed by a larger contingent of fighting troops sent directly from the United States.

At about the same time, also, a detachment of American Marines was sent to the Murman Coast and landed to

help the other Allies defend the great quantities of stores
at Kola from being seized by or for the Germans. The
Bolshevik government of Russia had, under German
pressure, ceded that region to Finland, and the latter
country was almost completely under German control and
largely under German occupation. This action of the
Allied troops was therefore the part of prudence. By
the Fourth of July, 1918, therefore, American troops were
in active co-operation with their allies on three fronts of
the war.

FOUR DRIVES REPULSED

Within the space of three months in the spring of 1918
the American troops assisted in the checking of four successive German drives on the Western Front, two of them
being toward the Channel ports and two toward Paris.
These drives cost the Allies much in territory, prisoners
and supplies. But they cost the Germans far more in
killed and wounded, and as they did not reach their objectives, and did not break the Allied line, they must be
accounted failures. The gains made by the Germans may
be recapitulated as follows, the table showing a decline in
those gains in the successive drives:

Scene and Date of Drive.	Maximum Advance.	Territory Won.	Prisoners Taken.	Guns Taken.
Amiens, March 21	35 miles	975 sq. m.	90,000	1,300
Ypres, April 9	10 miles	190 sq. m.	20,000	200
Champagne, May 27	32 miles	950 sq. m.	65,000	900
Oise, June 9	6 miles	180 sq. m.	15,000	150

FIRST ARMY CORPS FORMED

The rapid growth of the American Expeditionary Force,
as our army abroad is called, necessitated the organization
of it into divisions and corps. It was announced at the

middle of June that this would be done, and before the end of the month the First Army Corps was formed and was placed under the command of Major General Hunter Ligett. It comprised 220,000 men, in six divisions. These latter were the First, Second and Third regular army divisions, commanded by Major Generals Robert L. Bullard, Omar Bundy and Joseph T. Dickman, respectively, and the Pioneer National Guard divisions in Pershing's forces, the New England troops, commanded by Major General Clarence R. Edwards, and the Rainbow Division, made up of representatives from all but the New England states, in command of Charles T. Menoher, together with the marines, in command of Brigadier General James Harboard.

A MILLION MEN SENT OUT

Owing to the unprepared condition of the country, and the time consequently required to recruit and train and equip troops, the dispatching of troops abroad in 1917 was slow. But in the spring of 1918 the work was "speeded up" until more than 100,000 a week were sent. At the first of July, 1918, the Secretary of War was able to report that, counting non-combatants, more than a million men had left American ports for the war; as follows:

1917		1918	
May	1,718	January	46,776
June	12,261	February	48,027
July	12,988	March	83,811
August	18,323	April	117,212
September	32,523	May	244,345
October	38,259	June	276,372
November	23,016		
December	48,840	Marines	14,644
Aggregating			1,019,115

The total number of our troops returned from abroad, lost at sea and casualties was 8,165, and of these, by reason of the superbly efficient portection which the navy had given our transport system, only 291 had been lost at sea.

Following this, on July 3d there was made public a review of war preparations and work during the fifteen months since the declaration of war. This showed that there were in the army, at home and abroad 160,400 officers and 2,010,000 men, against only 9,524 officers and 202,510 men fifteen months before. More than 1,300,000 rifles had been made and delivered up to June 1st. Of fighting airplanes, 286 had been delivered by June 8th, and at that date 80 a week were being completed. More than 2,000 Liberty motors had been delivered and the weekly production was 115. At the end of June more than 10,000 rifles and 27,000,000 cartridges of all kinds were being turned out.

GROWTH OF THE NAVY

Early in June, 1918, several German submarines appeared off the Atlantic coast of the United States, preying upon commerce and destroying many vessels, chiefly those engaged in the coasting trade. This circumstance seemed greatly to stimulate enlistments in our navy, nearly 27,000 men enlisting in the first two weeks of that month. On June 23d the Secretary of the Navy announced that the strength of the naval service aggregated 26,285 officers and 423,808 men, a total of 450,093, as follows:

	Officers.	Enlisted Men.
Regular Navy	9,204	205,798
Naval Reserves	14,704	148,505
Marine Corps	1,364	48,505
National Naval Reserves	785	15,000
Coast Guard	228	6,000

SUPPLYING THE ARMY

The stupendous magnitude of the business of supplying the army with needful things may be estimated from this list of purchases by the Quartermaster Corps from the beginning of the war to June 15, 1918:

HARDWARE AND METALS.

Hammers, each	2,567,000
Axes, each	5,121,729
Files, each	10,870,000

VEHICLES AND HARNESS.

Halters, each	1,700,000
Escort wagons	120,000
Combat wagons	26,000

ANIMALS.

Horses and mules	339,593

CLOTHING AND MATERIAL FOR CLOTHING.

Shoes, pairs	27,249,000
Boots (rubber, hip), pairs	2,340,000
Overshoes (arctic), pairs	4,010,000
Cotton undershirts, each	43,922,000
Denim cloth, yards	103,028,000
Stockings (wool), pairs	104,333,000

Nearly 50,000 men were engaged, by June, 1918, in railway construction and operation in France. Said the Secretary of War:

"There have been produced for the railroad operations of the War Department in France more than 22,000 standard gage and 60-centimeter freight cars, and more than 1,600 standard gage and 60-centimeter locomotives. In addition to this, purchases of both cars and locomotives have been made abroad.

"A double line of railroad communication has been secured from the French by army engineers, extending from the coast of France to the battlefront, including the construction of hundreds of miles of trackage for yards and the necessary sidings, switches, etc."

Early in the war it was necessary for the American troops to depend upon the French and British for their artillery. Sixteen huge establishments were built here for the manufacture of cannon, and by the summer of 1918 they began to produce artillery in quantity. Thus on July 1st it was reported that one concern, which had never before made a single gun, was turning out ready for use ten 155-millimeter howitzers a day, in a factory standing on ground which less than a year before had been occupied as a cornfield.

THE LISTS OF LOSSES

Down to the Fourth of July, 1918, the total losses of the army and Marine Corps were as follows:

Killed in action	1,238
Died of wounds	508
Died of diseases	1,304
Died of accidents, etc.	481
Lost at sea	291
Total deaths	3,822
Wounded	5,141
Missing and prisoners	434
Grand total, all losses	9,397

CHAPTER XXXII

OUR PURPOSE IN THE WAR

The President's Definition of Our Aims and Ends, Made Eight Months after the Declaration of War — Prussian Militarism and Autocracy to be Crushed — Lands to be Freed from Prussian Conquest — No War against the German People nor Wrong to the German Empire — The Truth to be Told to Russia — War with Austria-Hungary — Women to be Included among Hostile Aliens — No Selfish Ambition for Conquest.

THE WAR Message of the President, in April, was largely devoted to an exposition of the causes which compelled us to take up the gage of battle which arrogant Prussian militarism had flung into the face of the nation, and gave only a suggestive outline of the purposes which we had in view and of the ends upon which we should insist for a satisfactory termination of the war.   There arose in both America and Europe some question and controversy as to what those purposes and aims really were in detail. Upon the subject American opinion was more or less divided. Our Allies were not entirely certain. As for Germany, she grossly misrepresented our purposes, and prosecuted an ingenious and persistent propaganda of falsehood concerning them, which so poisoned the minds of many Russians as largely to contribute to the disorder and collapse which occurred in that country a few months later.

The President, therefore, wisely deemed it desirable, at the re-assembling of Congress in December, 1917, to make a straightforward and explicit statement of our purposes in the war, so clearly and directly that there could be no excuse for misunderstanding or misrepresentation of it.   At the same time it was necessary to extend our declaration of the existence of a state of war so as to include Austria-Hungary as well as Germany. Accordingly a joint session of the two houses was held in the hall of the House of Representatives on Tuesday, December 4th, just eight months and two days after the declaration of war with Germany, and the President addressed it with all the added authority of the experience of that momentous period of time. He said:

THE PRESIDENT'S ADDRESS

Eight months have elapsed since I last had the honor of addressing you. They have been months crowded with events of immense and grave significance for us. I shall not undertake to detail or even to summarize those events. The practical particulars of the part we have played in them will be laid before you in the reports of the executive departments. I shall discuss only our present outlook upon these vast affairs, our present duties and the immediate means of accomplishing the objects we shall hold always in view.

I shall not go back to debate the causes of the war. The intolerable wrongs done and planned against us by the sinister masters of Germany have long since become too grossly obvious and odious to every true American to need to be rehearsed. But I shall ask you to consider again and with a very grave scrutiny our objectives, and the measures by which we mean to attain them; for the purpose of discussion here in this place is action, and our action must move straight toward definite ends. Our object is, of course, to win the war, and we shall not slacken or suffer ourselves to be diverted until it is won. But it is worth while asking and answering the question, When shall we consider the war won?

THE NATION UNITED

From one point of view it is not necessary to broach this fundamental matter. I do not doubt that the American people know what the war is about and what sort of outcome they will regard as a realization of their purpose in it. As a nation we are united in spirit and intention. I pay little heed to those who tell me otherwise. I hear the voices of dissent—who does not? I hear the criticism and the clamor of the noisily thoughtless and troublesome. I also see men here and there fling themselves in impotent disloyalty against the calm, indomitable power of the nation. I hear men debate peace who understand neither its nature nor the way in which we may obtain it with uplifted eyes and unbroken spirits. But I know that none of these speaks for the nation. They do not touch the heart of anything. They may safely be left to strut their uneasy hour and be forgotten.

But from another point of view, I believe that it is necessary to say plainly what we here at the seat of action consider the war to be for and what part we mean to play in the settlement of its searching issues. We are the spokesmen of the American people and they have a right to know whether their purpose is ours. They desire peace by the overcoming of evil, by the defeat once for all of the sinister forces that interrupt peace and render it impossible, and they wish to know how closely our thought runs with theirs and what action we propose. They are impatient with those who desire peace by any sort of compromise—deeply and indignantly impatient—but they will be equally impatient with us if we do not make it plain to them what our objectives are and what we are planning for in seeking to make conquest of peace by arms.

A THING TO BE CRUSHED

I believe that I speak for them when I say two things: First, that this intolerable Thing of which the masters of Germany have shown us the ugly face, this menace of combined intrigue and force, which we now see so clearly as the German power, a Thing without conscience or honor or capacity for covenanted peace, must be crushed, and if it be not utterly brought to an end, at least shut out from friendly intercourse of the nations; and, second, that when this Thing and its power are indeed defeated and the time comes that we can discuss peace, when the German people have spokesmen whose word we can believe, and when those spokesmen are ready in the name of their people to accept the common judgment of the nations as to what shall henceforth be the bases of law and of covenant for the life of the world—we shall be willing and glad to pay the full price for peace and pay it ungrudgingly. We know what that price will be. It will be full impartial justice—justice done at every point and to every nation that the final settlement must affect, our enemies as well as our friends.

384

THE VOICE OF HUMANITY

You catch, with me, the voices of humanity that are in the air. They grow daily more audible, more articulate, more persuasive, and they come from the hearts of men everywhere. They insist that the war shall not end in vindictive action of any kind; that no nation or people shall be robbed or punished because the irresponsible rulers of a single country have themselves done deep and abominable wrong. It is this thought that has been expressed in the formula, "No annexations, no contributions, no punitive indemnities." Just because this crude formula expresses the instinctive judgment as to right of plain men everywhere it has been made diligent use of by the masters of German intrigue to lead the people of Russia astray, and the people of every other country their agents could reach, in order that a premature peace might be brought about before autocracy has been taught its final and convincing lesson and the people of the world put in control of their own destinies.

THE DOOM OF AUTOCRACY

But the fact that a wrong use has been made of a just idea is no reason why a right use should not be made of it. It ought to be brought under the patronage of its real friends. Let it be said again that autocracy must first be shown the utter futility of its claims to power or leadership in the modern world. It is impossible to apply any standard of justice so long as such forces are unchecked and undefeated as the present masters of Germany command. Not until that has been done can right be set up as arbiter and peacemaker among the nations. But when that has been done—as, God willing, it assuredly will be—we shall at last be free to do an unprecedented thing, and this is the time to avow our purpose to do it. We shall be free to base peace on generosity and justice, to the exclusion of all selfish claims to advantage, even on the part of the victors.

THE WAR MUST BE WON

Let there be no misunderstanding. Our present and immediate task is to win the war, and nothing shall turn us aside from it until it is accomplished. Every power and resource we possess, whether of men, of money or of material, is being devoted and will continue to be devoted to that purpose until it is achieved. Those who desire to bring peace about before that purpose is achieved I counsel to carry their advice elsewhere. We will not entertain it. We shall regard the war only as won when the German people say to us, through properly accredited representatives, that they are ready to agree to a settlement based upon justice and the reparation of the wrongs their rulers have done. They have done a wrong to Belgium, which must be repaired. They have established a power over other lands and peoples than their own—over the great empire of Austria-Hungary, over hitherto free Balkan states, over Turkey, and within Asia—which must be relinquished.

WRONGS MUST BE RIGHTED

Germany's success by skill, by industry, by knowledge, by enterprise, we did not grudge or oppose, but admired rather. She had built up for herself a real empire of trade and influence, secured by the peace of the world. We were content to abide the rivalries of manufacture, science and commerce that were involved for us in her success, and stand or fall as we had or did not have the brains and the initiative to surpass her. But at the moment when she had conspicuously won her triumphs of peace she threw them away, to establish in their stead what the world will no longer permit to be established—military and political domination by arms, by which to oust where she could not excel the rivals she most feared and hated. The peace we make must remedy that wrong. It must deliver the once fair lands and happy peoples of Belgium and Northern France from the Prussian conquest and the Prussian menace, but it must also deliver the peoples of Austria-Hungary, the peoples of the Balkans and the peoples of Turkey, alike in Europe and in Asia, from the impudent and alien domination of the Prussian military and commercial autocracy.

NO MENACE TO THE EMPIRES

We owe it, however, to ourselves to say that we do not wish in any way to impair or to rearrange the Austro-Hungarian Empire. It is no affair of ours what they do with their own life, either industrially or politically. We do not purpose or desire to dictate to them in any way. We only desire to see that their affairs are left in their own hands, in all matters, great or small. We shall hope to secure for the peoples of the Balkan Peninsula and for the people of the Turkish Empire the right and opportunity to make their own lives safe, their own fortunes secure against oppression or injustice and from the dictation of foreign courts or parties.

And our attitude and purpose with regard to Germany herself are of a like kind. We intend no wrong against the German Empire, no interference with her internal affairs. We should deem either the one or the other absolutely unjustifiable, absolutely contrary to the principles we have professed to live by and to hold most sacred throughout our life as a nation.

The people of Germany are being told by the men whom they now permit to deceive them and to act as their masters that they are fighting for the very life and existence of their empire—a war of desperate self-defense against deliberate aggression. Nothing could be more grossly or wantonly false, and we must seek by the utmost openness and candor as to our real aims to convince them of its falseness. We are in fact fighting for their emancipation from fear, along with our own—from the fear as well as from the fact of unjust attack by neighbors or rivals or schemers after world empire. No one is threatening the existence or the independence or the peaceful enterprise of the German Empire.

TO SERVE THE GERMAN PEOPLE

The worst that can happen to the detriment of the German people is this, that if they should still, after the war is over, continue to be obliged to live under ambitious and intriguing masters interested to disturb the peace of the world, men or classes of men whom the other peoples of the world could not trust, it might be impossible to admit them to the partnership of nations which must henceforth guarantee the world's peace. That partnership must be a partnership of peoples, not a mere partnership of governments. It might be impossible, also, in such untoward circumstances, to admit Germany to the free economic intercourse which must inevitably spring out of the other partnerships of a real peace. But there would be no aggression in that; and such a situation, inevitable because of distrust, would in the very nature of things sooner or later cure itself by processes which would assuredly set in.

The wrongs, the very deep wrongs, committed in this war will have to be righted. That of course. But they can not and must not be righted by the commission of similar wrongs against Germany and her allies. The world will not permit the commission of similar wrongs as a means of reparation and settlement. Statesmen must by this time have learned that the opinion of the world is everywhere wide awake and fully comprehends the issues involved. No representative of any self-governed nation will dare disregard it by attempting any such covenants of selfishness and compromise as were entered into at the Congress of Vienna. The thought of the plain people here and everywhere throughout the world, the people who enjoy no privilege and have very simple and unsophisticated standards of right and wrong, is the air all governments must henceforth breathe if they would live. It is in the full disclosing light of that thought that all policies must be conceived and executed in this midday hour of the world's life.

THE CRIMES OF THE HOHENZOLLERNS

German rulers have been able to upset the peace of the world only because the German people were not suffered under their tutelage to share the comradeship of the other peoples of the world either in thought or in purpose. They were allowed to have no opinion of their own which might be set up as a rule of conduct for those who exercised, authority over them. But the congress that concludes this war will feel the full strength of the tides that run now in the hearts and consciences of free men everywhere. Its conclusions will run with those tides.

All these things have been true from the very beginning of this stupendous war; and I cannot help thinking that if they had been made plain at the very outset the sympathy and enthusiasm of the Russian people might have been once for all enlisted on the side of the Allies, suspicion and distrust swept away and a real and lasting union of purpose effected. Had they believed these things at the very moment of their revolution, and had they been confirmed in that belief since, the sad reverses which have recently marked the progress of their affairs toward an ordered and stable government of free men might have been avoided.

RUSSIA MUST KNOW THE TRUTH

The Russian people have been poisoned by the very same falsehoods that have kept the German people in the dark, and the poison has been administered by the very same hands. The only possible antidote is the truth. It cannot be uttered too plainly or too often.

From every point of view, therefore, it has seemed to be my duty to speak these declarations of purpose, to add these specific interpretations to what I took the liberty of saying to the Senate in January. Our entrance into the war has not altered our attitude toward the settlement that must come when it is over. When I said in January that the nations of the world were entitled not only to free pathways upon the sea, but also to assured and unmolested access to those pathways, I was thinking, and I am thinking now, not of the smaller and weaker nations alone, which need our countenance and support, but also of the great and powerful nations and of our present enemies, as well as our present associates in the war. I was thinking, and am thinking now, of Austria herself, among the rest, as well as of Serbia and of Poland. Justice and equality of rights can be had only at a great price. We are seeking permanent, not temporary, foundations for the peace of the world, and must seek them candidly and fearlessly. As always, the right will prove to be the expedient.

WAR WITH AUSTRIA-HUNGARY

What shall we do, then, to push this great war of freedom and justice to its righteous conclusion? We must clear away with a thorough hand all impediments to success, and we must make every adjustment of law that will facilitate the full and free use of our whole capacity and force as a fighting unit.

One very embarrassing obstacle that stands in our way is that we are at war with Germany, but not with her allies. I, therefore, very earnestly recommend that the Congress immediately declare the United States in a state of war with Austria-Hungary. Does it seem strange to you that this should be the conclusion of the argument I have just addressed to you? It is not. It is, in fact, the inevitable logic of what I have said. Austria-Hungary is for the time being not her own mistress, but simply the vassal of the German government. We must face the facts as they are and act upon them without sentiment in this stern business.

The government of Austria-Hungary is not acting upon its own initiative or in response to the wishes and feelings of its own peoples, but as the instrument of another nation. We must meet its force with our own and regard the Central Powers as but one. The war can be successfully conducted in no other way. The same logic would lead also to a declaration of war against Turkey and Bulgaria. They also are the tools of Germany. But they are mere tools and do not yet stand in the direct path of our necessary action. We shall go wherever the necessities of this war carry us, but it seems to me that we should go only where immediate and practical considerations lead us and not heed any others.

DEALING WITH ENEMY ALIENS

The financial and military measures which must be adopted will suggest themselves as the war and its undertakings develop, but I will take the liberty of proposing to you certain other acts of legislation which seem to me to be needed for the support of the war and for the release of our whole force and energy.

It will be necessary to extend in certain particulars the legislation of the last session with regard to alien enemies; and also necessary, I believe, to create a very definite and particular control over the entrance and departure of all persons into and from the United States.

"THE FEMALE OF THE SPECIES"

Legislation should be enacted defining as a criminal offense every wilful violation of the Presidential proclamations relating to enemy aliens, promulgated under Section 4067 of the Revised Statutes, and providing appropriate punishments; and women as well as men should be included under the terms of the acts placing restraints upon alien enemies. It is likely that, as time goes on, many alien enemies will be willing to be fed and housed at the expense of the government in the detention camps, and it would be the purpose of the legislation I have suggested to confine offenders among them in penitentiaries and other similar institutions, where they could be made to work as other criminals do.

ECONOMIC LEGISLATION

Recent experience has convinced me that the Congress must go further in authorizing the government to set limits to prices.

The law of supply and demand, I am sorry to say, has been replaced by the law of unrestrained selfishness. While we have eliminated profiteering in several branches of industry it still runs impudently rampant in others. The farmers, for example, complain, with a great deal of justice, that, while the regulation of food prices restricts their incomes, no restraints are placed upon the prices of most of the things they must themselves purchase; and similar inequities obtain on all sides.

It is imperatively necessary that the consideration of the full use of the water power of the country, and also the consideration of the systematic and yet economical development of such of the natural resources of the country as are still under the control of the Federal government, should be resumed and affirmatively and constructively dealt with at the earliest possible moment. The pressing need of such legislation is daily becoming more obvious.

The legislation proposed at the last session with regard to regulated combinations among our exporters, in order to provide for our foreign trade a more effective organization and method of co-operation, ought by all means to be completed at this session.

FISCAL ECONOMY

And I beg that the members of the House of Representatives will permit me to express the opinion that it will be impossible to deal in any way but a very wasteful and extravagant fashion with the enormous appropriations of the public moneys which must continue to be made, if the war is to be properly sustained, unless the House will consent to return to its former practice of initiating and preparing all appropriation bills through a single committee, in order that responsibility may be centered, expenditures standardized and made uniform, and waste and duplication as much as possible avoided.

Additional legislation may also become necessary before the present Congress adjourns in order to effect the most efficient co-ordination and operation of the railway and other transportation systems of the country; but to that I shall, if circumstances should demand, call the attention of Congress upon another occasion

WAR LEGISLATION

If I have overlooked anything that ought to be done for the more effective conduct of the war, your own counsels will supply the omission. What I am perfectly clear about is that in the present session of the Congress our whole attention and energy should be concentrated on the vigorous and rapid and successful prosecution of the great task of winning the war.

We can do this with all the greater zeal and enthusiasm because we know that for us this is a war of high principle, debased by no selfish ambition of conquest or spoliation; because we know, and all the world knows, that we have been forced into it to save the very institutions we live under from corruption and destruction. The purposes of the Central Powers strike straight at the very heart of everything we believe in; their methods of warfare outrage every principle of humanity and of knightly honor; their intrigue has corrupted the very thought and spirit of many of our people; their sinister and secret diplomacy has sought to take our very territory away from us and disrupt the union of the states. Our safety would be at an end, our honor forever sullied and brought into contempt were we to permit their triumph. They are striking at the very existence of democracy and liberty.

It is because it is for us a war of high, disinterested purpose, in which all the free peoples of the world are banded together for the vindication of right, a war for the preservation of our nation and of all that it has held dear of principle and of purpose, that we feel ourselves doubly constrained to propose for its outcome only that which is righteous and of irreproachable intention, for our foes as well as for our friends.

A HOLY WAR

The cause being just and holy, the settlement must be of like motive and quality. For this we can fight, but for nothing less noble or less worthy of our traditions. For this cause we entered the war and for this cause will we battle until the last gun is fired.

I have spoken plainly because this seems to me the time when it is most necessary to speak plainly, in order that all the world may know that even in the heat and ardor of the struggle and when our whole thought is of carrying the war through to its end we have not forgotten any ideal or principle for which the name of America has been held in honor among the nations and for which it has been our glory to contend in the great generations that went before us. A supreme moment of history has come. The eyes of the people have been opened and they see. The hand of God is laid upon the nations. He will show them favor, I devoutly believe, only if they rise to the clear heights of His own justice and mercy.

RESPONSE OF CONGRESS

This address was received with practically universal favor by Congress and the nation. Many members of Congress would have preferred to declare war against Turkey and Bulgaria also, so as to include all of Germany's allies, but they deferred to the President's judgment and wishes in the matter. On December 7th both houses adopted a resolution declaring the existence of a state of war between the United States and Austria-Hungary, the vote being unanimous save for a single negative vote cast by a Socialist Representative from New York, Mr. London, who was on principle opposed to any war whatever. The other legislation suggested by the President followed at an early date.

CHAPTER XXXIII

THE FINAL WORD

President Wilson's Definitive Statement of the Aims of the United States and Its Allies in the War, and the Only Acceptable Basic Principles of Peace — Prussian Militarism to be Beaten and World-Wide Democracy Vindicated — Belgium and Serbia to be Evacuated and Restored by Germany, and Alsace-Lorraine to be Returned to France — Poland to be Restored as It was Before the Partition — A "New Magna Charta for the World."

DESPITE THE explicit declarations of American and allied policy in the war, demands continued to be made for a definite statement on the subject, and this indeed appeared to be desirable for the enlightenment and encouragement of Russia, and also, if possible, of the German democracy which was restless under the yoke of Prussian militarism. On January 5, 1918, David Lloyd George, the British Prime Minister, made a noteworthy declaration on the subject, and three days later, on January 8th, President Wilson unexpectedly appeared before Congress and made an address to similar effect, which may be regarded as the final word of the United States concerning its aims and purposes in the war, and the only terms on which it will consider the making of peace. The full text of this address, one of the most epochal utterances ever made by an American President, is as follows:

THE PRESIDENT'S ADDRESS

Gentlemen of the Congress:

Once more, as repeatedly before, the spokesmen of the Central Empires have indicated their desire to discuss the objects of the war and the possible basis of a general peace. Parleys have been in progress at

394

Brest-Litovsk between Russian representatives and representatives of the Central Powers, to which the attention of all the belligerents has been invited, for the purpose of ascertaining whether it may be possible to extend these parleys into a general conference with regard to terms of peace and settlement. The Russian representatives presented not only a perfectly definite statement of the principles upon which they would be willing to conclude peace, but also an equally definite program for the concrete application of those principles. The representatives of the Central Powers, on their part, presented an outline of settlement which, if much less definite, seemed susceptible of liberal interpretation until their specific program of practical terms was added. That program proposed no concessions at all, either to the sovereignty of Russia or to the preferences of the population with whose fortunes it dealt, but meant, in a word, that the Central Empires were to keep every foot of territory their armed forces had occupied— every province, every city, every point of vantage—as a permanent addition to their territories and their power. It is a reasonable conjecture that the general principles of settlement which they at first suggested originated with the more liberal statesmen of Germany and Austria, the men who have begun to feel the force of their own people's thought and purpose, while the concrete terms of actual settlement came from the military leaders who have no thought but to keep what they have got. The negotiations have been broken off. The Russian representatives were sincere and in earnest. They cannot entertain such proposals of conquest and domination.

WHO ARE RESPONSIBLE?

The whole incident is full of significance. It is also full of perplexity. With whom are the Russian representatives dealing? For whom are the representatives of the Central Empires speaking? Are they speaking for the majorities of their respective parliaments or for the minority parties, that military and imperialistic minority which has so far dominated their whole policy and controlled the affairs of Turkey and of the Balkan States, which have felt obliged to become their associates in this war? The Russian representatives have insisted, very justly, very wisely, and in the true spirit of modern democracy, that the conferences they have been holding with the Teutonic and Turkish statesmen should be held with open, not closed, doors, and all the world has

been audience, as was desired. To whom have we been listening, then?
To those who speak the spirit and intention of the resolutions of the
German Reichstag of the 9th of July last, the spirit and intention of
the liberal leaders and parties of Germany, or to those who resist and
defy that spirit and intention and insist upon conquest and subjugation?
Or are we listening, in fact, to both, unreconciled and in open and
hopeless contradiction? These are very serious and pregnant questions.
Upon the answer to them depends the peace of the world.

ANSWERING THE TEUTONS

But whatever the results of the parleys at Brest-Litovsk, whatever
the confusions of counsel and of purpose in the utterances of the spokesmen of the Central Empires, they have again attempted to acquaint
the world with their objects in the war and have again challenged their
adversaries to say what their objects are and what sort of settlement
they would deem just and satisfactory. There is no good reason why
that challenge should not be responded to, and responded to with the
utmost candor. We did not wait for it. Not once, but again and again
we have laid our whole thought and purpose before the world, not in
general terms only, but each time with sufficient definition to make it
clear what sort of definite terms of settlement must necessarily spring
out of them. Within the last week Mr. Lloyd George has spoken with
admirable candor and in admirable spirit for the people and Government
of Great Britain. There is no confusion of counsel among the adversaries of the Central Powers, no uncertainty of principle, no vagueness
of detail. The only secrecy of counsel, the only lack of fearless frankness,
the only failure to make definite statement of the objects of the war,
lies with Germany and her allies. The issues of life and death hang
upon these definitions. No statesman who has the least conception of
his responsibility ought for a moment to permit himself to continue this
tragical and appalling outpouring of blood and treasure unless he is sure
beyond a peradventure that the objects of the vital sacrifice are part and
parcel of the very life of society and that the people for whom he speaks
think them right and imperative as he does.

THE NEED OF DEFINITION

There is, moreover, a voice calling for these definitions of principle
and of purpose which is, it seems to me, more thrilling and more compelling than any of the many moving voices with which the troubled

air of the world is filled. It is the voice of the Russian people. They are prostrate and all but hopeless, it would seem, before the grim power of Germany, which has hitherto known no relenting and no pity. Their power apparently is shattered. And yet their soul is not subservient. They will not yield either in principle or in action. Their conception of what is right, of what is humane and honorable for them to accept, has been stated with a frankness, a largeness of view, a generosity of spirit, and a universal human sympathy which must challenge the admiration of every friend of mankind; and they have refused to compound their ideals or desert others that they themselves may be safe. They call to us to say what it is that we desire, in what, if in anything, our purpose and our spirit differ from theirs; and I believe that the people of the United States would wish me to respond with utter simplicity and frankness. Whether their present leaders believe it or not, it is our heartfelt desire and hope that some way may be opened whereby we may be privileged to assist the people of Russia to attain their utmost hope of liberty and ordered peace.

THE NEW DIPLOMACY

It will be our wish and purpose that the processes of peace, when they are begun, shall be absolutely open, and that they shall involve and permit henceforth no secret understandings of any kind. The day of conquest and aggrandizement is gone by; so is also the day of secret covenants entered into in the interest of particular governments and likely at some unlooked-for moment to upset the peace of the world. It is this happy fact, now clear to the view of every public man whose thoughts do not still linger in an age that is dead and gone, which makes it possible for every nation whose purposes are consistent with justice and the peace of the world to avow now or at any other time the objects it has in view.

WHY WE ENTERED THE WAR

We entered this war because violations of right had occurred which touched us to the quick and made the life of our own people impossible unless they were corrected and the world secured once for all against their recurrence. What we demand in this war, therefore, is nothing peculiar to ourselves. It is that the world be made fit and safe to live in; and particularly that it be made safe for every peace-loving nation which, like our own, wishes to live its own life, determine its own institutions, be assured of justice and fair dealings by the other peoples of the world, as against force and selfish aggression. All the peoples of the world are in effect partners in this interest and for our own part we see very clearly that unless justice be done to others it will not be done to us.

The program of the world's peace, therefore, is our program, and that program, the only possible programme, as we see it, is this:

THE PROGRAMME OF PEACE

I.—Open covenants of peace, openly arrived at, after which there shall be no private international understandings of any kind, but diplomacy shall proceed always frankly and in the public view.

II.—Absolute freedom of navigation upon the seas, outside territorial waters, alike in peace and in war, except as the seas may be closed in whole or in part by international action for the enforcement of international covenants.

III.—The removal, so far as possible, of all economic barriers and the establishment of an equality of trade conditions among all the nations consenting to the peace and associating themselves for its maintenance.

IV.—Adequate guarantees given and taken that national armaments will reduce to the lowest point consistent with domestic safety.

V.—Free, open-minded, and absolutely impartial adjustment of all colonial claims, based upon a strict observance of the principle that in determining all such questions of sovereignty the interest of the population concerned must have equal weight with the equitable claims of the government whose title is to be determined.

RUSSIA TO BE SAVED

VI.—The evacuation of all Russian territory and such a settlement of all questions affecting Russia as will secure the best and freest co-operation of the other nations of the world in obtaining for her an unhampered and unembarrassed opportunity for the independent determination of her own political development and national policy, and assure her of a sincere welcome into the society of free nations under institutions of her own choosing; and, more than a welcome, assistance also of every kind that she may need and may herself desire. The treatment accorded Russia by her sister nations in the months to come will be the acid test of their good-will, of their comprehension of her needs as distinguished from their own interests, and of their intelligent and unselfish sympathy.

BELGIUM MUST BE RESTORED

VII.—Belgium, the whole world will agree, must be evacuated and restored, without any attempt to limit the sovereignty which she enjoys in common with all other free nations. No other single act will serve as this will serve to restore confidence among the nations in the laws which they have themselves set and determined for the government of their relations with one another. Without this healing act the whole structure and validity of international law is forever impaired.

ALSACE-LORRAINE

VIII.—All French territory should be freed and the invaded portions restored, and the wrong done to France by Prussia in 1871 in the matter of Alsace-Lorraine, which has unsettled the peace of the world for nearly fifty years, should be righted, in order that peace may once more be made secure in the interest of all.

IX.—A readjustment of the frontiers of Italy should be effected along clearly recognizable lines of nationality.

X.—The peoples of Austria-Hungary, whose place among the nations we wish to see safeguarded and assured, should be accorded the freest opportunity of autonomous development.

THE BALKAN STATES

XI.—Roumania, Serbia, and Montenegro should be evacuated; occupied territories restored; Serbia accorded free and secure access to the sea; and the relations of the several Balkan States to one another determined by friendly counsel along historically established lines of allegiance and nationality; and international guarantees of the political and economic independence and territorial integrity of the several Balkan States should be entered into.

XII.—The Turkish portions of the present Ottoman Empire should be assured a secure sovereignty, but the other nationalities which are now under Turkish rule should be assured an undoubted security of life and an absolutely unmolested opportunity of autonomous development, and the Dardanelles should be permanently opened as a free passage to the ships and commerce of all nations under international guarantees.

POLAND TO BE REDEEMED

XIII.—An independent Polish State should be erected which should include the territories inhabited by indisputably Polish populations, which should be assured a free and secure access to the sea, and whose political and economic independence and territorial integrity should be guaranteed by international covenant.

XIV.—A general association of nations must be formed under specific covenants for the purpose of affording mutual guarantees of political independence and territorial integrity to great and small States alike.

THE ALLIES UNITED

In regard to these essential rectifications of wrong and assertions of right, we feel ourselves to be intimate partners of all the governments and peoples associated together against the imperialists. We cannot be separated in interest or divided in purpose. We stand together until the end.

For such arrangements and covenants we are willing to fight and to continue to fight until they are achieved; but only because we wish the right to prevail and desire a just and stable peace, such as can be secured only by removing the chief provocations to war, which this program does remove. We have no jealousy of German greatness, and there is nothing in this program that impairs it. We grudge her no achievement or distinction of learning or of pacific enterprise such as have made her record very bright and very enviable. We do not wish to injure her or to block in any way her legitimate influence or power. We do not wish to fight her either with arms or with hostile arrangements of trade, if she is willing to associate herself with us and the other peace-loving nations of the world in covenants of justice and law and fair dealing. We wish her only to accept a place of equality among the peoples of the world—the new world in which we now live—instead of a place of mastery.

Neither do we presume to suggest to her any alteration or modification of her institutions. But it is necessary, we must frankly say, and necessary as a preliminary to any intelligent dealings with her on our part, that we should know whom her spokesmen speak for when they speak to us, whether for the Reichstag majority or for the military party and the men whose creed is imperial domination.

OUR FINAL WORD

We have spoken now, surely, in terms too concrete to admit of any further doubt or question. An evident principle runs through the whole program I have outlined. It is the principle of justice to all peoples and nationalities, and their right to live on equal terms of liberty and safety with one another, whether they be strong or weak.

Unless this principle be made its foundation, no part of the structure of international justice can stand. The people of the United States could act upon no other principle, and to the vindication of this principle they are ready to devote their lives, their honor, and everything that they possess.

The moral climax of this, the culminating and final war for human liberty, has come, and they are ready to put their own strength, their own highest purpose, their own integrity and devotion to the test.

THE MESSAGE APPROVED

This powerful statement was received by Congress and by the American people with practically unanimous approval, amounting to genuine enthusiasm. It was similarly received in Great Britain, France, Italy and elsewhere. Notably the British Labor Party, the attitude of which toward the war had been uncertain, gave to it most cordial sanction. It was hailed throughout the world as a new Magna Charta for world-wide democracy, and all the Allies were impregnably confirmed in their resolution to fight to the end on the lines and for the principles therein set forth.

Chapter XXXIV

UNIVERSAL MILITARY SERVICE

No "Peace at Any Price" Advocates Among the Founders of the Republic—The Volunteer System Discredited and Repudiated at the Very Beginning and Again in Every War We Have Ever Waged—Washington's Condemnation of the Volunteer Militia System — Its Disastrous Effects in the Revolution — Jefferson's Earnest Advocacy of Universal Military Training and Service — Disgraceful Results of the Militia System in the War of 1812 — Why the Traditional Policy of Washington and Jefferson Was Abandoned—Universal Service the True Democratic System — Examples in Switzerland and Other Republics — Advantages of the System for the United States — The Duty of the Citizen to Serve the State in Either Peace or War.

"I DIDN'T Raise My Boy to Be a Soldier" was not a popular song among the founders of the American Republic. The mothers of 1776 were proud and glad with a fearful gladness to buckle sword-belts about their sons and send them forth to battle with their blessing. The statesmen who resisted the misgovernment of the Mother Country and pledged their lives, their fortunes and their sacred honor to the achievement and maintenance of our national independence, were not believers in "peace at any price." The true spirit of America, the only spirit that could have made America a nation, the only spirit that can be worthy of the successors of those devoted men, was voiced in Henry's familiar words: "Is life so dear, or peace so sweet, as to be purchased at the price of chains and slavery? Forbid it, Almighty God!" That was and is the "traditional spirit" of America.

Washington, addressing the Congress of the young republic, on January 8, 1790, said: "To be prepared for war is one of the most effectual means of preserving peace."

FAILURE OF UNTRAINED VOLUNTEERS

Washington's meaning was that there should be universal military training and universal military service. He spoke from bitter personal experience. Again and again he testified, in the Revolution, in the "times that tried men's souls," that the greatest difficulty with which he had to contend was not the British Government, nor the German levies. No; but the untrained militia of which his army was so largely composed. Again and again he declared that he would actually be better off and have a stronger army without them. That was not because they were not good patriots and brave men. No; but because they were not trained soldiers. Loyalty and valor are not sufficient. There must be knowledge of arms and of tactics; there must be discipline and obedience; there must be such familiarity with war as will assure steadiness of nerves in the presence of the enemy; there must be the physical training which will enable men to endure the fatigues of campaign and battle. Without these qualities troops are ineffective, and to send them into battle is to imperil them far more than the enemy.

This latter point was repeatedly emphasized by Washington, who declared that it was nothing short of criminal to send untrained militiamen into battle against disciplined and expert soldiers. The same conviction was expressed by Washington's close friend and comrade in arms, "Light Horse Harry" Lee, when he said: "That government is a murderer of its citizens which sends them to the field uninformed and untaught, where they are to meet men of the same age and strength, mechanized by education and discipline for battle."

THE POLICY OF WASHINGTON

Washington left us in no doubt as to what he meant by being prepared for war. He meant compulsory universal military training and compulsory universal military service. This was made clear at the very beginning of his administration. It was in his first annual message or address to Congress, and at the beginning of that address, that he uttered the words already quoted. He said:

"Among the many interesting objects which will engage your attention that of providing for the common defense will merit particular regard. To be prepared for war is one of the most effectual means of preserving peace. A free people ought not only to be armed, but disciplined; to which end a uniform and well-digested plan is requisite; and their safety and interest require that they should promote such manufactories as tend to render them independent of others for essential, particularly military, supplies."

There was the whole gospel of preparedness and efficiency epitomized in a single sentence. But he did not stop with that. So important did this man—who was first in peace as well as in war—consider the project of universal preparation and service that only thirteen days later he sent to Congress a special message on the subject, urging immediate action and presenting a plan for adoption. This plan was Washington's own, though he modestly gave credit for it to his Secretary of War, General Knox. It provided that all able-bodied male citizens, with certain specified exemptions for cause, should be enrolled by conscription for military duty. They were to be divided into three classes. Those from 18 to 20 years of age were to form the advanced corps, or first line of battle; those from 21 to 45 were to form the main corps; and those from 45 to 60 were to form the reserve.

404

SERVICE ESSENTIAL TO CITIZENSHIP

It was an integral and essential part of this plan that service should be a prerequisite of complete citizenship. Unless specially exempted for cause, no man was to be permitted to vote or hold office of any kind unless he had served his term with the colors. Having served in the advanced corps for three years, on attaining the age of twenty-one the young man was to be received into full citizenship; but if he had not thus served, he was to be excluded from office and from the polls. This was Washington's conception of the functions of the advanced corps:

"The advanced corps are designed not only as a school in which the youth of the United States are to be instructed in the art of war, but they are, in all cases of exigence, to serve as an actual defense of the community. The whole of the armed corps shall be clothed, armed and subsisted at the expense of the United States, and encamped together if practicable, or by legions, which encampments shall be denominated the annual camps of discipline. The youth of 18 and 19 years shall be disciplined for 30 days successively in each year; and those of 20 years shall be disciplined only for 10 days in each year, which shall be the last 10 days of the annual encampment."

A FUTILE SUBSTITUTE

Congress rejected Washington's plan, and thereby entailed upon the country loss and disaster inestimable—as we shall see. Instead, it enacted the stupid and stultifying militia law of 1792, contemplation of which reminds us of the genius who was "in favor of the law but against its enforcement." In brief, it declared that all citizens were liable to be called for military service, but it omitted to provide any means for thus calling them, or for preparing them to render efficient service. It declared that every able-bodied male citizen between the ages of 18 and 45 was a member of the militia. Those who voluntarily formed themselves into military companies for training were called the organized militia, while all the rest were the unorganized militia. As not one in a thousand voluntarily entered the organized militia, the nation was practically left unprepared for war, and its citizens in a condition in which, as Lee said in the words already quoted, it would be murder to send them into the field.

The result of this fatuous policy was seen before that generation had passed away. In our second war with Great Britain, with two or three exceptions, the performances of our army of raw recruits were disgraceful. Poltroonery and rout were the order of the day. When a small British force approached the national capital, it found that city "defended" by two or three times its number of American troops. Yet the latter, under the eyes of the President himself, fired one volley and then fled in disgraceful rout, like frightened rabbits, abandoning the capital to the foe. The one real victory was won at the very end of the war, indeed after the treaty of peace had been signed; by which time, after two and a half years of war, the troops had become disciplined and hardened and therefore efficient. Had the troops at Washington been of the quality of those at New Orleans, the nation would not have suffered the indelible disgrace of having its capital betrayed into the hands of an invading foe. Yet with fatuous folly, in all the years since, we have busied ourselves with raging against the vandalism of the invaders in burning our public buildings, and have had nothing to say about the poltroonery of our own troops or the crass

406

stupidity of the system which thus entrusted the safety of the country to unprepared greenhorns.

JEFFERSON'S CHANGE OF POLICY

Jefferson was at first a pacifist, believing in neither army nor navy. So when a United States ship was attacked unawares by a British ship, riddled with shot and shell, and men were taken from it by force, his only reply was to order all American ships to stay in port, where they would not get hurt. Also, at first Jefferson opposed the building of cities, opposed the establishment of manufactures, opposed commerce, and hoped for a revolution every twenty years. But he got over all those crazy notions of his salad days. The disgraceful fiascoes of our militia warfare in 1812–14 opened his eyes. From his retirement at Monticello he wrote to Monroe, regretting that the latter's plan of introducing here Napoleon's conscription system had not been adopted:

"Nothing more *wise* or *efficient* could have been imagined than what you proposed. It would have filled our ranks with *regulars*, and that, too, by throwing a *just share of the burthen* on the purses of those persons who are exempt either by age or office; it would have rendered our *militia* . . . *a nation of warriors*. But the go-by seems to have been given to your proposition, and longer *sufferance* is necessary to *force* us to *what is best*. We seem equally *incorrigible*. . . ."

And again he wrote to Monroe:

"We must *train* and *classify* the *whole* of our male citizens, and make *military instruction* a part of collegiate education. *We can never be safe until this is done*."

OTHER AUTHORITIES FOR PREPAREDNESS

Both the Adamses, Madison and Monroe favored universal military training and service. So did Jackson, the founder of modern democracy. He urged in his message of December, 1835, that the whole body of the male population be organized and classified for training and service. "A classification of the population," he wrote, "offers the most obvious means of effecting this organization. Such a division may be made as will be just to all by transferring each at a proper period of life from one class to another and by calling first for the service of that class, whether for instruction or action, which from age is qualified for the duty and may be called to perform it with the least injury to themselves or the public.

"Should the danger ever become so imminent as to require additional force the other classes in succession would be ready for the call."

THE TRADITIONAL POLICY ABANDONED

Such was the policy of the founders of the republic. Such, then, was the traditional policy of the republic. But it was abandoned; or, rather, it was never fulfilled. The need of it was bitterly felt in the War of 1812, when the great majority of our land operations were as disgraceful and as disastrous as our achievements on the sea were brilliant. Despite these admonitions and that example, however, the policy was neglected and abandoned. There was little or no attempt made to give the militia universal training, and the standing army was reduced to a merely nominal strength.

The numbers of troops engaged in our various wars, including re-enlistments, have been as follows:

Revolution, 1775–83; 309,791. Northwestern Indian,

1790–95; 8,983. France, 1798–1800; 4,593. Tripoli, 1801–05; 3,330. Indian (Harrison), 1811–13; 910. War of 1812, 1812–15; 576,622. Creek Indian, 1813–14; 13,781. Seminole, 1817–18; 6,911. Winnebago (Wis.), 1827; 1,416. Sac and Fox (Ill.), 1831; ——. Black Hawk, 1832; 6,465. Cherokee removal, 1833–39; 9,494. Seminole (Fla.), 1835–42; 41,122; Sabine Indian, 1836–37; 4,429. Creek (Fla.), 1836–37; 13,418. "Patriot" (frontier), 1838–39; 1,500. Seminole (Fla.), 1842–58; Mexico, 1846–48; 112,230. Cayuse Indian (Ore.), 1848; 1,116. Texas Indian, 1849–56; 4,243. Apache (Utah), 1849–55; 2,561. California Indian, 1849–55; 265. Utah Indian, 1851–53; 540. Oregon-Washington Indian, 1851–56; 5,145. Comanche, 1854; 503. Seminole, 1855–58; 2,687. Civil War, 1861–66; 2,778,304. Spanish-American, 1898–99; 312,523. Philippine, 1899–1902; 140,038. Pekin (China) expedition, 1900–01; 6,913. Grand total, 4,371,839.

In the principal wars these figures represented chiefly volunteers, and the numbers were ludicrously disproportionate to the efficiency of the service. Thus in the Revolution and in the War of 1812 it is doubtful if at any one time we ever had of effective troops in the field more than one-tenth of the numbers mentioned.

ORIGIN OF THE VOLUNTEER DELUSION

We may trace the origin of the insane delusion concerning the efficiency of volunteers and raw levies to our first important battle, Bunker Hill. "The Americans," says Greene in his military history of the Revolution, "without proper organization, equipment, or supplies, had fought the best regular troops of Europe, and had repulsed them until their ammunition gave out . . . and they were convinced that they could do it again, and that *regular organization was not necessary*—a conviction which they tenaciously held to throughout the Revolution; and then *transmitted to their descendants, who have believed it almost to this day.*"

That delusion survived the disaster and disgrace of the War of 1812, because of the fine achievements of our navy, and because the fact that the British army was chiefly occupied with beating Bonaparte in Spain and Flanders enabled us to come out of that war without the sound drubbing that we otherwise would doubtless have received. Of course at Bunker Hill we won because of the monumental folly of the British in walking into a trap and of attempting to storm, with solid columns, an entrenched position. But in every war which we have fought we have suffered grossly and inexcusably, from lack of preparedness and from our fatuous dependence upon untrained men.

UNIVERSAL SERVICE DEMOCRATIC

It should of course be perfectly obvious, without argument or explication, that universal military service is not only quite compatible with democratic institutions but also is actually demanded by them. If all men are regarded as equal, in the sight of the law, they must be equal in responsibility and duties as well as in rights and privileges. If they are equal in their enjoyment of the service and the protection of the government, they must be equal in their service to and their support of the government, and they must be these things and do these things at all times, in war as well as in peace. These principles need no demonstration. They are axiomatic.

Moreover, since the republic prepares its citizens, by compulsory universal education, for the duties of citizenship in peace, it is similarly legitimate and indeed imperative for it to prepare them for their duties in war, by giving them universal military instruction and training.

THE SWISS EXAMPLE

An example of universal service in a democracy is presented by Switzerland. That republic has long been probably the most perfectly prepared nation in the world, for military defense. Yet in no other country has militarism less interfered with industry and social economy, and in no other land is the burden of military expenses lighter. Under the Swiss constitution, with the exceptions of certain specified classes, such as federal officials, postal employes, police, clergymen and teachers, etc., all men are liable for military duty between the ages of 20 and 48. The army is divided into three classes: The elite, from 20 to 32; the landwehr, from 32 to 40; and the landsturm, from 40 to 48 years of age. At 20 every young Swiss reports for admittance to service, and if he passes a satisfactory examination he is enrolled and receives a uniform, rifle and full equipment, which he takes home and keeps during his whole period of service, being responsible for their good care, under heavy penalty.

He is then sent to one of the schools for recruits, where he serves under an expert corps of instructors. Each day at the school means eight hours of hard drill and other work, including night-firing and entrenching. During the first year he serves thus 65 days if he is in the infantry and 90 days if he is in the cavalry. After that year he is called out for from 11 to 14 days every other year while he is in the elite. In the landwehr he is called out only once, for 11 days. In the landsturm he is called out only in case of war.

411

SCHOOLBOY TRAINING

The recruit on entering the service at 20 years of age is by no means raw material. Up to 15 years of age every boy is compelled to attend school, in which there is systematic physical training intended to give preparation for military service. There is also an elaborate cadet corps system, which boys are encouraged to join, and in which they are instructed in rifle-firing and other military details. At 20 the average young Swiss is already expert in the manual of arms and in many of the duties of a soldier's life.

The cost of all this to the nation is trifling, the total cost of the military establishment being only about $13,000,000 a year. The cost of each recruit, for training and maintenance during his first year's period of service, is $13. He serves without pay, save for 16 cents a day for spending money, and the government pays for his uniform, rifle and other equipment, transportation, lodgings and food. The net result is that Switzerland, one of the most peaceful and least militaristic countries in the world, is a nation of efficient, disciplined and expert soldiers.

Australia, New Zealand, and South Africa, though British colonies, are really republics; certainly they are no less democracies than the United States; and they have systems of universal service. In Australia military training and service is compulsory upon all boys and men between the ages of 12 and 26. From 12 to 14 they are junior cadets; from 14 to 18 senior cadets; and from 18 to 26 they are citizen forces, armed, equipped and disciplined precisely as in the regular British army.

The suggestion of what such a system would mean to this country—of what it would be meaning to us now, if it had been in force for the last score of years—is uncommonly profitable for consideration.

CHAPTER XXXV

THE MONROE DOCTRINE IN THE WAR

Fears that Our Participation in the War Might Compromise the Monroe Doctrine — Talk about Abandonment of Our "Policy of Isolation" — What the Monroe Doctrine Is, and What It Means — How It was Interpreted by Those Who Made It — No "Policy of Isolation" to be Found in It or Elsewhere — The United States a Full-sized Nation, "Able to Do All Things that Free and Independent States May of Right Do."

IS THE Monroe Doctrine abrogated by our entry into the war? The question is still asked, seriously if not wisely. So it was asked, years ago, if our conquest of Spain in the Philippines had not violated and abrogated that doctrine. Perhaps we might, Yankee fashion, answer the question by asking another. Did the Monroe Doctrine abrogate or forfeit our rights as a sovereign nation?

Beyond doubt, a certain fear that we should thus destroy that doctrine was conspicuous among the forces which so long restrained our government from declaring the war to which it had so abundant provocation. Even the President of the United States was troubled with such forebodings, when he intimated that we should perhaps have to abandon our traditional policy of isolation in order to take part in the affairs of the world for the sake of our own rights and of world-wide humanity.

NO ISOLATION POLICY

The fact is, however, that the United States has no "policy of isolation." It never had one. It never consistently practiced one. No trace of one is to be found,

413

in either the public pronouncements or the acts of the nation. Let us begin with the Declaration of Independence. It specifically asserts that the United States, "as free and independent States, have full power to levy war, conclude peace, contract alliances, establish commerce and to do all other acts and things which independent States may of right do." Certainly there is no hint of isolation there, but rather an assertion of our equal status as a nation among the nations of the world, competent to participate in any and all international affairs.

"NO ENTANGLING ALLIANCES'

Washington and Jefferson are named as sponsors for an isolation policy; but they were not. Washington warned the nation against permanent alliances with European powers, but he made it clear that his advice was intended merely for that time, while we were comparatively small and weak, and in the same breath he cordially sanctioned temporary alliances for special purposes. Jefferson also spoke epigrammatically against "entangling alliances," but in almost the next breath he advocated a hard and fast offensive and defensive alliance with Great Britain, and twenty years later, in the ripeness of his retirement as the "Sage of Monticello," he again recommended a permanent alliance with that country in order to detach it from the Continental system and to oppose the Holy Alliance with an Anglo-American alliance. His notable declarations of policy were thus at least two to one against "isolation."

THE MONROE DOCTRINE

If we come on down to the Monroe Doctrine, which is perhaps most frequently referred to as the basis of our

414

"isolation" policy, what do we find? Not a hint nor a suggestion of "isolation," either in the doctrine itself or in the authoritative comments upon it which were made at that time. In his message Monroe expressed ardent sympathy with Greece in her struggle for independence, and a deep interest in the unhappy condition of Spain and Portugal. There was no hint at isolation, or even at neutrality. Then he proceeded with the doctrine:

"In the wars of the European Powers, in *matters relating to themselves*, we have never taken any part, nor does it comport with our policy so to do. It is only when our rights are invaded or seriously menaced that we resent injuries or make preparations for our defense. . . . With the existing colonies or dependencies of any European Power we have not interfered, and shall not interfere. . . . Our policy in regard to Europe . . . remains the same, which is not to interfere in the *internal concerns* of any of its Powers, . . . and to preserve those relations by a frank, firm and manly policy, meeting in all instances the just claims of every power, submitting to injuries from none."

NEITHER ISOLATION NOR MEDDLING

There is no "policy of isolation" there, unless indeed it be isolation for a nation to refrain from being a busybody and a meddler in matters which are none of its business. It does not comport with our policy to take part in matters relating solely to other powers. Our policy is not to interfere "in the internal concerns" of other powers. All that is quite true. But how about matters which do not relate solely to European powers, and concerns which are not internal but external? The doctrine leaves us perfectly free to take any action which may be dictated by our own interest and welfare.

JEFFERSON'S VIEW OF THE DOCTRINE

So much for the doctrine itself, in letter and in spirit. In the Rush-Canning and Rush-Adams correspondence, which preceded and led to it, there was not the remotest hint at "isolation," but, rather, some very direct intimations of prospective alliance between America and Great Britain. Before issuing the doctrine Monroe sought the advice of Jefferson and Madison, and they both gave it, voluminously, but neither hinted at isolation. Instead, both directly and emphatically recommended and anticipated the contrary, and approved the proposed doctrine, because they regarded it as a step toward if not a practical achievement of a permanent alliance between America and Great Britain. It is true that Jefferson said that "our first and fundamental maxim should be never to entangle ourselves in the broils of Europe. . . . America has a set of interests distinct from those of Europe, and particularly her own. She should therefore have a system of her own, separate and apart from that of Europe." But that does not mean isolation, any more than it means isolation for one family not to meddle in the wrangles of another family, but to have its own domestic system, separate from that of any other household. To refrain from being a meddler one need not be a hermit.

A VIGOROUS POLICY

But note, further, what Jefferson said in the very next paragraph: "One nation, most of all, could disturb us in this pursuit; she now offers to lead, aid, and accompany us in it. . . . Great Britain is the nation which can do us the most harm of any or all on earth; and with her on our side we need not fear the whole world. With her, then, we should most sedulously cherish a cordial friendship; and nothing would tend more to knit our affections than to be fighting once more, side by side, in the same cause. . . . If we can effect a division in the body of the European powers, and draw over to our side its most powerful member, surely we should do it." In other words, we were to seek an Anglo-American alliance with which to oppose the Holy Alliance.

MADISON ON ALLIANCES

That was Jefferson's policy. Madison's was the same. "It is particularly fortunate," he said, "that the policy of Great Britain has presented a co-operation for an object the same with ours. With that co-operation we have nothing to fear from the rest of Europe. There ought not, therefore, to be any backwardness in meeting her in the way she has proposed . . . Will it not be honorable to our country to invite the British Government to extend the 'avowed disapprobation' of the project against the Spanish colonies to the enterprise of France against Spain herself, and even to join in some declaratory act in behalf of the Greeks?"

Thus while Jefferson was advocating an alliance with Great Britain, Madison, the most scholarly and thoughtful of men, was suggesting that we should utilize that alliance not merely for the protection of the new republics in Spanish America, but also for intervention—Anglo-American intervention—between France and Spain, and between Turkey and Greece. For while he spoke primarily of mere words of "disapprobation" of France's aggressions upon Spain, and of a mere "declaratory act" in favor of Greece, he recognized the fact that such declarations might imply a pledge to follow them up with war; in which case, he said, "we ought to compare the good to be done with the little injury to be apprehended to the United States, shielded as their interests would be by the power and the fleets of Great Britain united with their own." In short, we were to join Great Britain in waging war against France for the protection of Spain, and in waging war against Turkey for the liberation of Greece! Yet people prate about our "traditional policy of isolation!"

NATIONAL ACTS AND PRACTICE

If from these most weighty and authoritative declarations, which however are nothing but declarations, we turn to concrete acts, not only performed by the President but also approved by Congress or by the Senate, what do we find? Note the case of Morocco. In 1880 we united with the European powers in a formal treaty for the protection of foreigners in that empire, and in 1906 we entered at Algeciras that monstrous embroilment of the powers which was one of the most direct preludes to the present European war, and we took almost a predominant part in defining and regulating the rival interests of European powers in that African country. Or what shall we say of the two treaties, or sets of treaties, at The Hague? The United States took a leading part in those conferences and in the making of those treaties, side by side with the European powers; and they were and are treaties relating not merely to our own concerns but to the general international interests of the whole world. Surely, it was not an empty form for this country to sign and ratify those treaties. And surely in our doing so there could not have been the slightest trace of "isolation."

THE TRUE RULE OF CONDUCT

It is not to be contended that we should embroil ourselves in purely European affairs, or that we should hastily enter into alliances with any other powers in the world. But it cannot be too strongly insisted upon that the Declaration of Independence is not mere "buncombe" when it says that this country has "full power to contract alliances," and that it was not a purposeless form for the Constitution to invest the President with the power "to make treaties" in the unlimited sense of the term. It may not be expedient for us to enter into alliances. A great authority of old reminded us that things which are lawful are sometimes not expedient. But nothing can be more certain than that there is and has been no "policy of isolation" which may now be abandoned, and that there is nothing in tradition or precedent or declaration or theory or practice to restrain us for one moment from making any alliances or doing any other lawful act which may be expedient and for the interest of our own security and welfare. The United States is not a dwarf nor a cripple, nor yet a hermit, among the nations of the world.

Chapter XXXVI

THE FLAG AND ITS ANTHEM

THE STARS AND STRIPES are on the firing line of the European war, and will be "in at the death" when Hohenzollern despotism and Prussian militarism and all the bestial anarchism of "Kultur" are finally rounded up and crushed by the triumphant democracy of both hemispheres. The entry of our banner into the world war was signally welcomed by our allies, particularly in its being raised to the highest place of honor above the Parliament Houses and all the government offices in London. During the great public demonstrations of "American Day" in the British capital, April 20, 1917, the King of England was heard to join heartily in the singing of "The Star Spangled Banner," an anthem which had been written as the American war song in a war waged against England more than a century before

These stirring and epochal incidents make it fitting to recall the story of the flag and of the anthem; the one conceived and born during our first war and the other during our second war; and the two associated with peculiar

420

intimacy because of the fact that the anthem, alone among the important national anthems of the world, was inspired by and is indeed essentially a tribute to the flag.

KEY'S MISSION TO THE BRITISH FLEET

The story of the song is briefly told. Francis Scott Key, a brilliant member of a noted family, the son of a gallant officer in the Revolution, was at that time thirty-five years old and had already risen into eminence as a lawyer at the national capital. He was looked upon as one of the most important and influential men in his part of Maryland. Now at Upper Marlboro there was a somewhat choleric old physician, of excellent skill and abundant patriotism, Dr. William Beanes. To his house came some of the British forces which raided the shores of the Chesapeake and burned the capitol at Washington, and the officers insisted upon dining at his table and making his office their headquarters. This he was unable to prevent, and so he acquiesced, at heart grudgingly and indignantly, but outwardly with true Maryland hospitality. But after the officers had gone, there came some scurvy stragglers and camp followers, much the worse for firewater, free with insults and inclined toward loot. These Dr. Beanes properly clapped into jail for safe keeping. But when the British learned this they sent back a strong force, released the captives, and took Dr. Beanes aboard the flagship of their fleet, with the cheerful assurance that in a day or two he would infallibly be hanged at the yardarm. At this Key was besought to go to Admiral Cochrane and secure the doctor's release. It was a perilous and unpromising errand, but Key undertook it. He reached the British fleet under a flag of truce on the morning of September 6, 1814, and was well received. It did not take him long to secure the release of Dr. Beanes. But just at that time the British were preparing for an attack upon Baltimore which they meant to make a surprise, and in order that they might not disclose what they had seen of these preparations, both Key and Beanes were required to remain aboard the flagship until after the attack had been made, and they were told that they would thus have an unsurpassed opportunity to witness the reduction of Fort McHenry and the capture of the city.

"OUR FLAG WAS STILL THERE"

That attack was made as per schedule on September 13th, in the evening, but it did not result as the British had expected. On the contrary, the fort, under the command of the gallant Armistead, repulsed the fleet and kept its flag flying in triumph all through the night of battle. It was while he anxiously watched this fight from the deck of the British flagship that Key conceived the song, and jotted down rough notes of it on the back of an old letter, to be completed the next day. It may be observed that the song was made quite realistic. The "rockets' red glare, the bombs bursting in air" were very real and numerous that night, and they gave ample proof that "our flag was still there;" and the return of daylight confirmed that proof.

The next day the British realized that their attack had failed; and if, made as a surprise, it had been unsuccessful, there would be no hope of success in openly renewing it. So they sent Key and Dr. Beanes ashore, and sailed away. Key went to Baltimore and showed Judge Nicholson the draft of the song, and at Nicholson's urging it was at once given to a printer and handbill copies of it were struck off and distributed about the city and in the American army, where, sung to the English air of "To Anacreon in Heaven," it quickly gained great popularity. It was published in *The Baltimore American* on September 21st, with a note setting forth the circumstances of its origin but not mentioning the name of the writer.

THE GRAND UNION FLAG

The evolution of the Stars and Stripes from the British flag began in 1774, at Taunton, Mass., when the patriots raised the British flag with the motto "Liberty and Union" added; union then meaning continued union with Great Britain, and liberty meaning the same liberty for the colonists as the people of England enjoyed.

Next came the memorable step of January 2, 1776, when George Washington, who six months before had assumed chief command of the united colonial armies at Cambridge, raised there a new flag of his own devising. This was the so-called Grand Union flag, and it consisted of thirteen stripes, alternately red and white, with the union jack in canton. That is to say, it was exactly like the Stars and Stripes, with the union jack in place of the stars; or it was like the British flag, with stripes instead of the plain red field. In brief, it was half British and half American.

That Grand Union flag was carried for more than a year at the beginning of the Revolution: at Boston, at New York, Long Island, Harlem Heights, White Plains, Trenton and Princeton. Leutze's fine painting of "Washington Crossing the Delaware" shows the Stars and Stripes carried on his boat, but the Stars and Stripes did not then exist and did not come into being until months later

THE FIRST STARS AND STRIPES

But after Trenton and Princeton it was deemed by Congress necessary that we should have another national flag, without the British feature of the union jack, and Washington, then spending the winter between Bound Brook and Morristown, N. J., was commissioned to design one, with Robert Morris and Colonel George Ross as his colleagues. Washington simply took the Grand Union flag, struck out the union jack from the canton, and substituted a circle of thirteen white stars on a blue canton, and the Stars and Stripes stood revealed. This was the second step in the evolution from the British flag.

There is no reason for doubting that the first sample flag was made by Mrs. Elizabeth Ross, widow of John Ross, at No. 239 Arch Street, Philadelphia. We may also accept the entirely plausible story that Washington drew the design with the six-pointed stars of English heraldry, and that Mrs. Ross suggested the change to five-pointed stars; for which we have much cause to be grateful to that clever woman. It is indisputable that on June 14, 1777, John Adams proposed and the Continental Congress adopted a resolution that

"The flag of the thirteen United States be thirteen stripes, alternate red and white; that the union be thirteen stars, white on a blue field, representing a new constellation."

FIRST USE OF THE FLAG

There has been some dispute as to when the flag was first publicly displayed and used, but the overwhelming weight of evidence indicates that it was at Fort Schuyler, formerly called Fort Stanwix, on the site of the present city of Rome, N. Y.

The flag was not officially promulgated until September

424

3, 1777, after which date it speedily came into general use in both the army and navy, as well as in civil life. It was first raised at sea on a warship when John Paul Jones sailed with the sloop Ranger from Portsmouth, N. H., on a memorable raid upon the coasts of the British Isles. That was on November 1, 1777, and the flag was specially made for Jones by some of the ladies of Portsmouth. Thirty days later he was at Nantes, France, first carrying the flag into a European port and securing for it recognition and a salute from a foreign power.

THE FLAG OF FIFTEEN STRIPES

The flag presently began to increase and multiply. Vermont came into the Union in 1791, and Kentucky in 1792, and wanted some recognition; wherefore on January 13, 1794, it was enacted that the flag should thereafter consist of fifteen stars and fifteen stripes, with the blue canton resting on the fifth red stripe and the stars in three horizontal rows of five each. That was our flag for twenty-three years, including some of the most heroic and historic in our national life. When "The Star Spangled Banner" was written, ours was a flag of fifteen stars and fifteen stripes. The painting of Perry's victory, which hangs in the Capitol, shows another anachronism, the flag having only thirteen stripes.

THE FINAL DESIGN OF THE FLAG

But even when that change was made in 1794 there were those who perceived its folly, and protested against it, on the ground that further changes would have to be made, so that for a hundred years the flag would be unsettled and varying. Surely enough, in 1796 Tennessee was admitted to the Union, Ohio in 1803, Louisiana in 1812, Indiana in 1816, and Mississippi in 1817; so that there were five new states without representation in the flag. That would not do, and so Peter H. Wendover, a Representative of New York, secured the appointment of a committee, which on January 2, 1817, reported a bill for remodeling the flag. This report was based upon suggestions which were made to the committee at Wendover's request by Captain Samuel Chester Reid, of the navy, the commander of the famous privateer General Armstrong in the War of 1812; and it provided for a flag of thirteen stripes, as at first, representing the thirteen original states, and of twenty stars, representing the increased number of states, a new star to be added thereafter for each new state, the star to be added on the Fourth of July following the admission of the state. That was enacted on April 4, 1818, and remains to this day the flag law of the nation.

Thus on July 4, 1818, the flag assumed the form of thirteen stripes and twenty stars. The number of stars thereafter increased automatically on the Fourth of July of each year named, on account of the admission of the states named, as follows: Twenty-one in 1819, for Illinois; 23 in 1820, Alabama and Maine; 24 in 1822, Missouri; 25 in 1836, Arkansas; 26 in 1837, Michigan; 27 in 1845, Florida; 28 in 1846, Texas; 29 in 1847, Iowa; 30 in 1848, Wisconsin; 31 in 1851, California; 32 in 1858, Minnesota; 33 in 1859, Oregon; 34 in 1861, Kansas; 35 in 1863, West Virginia; 36 in 1865, Nevada; 37 in 1867, Nebraska; 38 in 1877, Colorado; 43 in 1890, North Dakota, South Dakota, Montana, Washington and Idaho; 44 in 1891, Wyoming; 45 in 1896, Utah; 46 in 1908, Oklahoma; 48 in 1912, Arizona and New Mexico. Thus in 140 years the Stars and Stripes has assumed no fewer than twenty-five different forms. As it is today, LONG MAY IT WAVE!

EPILOGUE

THE STAR SPANGLED BANNER

Oh! say, can you see, by the dawn's early light,
  What so proudly we hailed at the twilight's last gleaming?
Whose broad stripes and bright stars thro' the perilous fight,
  O'er the ramparts we watched, were so gallantly streaming.
And the rockets' red glare, the bombs bursting in air,
Gave proof thro' the night that our flag was still there.
  Oh! say, does the Star Spangled Banner yet wave
  O'er the land of the free and the home of the brave?

On the shore, dimly seen thro' the mist of the deep,
  Where the foe's haughty host in dread silence reposes,
What is that which the breeze, o'er the towering steep,
  As it fitfully blows, half conceals, half discloses?
Now it catches the gleam of the morning's first beam,
In full glory reflected, now shines on the stream.
  'Tis the Star Spangled Banner, oh! long may it wave
  O'er the land of the free and the home of the brave!

Oh! thus be it ever when freemen shall stand
  Between their lov'd homes and the war's desolation,
Blest with vict'ry and peace, may the Heav'n-rescued land
  Praise the Pow'r that hath made and preserved us a nation.
Then conquer we must, when our cause it is just,
And this be our motto, "In God is our trust."
  And the Star Spangled Banner in triumph shall wave
  O'er the land of the free and the home of the brave!